Pretend You *...*

'Touching, funny, ... ill

Winter *... Sheridan*

'Full of passages of astonishing writing... unbearable to watch but unforgettable; strange yet completely recognisable'
Guardian

Three Birds by Janice Okoh

'Deals in harsh realism but hovers, brilliantly suspended, between dark comedy, thriller and an expressive human sympathy worthy of Tennessee Williams' *The Times*

Wish List by Katherine Soper

'A beautifully compassionate, tender and at times gently humorous piece of work... in its clear-eyed look at the interplay between two dehumanising systems, it arouses due political indignation' *Independent*

untitled f*ck m*ss s**gon play by Kimber Lee

'Ferociously funny... dissects years of racist, imperialist and misogynistic tropes... punky, polemical and stingingly fresh'
Guardian

Other Titles in this Series

David Adjmi
STEREOPHONIC

Waleed Akhtar
THE ART OF ILLUSION
 with Alexis Michalik
KABUL GOES POP: MUSIC TELEVISION
 AFGHANISTAN
THE P WORD
THE REAL ONES

Mike Bartlett
THE 47TH
ALBION
BULL
GAME
AN INTERVENTION
KING CHARLES III
MIKE BARTLETT PLAYS: TWO
MRS DELGADO
SCANDALTOWN
SNOWFLAKE
UNICORN
VASSA after Gorky
WILD

Jack Bradfield
THE HABITS

babirye bukilwa
...BLACKBIRD HOUR
...CAKE

Billie Collins
PEAK STUFF
TOO MUCH WORLD AT ONCE
THE WALRUS HAS A RIGHT TO
 ADVENTURE

Mohamed-Zain Dada
BLUE MIST
DIZZY
SPEED

Lucy Kirkwood
BEAUTY AND THE BEAST
 with Katie Mitchell
BLOODY WIMMIN
THE CHILDREN
CHIMERICA
HEDDA after Ibsen
THE HUMAN BODY
IT FELT EMPTY WHEN THE HEART
 WENT AT FIRST BUT IT IS
 ALRIGHT NOW
LUCY KIRKWOOD PLAYS: ONE
MOSQUITOES
NSFW
RAPTURE
TINDERBOX
THE WELKIN

Anna Jordan
CHICKEN SHOP
CLOSER TO GOD
FREAK
POP MUSIC
THE UNRETURNING
WE ANCHOR IN HOPE
YEN

Benedict Lombe
LAVA
SHIFTERS

Charley Miles
BLACKTHORN
DAUGHTERHOOD
THERE ARE NO BEGINNINGS

Suzie Miller
INTER ALIA
PRIMA FACIE

Chloë Moss
CHRISTMAS IS MILES AWAY
CORRINA, CORRINA
FATAL LIGHT
THE GATEKEEPER
HOW LOVE IS SPELT
RUN SISTER RUN
THIS WIDE NIGHT
THE WAY HOME

Chinonyerem Odimba
AMONGST THE REEDS
BLACK LOVE
PRINCESS & THE HUSTLER
UNKNOWN RIVERS

Ava Pickett
1536

Iman Qureshi
THE FUNERAL DIRECTOR
THE MINISTRY FOR LESBIAN AFFAIRS

Mark Rosenblatt
GIANT

Sam Steiner
KANYE THE FIRST
LEMONS LEMONS LEMONS LEMONS
 LEMONS
A TABLE TENNIS PLAY
YOU STUPID DARKNESS!

Joel Tan
NO PARTICULAR ORDER
SCENES FROM A REPATRIATION

debbie tucker green
BORN BAD
DEBBIE TUCKER GREEN PLAYS: ONE
DIRTY BUTTERFLY
EAR FOR EYE
HANG
NUT
A PROFOUNDLY AFFECTIONATE,
 PASSIONATE DEVOTION TO
 SOMEONE (– *NOUN*)
RANDOM
STONING MARY
TRADE & GENERATIONS
TRUTH AND RECONCILIATION

Tom Wells
BIG BIG SKY
BROKEN BISCUITS
DRIP *with* Matthew Robins
FOLK
JUMPERS FOR GOALPOSTS
THE KITCHEN SINK
ME, AS A PENGUIN

BRUNTWOOD AT 20:

Five Plays from the Bruntwood Prize for Playwriting

Pretend You Have Big Buildings
by Ben Musgrave

Winterlong
by Andrew Sheridan

Three Birds
by Janice Okoh

Wish List
by Katherine Soper

*untitled f*ck m*ss s**gon play*
by Kimber Lee

NICK HERN BOOKS
London
www.nickhernbooks.co.uk

A Nick Hern Book

Bruntwood at 20 first published in Great Britain in 2025 as a paperback original by Nick Hern Books Limited, The Glasshouse, 49a Goldhawk Road, London W12 8QP, in association with the Royal Exchange Theatre, Manchester, and Bruntwood

Foreword copyright © 2025 Sarah Frankcom
Introduction copyright © 2025 Rachel Clements
Pretend You Have Big Buildings © 2014, 2025 Ben Musgrave
Winterlong © 2011, 2025 Andrew Sheridan
Three Birds © 2013, 2025 Janice Okoh
Wish List © 2016, 2025 Katherine Soper
*untitled f*ck m*ss s**gon play* © 2023, 2025 Kimber Lee

The authors have asserted their moral rights

Cover image design: Stanley Chow
Designed and typeset by Nick Hern Books, London
Printed in the UK by Mimeo Ltd, Huntingdon, Cambridgeshire PE29 6XX

A CIP catalogue record for this book is available from the British Library

ISBN 978 1 83904 498 4

CAUTION All rights whatsoever in these plays are strictly reserved. Requests to reproduce the texts in whole or in part should be addressed in the first instance to the publisher.

Amateur Performing Rights Applications for performance, including readings and excerpts, by amateurs in the English language throughout the world should be addressed to the Performing Rights Department, Nick Hern Books, The Glasshouse, 49a Goldhawk Road, London W12 8QP, *tel* +44 (0)20 8749 4953, *email* rights@nickhernbooks.co.uk, except as follows: *Australia*: ORiGiN Theatrical, *email* enquiries@originmusic.com.au, *web* www.origintheatrical.com.au; *New Zealand*: Play Bureau, PO Box 9013, St Clair, Dunedin 9047, *tel* (3) 455 9959, *email* info@playbureau.com; *United States of America and Canada*: see details below

Professional Performing Rights Applications for performance by professionals in any medium throughout the world (and by amateurs in the United States of America and Canada), should be addressed as follows: *Pretend You Have Big Buildings*: United Agents Ltd, 12–26 Lexington St, London W1F 0LE, *tel* +44 (0)20 3214 0800, *email* info@unitedagents.co.uk; *Winterlong*: Casarotto Ramsay and Associates Ltd, *email* rights@casarotto.co.uk, www.casarotto.co.uk; *Three Birds*: Independent Talent Group Ltd, 40 Whitfield Street, London W1T 2RH, *tel* +44 (020) 7636 6565; *Wish List*: The Agency (London) Ltd, 24 Pottery Lane, Holland Park, London W11 4LZ, *fax* +44 (0)20 7727 9037, *email* info@theagency.co.uk; *untitled f*ck m*ss s**gon play* (both amateur and professional): The Gersh Agency, 41 Madison Avenue, 33rd Floor, New York, NY 10010 USA, *tel* +1 (212) 634 8124, *email* sglewen@gersh.com

No performance of any kind may be given unless a licence has been obtained. Applications should be made before rehearsals begin. Publication of these plays does not necessarily indicate their availability for performance.

www.nickhernbooks.co.uk/environmental-policy

Nick Hern Books' authorised representative in the EU is
Easy Access System Europe – Mustamäe tee 50, 10621 Tallinn, Estonia
email gpsr.requests@easproject.com

Contents

Foreword by Sarah Frankcom	vii
Introduction: 'Head, Heart and Guts' by Rachel Clements	ix
Pretend You Have Big Buildings by Ben Musgrave	1
Winterlong by Andrew Sheridan	125
Three Birds by Janice Okoh	225
Wish List by Katherine Soper	319
untitled f*ck m*ss s**gon play by Kimber Lee	413
A Timeline	483

Foreword
Sarah Frankcom

On a humid summer evening in 2005 I was asked to attend a dinner in an Italian restaurant in Manchester hosted by Braham Murray, one of the founding Artistic Directors of the Royal Exchange Theatre. In my capacity as the theatre's New Work Associate, I pitched an idea for a prize for Northern playwrights to Michael and Jean Oglesby from Bruntwood, a Manchester-based property company who were supporters of the theatre. I was totally unprepared for Mike's forensic interrogation of my modest proposal. I remember him asking, why would we want it to be limited by geography and not seize the opportunity to do something of national significance from here in Manchester? I didn't disagree with him. Mike was really inspiring (and determined) when he grabbed hold of an idea. I was charged with dreaming up something bigger and bolder. And so it began.

I can't quite believe that the prize is now twenty years old. It seems amazing that it's still here and unearthing plays and helping them find their way to theatres and audiences. Over 17,325 plays have been submitted and, as of 2025, over £394,000 has been distributed in prize funds.

At the heart of the prize has always been a very simple belief that anyone anywhere can write a play and that the prize should provide tools, support and, most importantly, a deadline for playwrights. As the prize has grown up it's been brilliant to see a community of playwrights emerge who have been through the Bruntwood experience as longlisted and shortlisted writers, winners and now judges. The prize has always seen itself as an investor in the playwright and the money that it has distributed has in many instances bought emerging playwrights the time to write at a critical moment in their career development.

Later when I became Artistic Director of the Royal Exchange Theatre, the prize and the plays it generated were central to my programming and partnerships. My relationship with Mike and Jean and latterly their daughter Kate deepened. Mike was very involved in all stages of the prize. He absolutely loved the ceremony and meeting the shortlisted writers and seeing their plays develop as they moved into production. Mike had an eye for an interesting play: he always claimed to not really know what made a good play, but this didn't stop him passionately championing the plays he fell in love with as a judge. He felt he represented the audience and believed that a new play was the lifeblood of the theatre, and that there was nothing more exciting than seeing a new play meet an audience for the first time.

I'm writing this at a time when the world needs new plays more than ever, but the climate for them is very challenging and the new-writing ecology is in a critical condition. Over the years I have found myself moved by the impact of the prize. I've had the privilege of working with some amazing playwrights and directing some brilliant first plays that have shown me the world in a new way and deepened my understanding of what it is to be alive. I continue to meet writers who tell me that making the longlist was the first moment they felt recognised as a writer. But mostly I am still moved by the simple fact that every few years, thousands of people take a leap of imagination and embark on the journey of crafting a play.

The prize is still and has always been built on the work of many people who are passionate about what new plays can be and do. I'd like to acknowledge all the readers who've worked tirelessly to make sure every play is considered fairly, the judging panels, all the theatres who have been partners over the years, and all the audiences who have seen Bruntwood Prize-winning plays in theatres in Manchester, around the country and all over the world. I'd particularly like to thank Jo Combes, Sam Pritchard and Suzanne Bell who looked after and shepherded the prize at the Royal Exchange. And finally express my gratitude to Mike and Jean Oglesby and Kate Vokes who generously supported a nascent idea with such determination, passion and unwavering commitment.

Head, Heart and Guts:
Twenty Years of the Bruntwood Prize for Playwriting
Rachel Clements

It's January 2016, and Erin Doherty is standing on the Royal Exchange Theatre's Studio Stage, singing Meat Loaf's 'I'd Do Anything for Love (But I Won't Do That)'. Her character, Tamsin, has been cajoled into song by Luke (played by Shaquille Ali-Yebuah). Unaccompanied, self-conscious, Tamsin's voice shakes and falters. Gradually, she finds her feet and, all of a sudden, the backing track kicks in. The world tilts. For a moment, Tamsin is supported by the full daft grandeur of a power ballad, and by the laughter and tears of the audience. And she soars: air guitar high kicks shed the tension of financial precarity and the constant worry that have smothered her throughout Katherine Soper's *Wish List*. She is glorious. The song ends, and we're back in Tamsin's flat. It is awkward, silly and sad; it is hopeful, resilient and desperate; a one-two emotional and political gut-punch. It's a kind of moment – urgent, original and deeply theatrical – which happens in many Bruntwood Prize-winning plays.

Writing in *The Stage* on 24 October 2024, theatre critic Anya Ryan argued that the Bruntwood Prize for Playwriting has become 'an integral part of the theatre landscape, propelling the careers of some of our most exciting writers', in a piece whose headline declared that the prize is 'vital to the UK's new-writing ecology'. This collection brings together a selection of five of the thirty-eight winning plays to date, including *Wish List*. The texts gathered here are not presented as 'best of the bests', but offered as a curated group which aim to give readers a sense of the prize's aims, development, values and impact over the past two decades.

The Bruntwood Prize has mattered to the theatre scene of the UK and beyond because, since its inception, it has been about much more than handing awards to a few exceptional plays. It has centred and celebrated the craft and creativity of the playwright, but in a way that understands the complex, interconnected network of the art and the ecology of the theatre. The plays published here are not the versions submitted to the prize but the texts as developed for production. Bruntwood Prizes, then, are the tip of a bigger iceberg: the most visible part, perhaps, but only part of the dramaturgical and developmental facilitation, and the support across the wider theatre ecology that Bruntwood and the Royal Exchange have offered to writers over the past two decades. Each of the plays in this volume is interesting and distinctive in its own right; each is committed to its own unique theatrical gesture. As dramaturg Suzanne Bell, whose involvement with the prize has been extensive, says, like many of the winning plays, they contain 'a marriage of head, heart and guts'. Together, they speak to the theatrical boldness, the social conscience, and the connection to their moment which has characterised Bruntwood Prize plays since 2005.

Large-scale ambitions: *Pretend You Have Big Buildings* by Ben Musgrave

Ben Musgrave's *Pretend You Have Big Buildings* won the inaugural Bruntwood Prize in 2005. Musgrave had not had a professional production staged before winning the prize, although he had completed an MA Writing for Performance at Goldsmiths College, University of London; he has gone on to a successful scriptwriting career across multiple dramatic forms, and also one that – via his longstanding work teaching at the University of East Anglia – has supported many other writers. *Pretend You Have Big Buildings* is distinctive for the way it combines a precise time and place (November–December 1995, Romford) with a story which has global as well as local implications, and for its negotiation of intertwined themes around grief, racism, family history, class and adolescence. In the central relationship between Danny (played in the 2007 Royal Exchange Theatre production by Sacha Dhawan) and

Leon (played by Jonathan Bailey), Musgrave dramatises the fallout of disintegrating marriages, and the impact of environment on teenagers' understandings of, and ability to inhabit, their own identities.

The play inherits and pushes at the strong social-realist tradition in British playwriting, as do *Monster* by Duncan Macmillan and *The Cracks in My Skin* by Phil Porter which also received prizes in the inaugural year. There is a strong social conscience in Musgrave's play which can also be seen in the rest of this collection, as well as many other Bruntwood plays, particularly those which are concerned with the challenges facing young people – especially those who have been pushed to the margins (Vivienne Franzmann's *Mogadishu*, which won a prize in 2008, and Anna Jordan's *Yen*, which won in 2013, are also good examples of these). Writing in the *Daily Telegraph*, Dominic Cavendish described Musgrave's play as 'touching, funny, immensely assured', while Dominic Maxwell, writing for *The Times*, praised it for having 'a scope and sense of recent history that too many new plays lack'.

Although much has developed and shifted in the prize since 2005, some fundamental principles have been established from the beginning. The anonymised, multi-stage reading process is one: plays are cut loose from any assumptions that a writer's name or biography might carry. Equally significant is the commitment not just to awarding money – important, even career-altering, as that has been – but to supporting plays through development and aspiring (though not guaranteeing) to take them into production. At twenty-six years old, Musgrave was the youngest writer to have had a play on in the 750-seater, in-the-round, main space of the Royal Exchange. *Pretend You Have Big Buildings*, and the Bruntwood Prize, opened doors at the Royal Exchange for early career writers. Musgrave and other prize-winning playwrights have shown that it is worth taking a risk with, and providing resources at scale for, the work of new artists, and demonstrated a confidence in new plays and in the audiences that come to see them.

Bruntwood and the North West: *Winterlong* by Andrew Sheridan

Winterlong, which won a prize in 2008, was Andrew Sheridan's first play as a writer. It combines an unflinching depiction of a cruel, damaged world (via the behaviour and language of its characters) with moments of sharp tender beauty, and shards of hope that are almost too hard to hold. Lyn Gardner, reviewing the first production in the *Guardian*, directed by Sarah Frankcom in the Exchange's Studio (transferring to London's Soho Theatre), called *Winterlong* a 'dense, difficult and brave' play. Its movement across fifteen years of protagonist Oscar's life means it's non-naturalistic in its theatrical strategy and, although it's oriented around a clear central figure, its social vision is expansive. There's a poetry to its violence and horrors which allows it to shuttle between a tight focus on character and their wider situation.

The confidence of the play's dialogue and voices owes a lot to Sheridan's experience and craft as an established actor (particularly on stage, including at the Royal Exchange). Several other prize-winning writers including Nathan Queeley-Dennis, Fiona Peek, Gareth Farr, Luke Norris, Chris Urch and Rebecca Callard also came to writing as or after being actors, though their plays are wildly different from one another. Indeed, Callard played Helen in the first production of *Winterlong*, before writing *A Bit of Light*, which received a commendation in 2017 (and which she has adapted into a film). This connection highlights the fact that a growing awareness of the Bruntwood Prize – and of the writers who had been recognised by it – has become a significant driver for subsequent submissions to the prize.

The Mancunian genesis and location of the Bruntwood Prize matters in several ways. A writer-centred approach to and understanding of theatre-making has a long history in the UK. But from the establishment of the English Stage Company at the Royal Court in the 1950s and the development of London's fringe theatres in the 1970s to the proliferation of 'new writing' in the 1990s, London has loomed large in the playwriting scene: for many, it has exerted a gravitational force. As Sarah Frankcom notes in her foreword to this volume, making Manchester another important hub for the development of plays and playwrights was a key ambition of both Bruntwood and the Royal Exchange. Reorienting or diversifying the map means that – though some Bruntwood Prize writers are London-based – a significant number of prize-winning plays come from right across the UK. Katherine Chandler's *Bird* and *How My Light is Spent* by Alan Harris (Judges' Award winners in 2013 and 2015) are both set in Wales; Michael John O'Neill's *Akedah*, which received the Original New Voice Award in 2019, is set in Northern Ireland. There is a strand of distinctly 'Northern' voices in the prize's history, too: *Electric Rosary* by Tim Foley, which won a Judges' Award in 2017, is set in Northumberland. Alistair McDowall's *Brilliant Adventures* is set in Middlesbrough; Gareth Farr's *Britannia Waves the Rules* in Blackpool. Both won Judges' Awards in 2011, the same year that *Winterlong*, the most emphatically Mancunian of the prize-winning plays to date, was first produced in the Royal Exchange's Studio. And in the 2022 cycle, the North West Original New Voice Award (given to Patrick Hughes) came with a year-long paid residency at the Royal Exchange, providing a theatrical home for a writer in the region.

Co-productions and development opportunities: *Three Birds* by Janice Okoh

Janice Okoh's *Three Birds* – which won the Bruntwood Prize in 2011 – also has vulnerable teenagers at the heart of the play, but there is more dark comedy in her play than in Sheridan's or Musgrave's, and a completely different approach to setting. Located in the flat that siblings Tiana, Tionne and Tanika live in, Okoh's work was described by Libby Purves in *The Times* as '[t]ough stuff, but no bleak social misery lecture', which 'deals in harsh realism but hovers, brilliantly suspended, between dark comedy, thriller and an expressive human sympathy worthy of Tennessee Williams'. When the play moved from the Royal Exchange's Studio to London's Bush Theatre, Sarah Hemming commended Okoh's 'vivid depiction of the children, her keen ear for demotic dialogue and her moving illustration of the need for love' in the *Financial Times*. It is a good example of the co-production model which has increasingly served both Bruntwood playwrights and the wider industry, making it possible for text to reach the stage. Finding suitable partner producing venues, has been crucial to the staging of Bruntwood Prize-winning plays – and to the fostering of relationships between writers and venues which might be good homes and stages for their works.

One of the main criteria for Bruntwood Prize readers to consider is whether a script is making distinctly theatrical gestures. Okoh's play does that: the flat feels less and less safe as *Three Birds* progresses, and the text makes particularly deft use of the possibilities of doors and entrances on stage, as the siblings struggle to hold themselves together and keep the outside world at bay. Director Sarah Frankcom worked with young adult actors Michaela Coel, Jahvel Hall and Susan Wokoma who played the teenagers and child of the piece, thereby mobilising the collective imagination of the production and its audience. There was a related but different iteration of total confidence in collective imagining in Alistair McDowall's *Brilliant Adventures* (which also won a prize in 2011), in which a large cardboard box becomes a time machine. The 'Meat Loaf moment' in *Wish List* was another. Understanding the co-creation that is happening with an audience is a key feature of a playtext, and the plays in this volume all let the audience in to their world-building.

Okoh has also successfully developed *Three Birds* into the six-part television series *Just Act Normal*, broadcast on the BBC in March 2025. Her writing was praised by Lucy Mangan of the *Guardian* for being 'beautifully structured and hold[ing] its many strands in perfect tension'. Other Bruntwood writers – notably Anna Jordan, Phoebe Eclair-Powell (*Shed: Exploded View,* winner in 2019), and James Fritz (*Parliament Square,* Judges' Award winner in 2015) – write for television and audio formats as well as for the stage. The creative industries are interconnected rather than siloed, and the Bruntwood Prize's impact reaches beyond the stage. The prize has also forged a number of 'legacy opportunities', including residencies at the Banff Playwrights Lab in Canada, Melbourne Theatre Company and the National Theatre Studio to support writers to go on to develop their next plays.

Writing the contemporary moment: *Wish List* by Katherine Soper

Katherine Soper's *Wish List* won the Bruntwood Prize in 2015, at a point where the public profile of the prize was such that it generated significant press interest. *Wish List* is one of the prize-winning plays which speaks most directly and critically to its social and political moment. Its two strands, connected by the beautifully drawn character of Tamsin (played in the first production by Erin Doherty), interrogate the impacts of zero-hours contracts in austerity Britain, and the effects of changes to a benefits system that is already failing to adequately support Tamsin's brother Dean (played by Joseph Quinn). Lyn Gardner, writing in the *Guardian*, called it 'a quietly essential and moving play that makes us empathise with the lives of the desperate and the unseen', while Paul Taylor, in the *Independent*, praised Soper's ability to take a 'clear-eyed look at the interplay between two dehumanising systems' and to arouse 'due political indignation'. In 2015, the impacts of austerity politics were biting particularly hard. That the Oglesby family and Bruntwood maintained their commitment to supporting the arts throughout this period, and again during the Covid-19 pandemic, was a testament to their values which (particularly in the wake of the global financial crisis) seems particularly important.

Like Musgrave, Soper's route into playwriting was via an MA (at the Royal Central School of Speech and Drama). The prize led to the development of a co-production of *Wish List* between the Royal Exchange and the Royal Court, directed by Matthew Xia, in 2016. It was described as a 'smashing debut play' by Matt Wolf in the *International New York Times,* suggesting that the collaboration between Bruntwood and the Royal Exchange was registering in the theatre landscape beyond the UK. *Wish List* is a great example of how the Bruntwood Prize has provided opportunities for fostering professional relationships and providing a springboard for those with huge creative skill who don't yet have industry connections. In a similar vein, Kendall Feaver's working relationship with director Katy Rudd was forged through staging *The Almighty Sometimes* (Judges' Award winner, 2015), and the pair have since created a hugely successful adaptation of Noel Streatfield's *Ballet Shoes* at the National Theatre (2024).

International connections: *untitled f*ck m*ss s**gon play* by Kimber Lee

As the prize moved towards its fifteenth year, two new awards were added: the Original New Voice Award (which became the North West Original New Voice Award and Residency in 2022), and the International Award. This second award was won, in 2019, by New York-based playwright Kimber Lee, whose brilliantly satirical *untitled f*ck m*ss s**gon play* sets out to critique and explode decades upon decades of racist and sexist stereotypes of Asian women. Matt Barton, reviewing for the *Financial Times* described Roy Alexander Weise's 2023 co-production between the Royal Exchange, Factory International for the Manchester International Festival, the Young Vic, and Headlong, as 'a show that's like a lit stick of dynamite', while Claire Allfree called it a 'spoofy spiky brickbat' of a play in the *Telegraph*. The International Award of the prize involves a set of partnerships with a network of new-writing companies in the United States, Canada and Australia who invite playwrights from their development programmes to submit eligible work anonymously. Already, this is facilitating the introduction to the UK theatre scene and production of writers like Lee and Dave Harris, who received a commendation in 2019 for *Tambo & Bones* (produced by the Actors Touring Company and Stratford East). *untitled* is a great example of a piece which is tackling issues that play out across, and therefore need to be addressed in, multiple different cultural landscapes.

As the Bruntwood Prize has grown and developed over twenty years – in terms of the number of entries, range of satellite activities, types of awards, and its international reach – it has both connected to and embraced an international scope and vision, and recognised the globalised awareness of emerging writers, while remaining a distinctly Mancunian engine room for new writing with a commitment to its region. As Anya Ryan noted, it directly propels and nurtures an increasing number of writers' careers and supports the UK's new-writing theatre ecology. What's more, it increasingly connects with playwriting cultures in the English-speaking theatre world beyond the UK. The Bruntwood Prize is a call from Manchester to a national and international writing community, celebrating plays that are ambitious, bold and compellingly current.

Sarah Frankcom is an acclaimed director and dramaturg. After joining the Royal Exchange Theatre as Literary Manager, she created the Bruntwood Prize for Playwriting alongside the Oglesby family in 2005. Sarah was joint Artistic Director of the Royal Exchange Theatre from 2008–2013, and was sole Artistic Director from 2014–2019. She has directed extensively for the Exchange and in venues across the UK, including several world premieres of Bruntwood Prize-winning plays: *Pretend You Have Big Buildings*, *Winterlong* and *Three Birds*.

Rachel Clements is a lecturer in Drama, Theatre and Performance at the University of Manchester. She convened the MA Playwriting for its first three years, works closely with early-career playwrights, and has published widely on contemporary British theatre.

the bruntwood
prize for playwriting

in partnership with the **Royal Exchange Theatre**

A cross-sector partnership between the Royal Exchange Theatre, property company Bruntwood and the Oglesby Charitable Trust, the Bruntwood Prize is an opportunity for writers of any background and experience to enter unperformed plays to be judged by a panel of industry experts.

Since its inception in 2005 over 17,000 scripts have been entered, £344,000 has been awarded to thirty-eight prize-winning writers, and twenty-seven winning productions have been staged in venues across the UK. At the heart of the Bruntwood Prize for Playwriting is the principle that anyone can enter – through an entirely anonymous submissions process, scripts are judged purely based on the merit of the work alone and with no knowledge of the identity of the playwright.

Each winner enters into a development process with the Royal Exchange Theatre in an endeavour to bring their work to production. There have been co-productions with the Bush Theatre, Ellie Keel Productions, HighTide, Live Theatre, Lyric Hammersmith, Manchester International Festival, Mercury Theatre Colchester, Orange Tree Theatre, Paines Plough Theatre Company, Royal Court Theatre, Sherman Theatre, Soho Theatre and the Young Vic Theatre. Work has also gone on to be produced internationally from Australia, Canada, France, Germany, Sweden and the USA.

The Bruntwood Prize for Playwriting is a genuine endeavour to discover new stories and support playwright to develop their craft, providing everybody and anybody with the opportunity to explore their creativity and write a play. It offers a fantastic opportunity to hone your writing skills, whether or not you have written for the stage before.

writeaplay.co.uk

Manchester's Royal Exchange Theatre Company transforms the way people see theatre, each other and the world around them. Our historic building was taken over by artists in 1976, and today it is an award-winning cultural charity that produces new theatre in-the-round, in communities, on the road and online.

Exchange remains at the heart of everything we make and do. Our currency is brand new drama and reinvigorated classics, the boldest artists and a company of highly skilled makers – all brought together in an imaginative endeavour to share ideas and experiences with the people of Greater Manchester (and beyond).

The Exchange's unique auditorium is powerfully democratic, a space where audiences and performers meet as equals, entering and exiting through the same doors. It is the inspiration for all we do: inviting everyone to understand the past, engage in today's big questions, collectively imagine a better future, and lose themselves in the moment of a great night out.

In 2026 our iconic theatre celebrates fifty years of producing award-winning plays, creating work that is ambitious in ideas, form and scale right in the heart of Manchester's city centre.

royalexchange.co.uk

bruntwood

Bruntwood, including Bruntwood SciTech, is one of the UK's leading and largest property providers and developers, committed to creating thriving cities and town centres for almost fifty years.

Bruntwood and Bruntwood SciTech have over £1.8bn in assets and more than 100 properties across Greater Manchester, Cheshire, Leeds, Liverpool, Birmingham Cambridge and London.

They provide workspace, residential, retail and leisure space, including the independent shopping emporium, Afflecks in Manchester City Centre.

Focused on forming long-term, consultation-led partnerships to revitalise town centres, Bruntwood has a portfolio of town centre regeneration projects with Trafford and Bury Councils. Through a community-focused approach to regeneration, Bruntwood aims to ensure social, economic and environmental sustainability and to create vibrant places that are dynamic, inspirational and futureproof.

Since 2018, Bruntwood has had a joint venture in Bruntwood SciTech alongside Legal & General, and was joined by Greater Manchester Pension Fund in October 2023. Bruntwood SciTech is the UK's leading developer of city-wide innovation ecosystems and specialist environments helping companies – particularly those in the science, technology and innovation sectors – to form, scale and grow. It is also the largest dedicated property platform serving the growth of the UK's knowledge economy to become a global science and technology superpower.

Recognising the urgency of the climate crisis, Bruntwood is committed to a sustainable and fair future, and was the UK's first commercial property company to sign up to the UK Green

Building Council's Advancing Net Zero Programme. By 2030, Bruntwood's entire portfolio will operate at net zero carbon in the areas under its direct control and in the construction of new builds and major redevelopments, and will be a net zero business by 2050. As of 2024, both Bruntwood and Bruntwood SciTech's workspaces are powered 100% by renewable energy.

Bruntwood also actively collaborates with ambitious and ground-breaking arts and cultural organisations, in addition to supporting environmental, civic and charitable initiatives through the Oglesby Charitable Trust.

bruntwood.co.uk

The Oglesby Charitable Trust (OCT) is an independent grantmaking charity dedicated to creating thriving communities across the North of England.

Established in 2001 by the late Michael Oglesby CBE DL – founder of Bruntwood – and Jean Oglesby CBE, the Trust has since donated over £35 million, supporting organisations that deliver measurable impact in arts, education, health and social inequalities.

The organisation's Trustees – family members and professional advisors – have been passionate ambassadors of arts and culture since the Trust was founded, and believe that philanthropy has a major role to play in the future of the sector. They support work that focuses on broadening who engages with arts and culture – as learners, performers, artists and audiences – and on increasing the use of arts and culture for learning, personal development and, crucially, social change. Excellence in the arts requires, and drives, investment, and the OCT has long committed support to artists and work of the highest standard.

The financial capacity of the OCT comes from both the philanthropic generosity of the Trust's founders, as well as the success of Bruntwood.

oglesbycharitabletrust.org.uk

PRETEND YOU HAVE BIG BUILDINGS

Ben Musgrave

BEN MUSGRAVE

Ben Musgrave grew up in Bangladesh, India and Essex. He won first prize in the inaugural Bruntwood Prize for *Pretend You Have Big Buildings*, which premiered at the Royal Exchange Theatre, Manchester, as part of the 2007 Manchester International Festival. He was subsequently commissioned by the National Theatre. His play *Crushed Shells and Mud*, developed on attachment at the National Theatre Studio, opened at Southwark Playhouse, London, in 2015.

Other work includes *Exams Are Getting Easier* (Birmingham Rep); *His Teeth* (Only Connect), an Evening Standard and Time Out Critics' Choice, nominated for an OffWestEnd Award for Best New Play; *Politrix* (The Big House); *Across the Dark Water* (The Point, Eastleigh); and *Indigo Giant*, produced in Bangladesh in 2022 and on tour in the UK in 2024, where it was nominated for an OffWestEnd Award for Best New Play. He is currently working on a new stage adaptation of LP Hartley's *The Go-Between* with Eastern Angles.

For radio, his credits include *The British Club*; *The Last Missionary of Kanaipur* and *Vital Signs* (all BBC Radio 4). He is a Lecturer in Scriptwriting at the University of East Anglia, and his work has been supported by the Peggy Ramsay Foundation, the Royal Society of Literature, and the British Council.

Introduction
Ben Musgrave, 2025

I wrote *Pretend You Have Big Buildings* in 2004. I was doing an MA in Writing for Performance at Goldsmiths, where I had spent a year immersing myself in possibilities of how I might be as a writer – watching Pina Bausch videos, following hunches, coming to understand more about what had a charge for me (I wanted my work to be joyful and colourful and international).

I had grown up in Bangladesh and India, but returned to the UK in 1994, and ended up going to school in Romford, in Essex. This was a massive culture shock. Romford was not the England I had spent my childhood dreaming about, but there was also something fascinating and alive about it.

I spent a long time resisting writing about Romford – but one day I just started; and something flowed quickly and easily in a way that hadn't happened before. I had an instinct about a feeling I wanted to explore, something to do with the experience of moving between worlds, and the feeling of 'becoming yourself'. And I ran with that. And that became *Pretend You Have Big Buildings*.

About six months later, I'd sent the play around a bit, and it was getting nowhere, but I saw there was a new playwriting prize called the Bruntwood Prize being launched. I did another draft of the play, and I remember reading it on a National Express coach and thinking that the play still 'gave me that feeling'. I sent it to the competition.

Since I'd first written the play, I'd got a job with the literary department at the Birmingham Rep. It was amazing to work with writers every day, but I was barely doing any writing at all. Then, out of the blue, I got a phone call from Royal Exchange Associate Director Jo Combes telling me I'd been shortlisted for the prize. I decided to leave the Rep to focus on writing.

A few weeks later I was standing in front of a load of people, holding an impossibly heavy glass trophy, knees buckling, and it felt like the universe was supporting that decision to commit to writing. That was the first meaning of the prize.

Bruntwood really did change my life. It gave me my break – I was quickly given a studio commission by the National Theatre – but it also gave me an extraordinary first experience of playwriting as a wonderfully collaborative process – working with wise and brilliant theatremakers – not least Sarah Frankcom and Jo Combes – who nurtured me and mentored me through it, and many wonderful actors, including Jonathan Bailey, Sacha Dhawan, Shobna Gulati and Tanya Franks. During previews, the play felt precarious, but something remarkable happened on press night – the play became the world that had been inside my head, and also gave me that feeling – something to do with people becoming themselves – that resonated with me. And that was such a privilege.

Something else I want to say about the meaning of the prize. It's tempting to think of a prize like the Bruntwood as a miracle-making machine for lifting writers 'out of nowhere' – as if their work developed in complete isolation. I do think the Bruntwood Prize is a miracle, and the miracle is bringing to the light wonderful work that might not have found a life elsewhere.

Sometimes, no doubt, the work has developed in isolation, but more often I think the work of the winners, and the shortlist, and the longlist… has not developed in a vacuum. Often that work has been nourished all over the country by mentors, teachers, dramaturgs, actors, fellow writers – through workshops (not least the Bruntwood Roadshows and workshops themselves), or attachments, or writing programmes, or informal chats in the bar. I wrote *Big Buildings* on an MA programme, and twenty years later I now teach on the scriptwriting programme at the University of East Anglia. I've been proud to see our writers amongst the Bruntwood shortlists and winners over the years – and I love the day the Bruntwood shortlist comes out because it's so often a moment when writers who've been working at it a little while – and working with others for a while – get the break they deeply deserve. I want to celebrate the way that Bruntwood is now a (vital) part of a new-writing theatre ecology – an ecology that feels a little endangered at the moment but one that has often worked well, and changed lives. The astonishment that Bruntwood readers always express about the sheer quality of the submissions is a sign that across the country something is going right.

Pretend You Have Big Buildings was first performed at the Royal Exchange Theatre, Manchester, on 11 July 2007, with the following cast:

DANNY	Sacha Dhawan
LEON	Jonathan Bailey
RUKHSANA	Shobna Gulati
ROB	Steve North
KAREN	Tanya Franks
STEVEN	Billy Seymour
ANNIE	Susan Twist
Directors	Sarah Frankcom and Jo Combes
Designer	Jaimie Todd
Lighting Designer	David Holmes
Sound Designer	Ian Dickinson

Acknowledgements

Pretend You Have Big Buildings began life during my MA in Writing for Performance at Goldsmiths College in 2005, and I am indebted to the MA group: Eric Bland, Duncan Chalmers, Jodi Gray, Kenny Emson and Pip Mayo; to Deborah Paige, who conducted a fruitful initial workshop; and especially to John Ginman, whose expert dramaturgy guided the play to its first incarnation at BAC in July 2005. Later, Act One was staged by acting students from E15 at the Actors Centre in 2006, and I am very grateful to them (and to Caroline Eves and Abigail Gonda for the opportunity), but especially to Meriel Baistow-Clare, who directed the play, and whose work on the script set the scene for the next phase of development. I would like to thank the Dog House Group for their support, rigour and friendship: Robin Booth, Lucy Caldwell, Nick Harrop, Matt Morrison, Jennifer Tuckett, Paul Amman Brar. And many thanks also to those who have read and discussed the script with me: Steve King, Lucy Morrison, Ben Jancovich, Chris Hannan, Nicholas Hytner, Jenny Marshall, Billy Dosanjh.

Thanks to Alex Marshall and Mark Willingham for development of the Essexman routines. To Ioannis Iordanidis, Amanda Washbrook, and Alex Haughey for advice on motorbikes. To the late Jim Reed for technical support. To all at Havering Libraries, especially Simon Donaghue for introducing me to local history. To Skye Wheeler. To Nick Hern and all at Nick Hern Books. To Mel Kenyon. To my parents.

And of course to Bruntwood and the Royal Exchange, without whom none of this extraordinary business would have come about. Finally, and especially, to Jo Combes and Sarah Frankcom, whose exemplary stewardship of the play's development has brought the script on no end.

And – an update for 2025: to Selene Burn, who was such a wonderful person in my life before even 2007.

B.M.

Historical Note

Havering Council built the Dolphin, the swimming pool referred to by the characters, in the eighties. Its distinctive pyramidal roof – which looked a little like the top of Canary Wharf – was the most remarkable architectural feature of Romford town centre. When pieces of roof panelling began to fall off, the pool was closed down, and remained derelict for ten years. In 2003, the Dolphin was finally razed to the ground, and an enormous ASDA began to take shape.

Characters

DANNY, *fifteen, mixed heritage*
LEON, *fifteen, white, Essex*
RUKHSANA, *thirty-seven, Indian*
ROB, *forty, white, Essex*
KAREN, *forty, white, Essex*
STEVEN, *fifteen, white, Essex*
ANNIE, *forty-two, white, Essex*
Various recorded voices

Act One *takes place in November to mid-December 1995.*

Act Two *takes place in the hours after Act One.*

Notes on the Text

A new line indicates a new impulse of thought or speech, and may replace a comma.

A blank line within speech generally replaces a beat.

A forward slash [/] indicates the point at which the next designated speech begins.

Italics within speech indicate added emphasis (*except when in parentheses*, which indicate a stage direction).

However, speech within parentheses is generally to be regarded as internal – or at any rate exclusive of other characters in the scene.

ACT ONE: Canary Wharf

Scene One

An aeroplane.

RUKHSANA *and* DANNY, *side by side.*

DANNY *looks out of the window. He generally addresses the landscape.*

DANNY Hey, London

    RUKHSANA *holds a claret UK passport. She generally addresses the audience.*

RUKHSANA Look of this, this

DANNY (*To the landscape.*) Look at you
The light on the loop of the river

RUKHSANA And the embassy took his.
Yours. Yours. They took it away
I remember the picture but it's
Fading it's all dammed up in my head.

DANNY The Thames.

    The PILOT *makes an announcement.*

PILOT'S VOICE
    It's a bit chilly down on the ground, ladies and gents, about three degrees Celsius

RUKHSANA Oh my God.

PILOT'S VOICE
    And quite a strong north wind so / do

DANNY (*Imitating the* PILOT.)
'Do wrap up warm, ladies and gents.'
Do wrap up warm.
Or you won't know what's hit you.

    DANNY *looks out of the window.*

RUKHSANA   And there's a list of things I have to remember.
           Just to get us from the airport.
           Things about staying calm and being strong and
               not being offended by coldness

DANNY   And England.
           From the way you're looking
           From the sky over the coast so green… !
           I think you're going to be just right.

           A judder of violent turbulence. RUKHSANA
           reacts badly.

           Mum
           It's normal

RUKHSANA   We're falling?

DANNY   It's perfectly normal.
           He'll announce it. Like this:
           'Just a spot of turbulence, ladies and gentlemen'
           With his English voice.

PILOT'S VOICE
           Just entering a patch of turbulence there, ladies
               and gents, we should be clear shortly.

RUKHSANA   (*To the audience.*)
           I know where I'm going no more
           Than the poor bastards to my right.
           The wide-eyed family in their best clothes
           Who packed their lunch in Bombay
           And eat it with their hands.

           The lights flicker out. The plane is landing.

DANNY   Hold my hand

RUKHSANA   Are we landing?

DANNY   Yes. We're landing.

           She holds his hand. The plane touches down.

RUKHSANA   And this family
           They will have relations waiting
           Seven little cousins

Waving
Miraculous placards
And I have no placard.
Only this strange son
Who's dreamed of this day for fifteen years.
Who thinks he knows
How to hail a taxi.

ROB *stands by the Canary Wharf Tower. By his car. A smart suit. He speaks as if to a companion.*

ROB I tell you
I can't take my eyes off that!
And by Christmas they reckon all the office space will be taken
And all the lights turned on again.
The company's just moved the HQ right up there.
And they got all of us supervisors, the white-collars and that, they brought us all in to talk about the future.
They ask me what I think of the new locale.
I say, (*A joke.*) 'Well it's not small'
They laugh
(*A cheeky smile.*) 'It's not small'
This bloke says: 'D'you know how big it is?'
'No.'
'It's taller than the Telecom Tower.
It's taller than the *Natwest* Tower.'
(*A cheeky nonchalance.*) 'Oh yeah?'
'It's the *tallest* structure in the *country*.'
(*Coolly.*) 'Oh yeah?'
Nice and cool. Don't give it away. Don't give nothing away.
'Fucking stupid name for a tower,' I proceed, 'Canary Wharf'.

RUKHSANA *and* DANNY *are now in a taxi zooming east. They gaze out of the window.*

DANNY Look at it.

RUKHSANA	And the roads are smooth here, Danny, you'll notice that and nobody uses their horn so the roads are quiet and
DANNY	It's
RUKHSANA	And at this stage of a city it always looks like this
DANNY	Concrete and pebbledash
ROB	Course I was burning ta say 'I was born two minutes walk away from here.' I was actually born *two minutes* away from the *tallest* structure in the *country*.
RUKHSANA	Look at that!

It is Canary Wharf. DANNY *is impressed.*

DANNY	Is it near here?
RUKHSANA	Maybe.
DANNY	I hope it's near here.

ROB *is still at Canary Wharf.*

ROB	And our house. All gone. Wiped away. Pwwwhhht. And up comes this fackin (*Tower.*) This I mean I'm not a socialist I'm not sayin I mean it sure as fuck's an improvement but what I wanna know is Who's been made the mug in all this?

Relax. He gets his keys out and zaps the remote locking system. The car makes its unlocking sound and light. He gets in.

Remote central-locking.

He puts on a pair of chamois gloves, and some driving glasses.

He shuts the door.

PRETEND YOU HAVE BIG BUILDINGS 13

	Electric Windows.
	He puts on some music, which continues to the end of the scene.
	CD player, as standard.
	On the passenger seat is a bag from an expensive shopping boutique.
	And something for the lady.
	Ignition. His car growls into life. He zooms off.
DANNY	Is this right?
RUKHSANA	What?
DANNY	(*To the taxi driver.*) Excuse me.
RUKHSANA	Relax.
DANNY	Excuse me, we've moved past the centre. That sign that green sign It says we're headed east. Excuse me.
	ROB *is driving east. He loosens his tie.*
ROB	Royal Hospital on the right. St Clem's. Where Leon was born. Which was just before (*A complicated manoeuvre.*) Excuse me It's a 'mare this. Just before we moved out to Romford. Nah, it weren't too bad growing up in the East End. It was a good community spirit. But, er Well things change, don't they? The people change.
	Something up on the road.
	Here we go… (*To an errant motorist.*) Come on, mate. Are you going?

YOU GONNA BE A PRAT ALL YER LIFE?
Well GO then!
Dickhead fucking dickhead.

ROB beeps his horn. He can't take it any more.

This isn't the fucking day for this.

DANNY   I don't believe it. Did you know?

RUKHSANA   No.

DANNY   He said

RUKHSANA   He never showed me!

DANNY   He said it is always warmer, it is always warmer in the centre of the city.

ROB is now at Forest Gate.

ROB   West Ham down there.
Funnily enough. Funnily enough
You do not see a white face round there except on a match day.

RUKHSANA   Never showed me any of this.

ROB   I don't have a problem. That was how I was raised.

The taxi screeches to a halt at the lights.

DANNY   And after all he said

ROB   And there is a moment.

DANNY   After all those stories

ROB   And we're coming up to it. Just past the tollgate.
Just after the point where the London Road meets Whalebone Lane:
A farm.
A strip of countryside that stretches north to south.
It's the end of London. And this is Romford.

RUKHSANA   This is what you are.

ROB	It don't last long
	LEON *enters. The Dolphin appears, a pyramidal structure housing a broken-down swimming pool. He speaks directly to the audience.*
LEON	But just pretend
ROB	The roundabouts, the ring road, the swimming pool they built and closed down.
LEON	Just pretend you havvem
ROB	This is it.
LEON	That you got the big buildings that make you proud.
ROB	This is where we moved. This is where we can breathe. Raise a family.
	ROB *stops his car, and gets out.*
LEON	Just lie. Just dream. It don't matter. Fuckin pretend it One day, in nineteen ninety-five, it came out that shithole swimming pool. That broken down swimming pool they called the Dolphin That pyramid they built and closed down. It burst outta there. Like you know one of those fairy-tale oak trees: Romford Castle Like someone had wished it, you know? Pretend Just pretend. There's no harm I swear That it cracked through dirty glass, asbestos, corrugated steel. Romford Castle Cutting off the ring road. This massive tower and a moat that joined the river Lovely.

Our own
Proper
Fuck-off
Castle.

Scene Two

Man and Boy

LEON *and* ROB. *The living room of* ROB*'s house. They are both nervous.*

ROB   Where's your mother?

LEON   She's out.
             With friends, she said. She won't be long.

ROB   She alright today, is she?

LEON   Yeah.

ROB   She okay?

LEON   Oh yeah, she was chattin away.
             No problem.

ROB   She had her tea?

LEON   Sort of.

ROB   Here we go.

LEON   Nah – I put cheese 'n' ham toast on, right?

ROB   Oh no.

LEON   For her birthday!

ROB   I thought I could smell something burnin.

LEON   Dint burn too bad.

ROB   What are you two like?

LEON   (*Over-defensive.*) What have I done?

ROB   Nothing.

Beat.

LEON	What's that, then? (*In the bag.*)
ROB	For her birthday.

He pulls an expensive dress from the bag.

It's what she wanted.

LEON	Let's have a look then?

LEON *examines it.*

No, it's nice. It's nice.

ROB	So you gonna behave yerself tonight?
LEON	Course I am.
ROB	Pictures with Steven?
LEON	Yeah.
ROB	Because your mum and me, we're going out tonight.
LEON	I know.
ROB	I don't want a repeat of last time.
LEON	Shut up, man.
ROB	*Don't* / you
LEON	Just / leave it
ROB	Tell me / what to say
LEON	So are they gonna sack you all then?
ROB	Oh fuckssake, Leon Don't ask me don't ask me.
LEON	What did you tell them?
ROB	Ar
LEON	Well?
ROB	(*Explodes.*) I told those wankers Head-office papershufflers.

	I said 'We shouldn't even be discussing this. It's ridiculous we're even discussing this.'
LEON	That's right!
ROB	'And it's not just us who gets fucked if we take the package. There's hundreds who'll lose their jobs if we give way. You know – black *and* white. And not just the boys on the floor. The whole supply chain.'
LEON	That's right.
ROB	It's all joined up. This bloke Nathaniel come in. Brown-skinned, but you can tell he's money. 'You take redundancy now, it'll be easier in the long term. We could lay before you some very interesting offers.' I say, 'How long have you been in this country, Nathaniel?' Coz I I gave this *company* twenty years of my life.' He turns to me. Looks me right in the eyes. Smiles. 'We've already structured very attractive terms For those in long service Who voluntarily accept the redundancy package.' But then the union guys take over and we just have to sit there. And Nathaniel comes back. 'Gents… do you want the good news or the bad news?' *Pause. Okay.* 'We're not going to make anyone redundant, for the moment.'
LEON	Fuckin A!

ROB	And we're nearly jumpin up an down, Lee, we think we're laughin then he goes 'Here's the bad news.'

                        Four-day week. Even supervisors.

                        No more overtime.

                        We're taking a pay cut.
                        We had to sign it.

                        I ain't gonna let it go, Lee!
                        This is your job in three, four years' time.
                        If we can just hang on, fings'll perk up.
                        This is your future. I want you
                        To have a future.

                        They don't hug.

Scene Three

Hot Water

That evening. A lounge/kitchen, Romford, in darkness. ANNIE, DANNY's *aunt, is showing* RUKHSANA *and* DANNY *the house.* ANNIE *wears motorbike leathers, and has placed her helmet close by her. There is a basin in the room, a trunk and a few other packing boxes lying around.*

ANNIE *slowly increases the intensity of the light.*

ANNIE	That's the dimmer switch there. That lets you change the brightness. He was good with wires that much I'll say for him. He did it all when he was seventeen. Rigged it all up. Saved her a fortune.

                        Well, don't just stand there, come in.
                        But mind out for the boxes.
                        It's just old stuff I'll be getting rid of it.

                        ANNIE *turns the tap on. High pressure.*

                        Hot.

RUKHSANA *runs her hand under.*

RUKHSANA Very hot!

ANNIE Bet you didn't have hot water where you was from?

DANNY There was

RUKHSANA In some places.

DANNY In most places.

RUKHSANA I'm looking forward to a bath!

ANNIE *jams the tap off.*

I always liked a good English bath!

ANNIE Do you speak Indian, then, Danny?

RUKHSANA Not much.

ANNIE Did you not teach him it?

RUKHSANA Everyone spoke English.

ANNIE That's funny coz the Indians in Forest Gate, they don't speak it.

I never understood why Simon took off in the first place. Globetrotting.
Fine. It's different. It's hot. Or it's cold. New food. New drink.
But I coulda told you something shit like this would happen.
I coulda told you that for nothing.

Most of the time we don't even know what country you're in.
Mum's on her deathbed, I can't reach him for weeks.

(*To* DANNY.)
Did you even know your dad had a sister?

(*To* RUKHSANA.)
Did *you* cut Danny off from *your* family as well?

Did you take him to see *them*?

(*Realising.*) Oh…
You didn't, did you?

What did you think about that, Danny?

I mean I couldn't understand it. This was my
   brother.
My nephew and I never see him. That's not
   right, is it?
What a bastard he was.

RUKHSANA You made your views plain

ANNIE You weren't there.

RUKHSANA What you stood for.

ANNIE You weren't there what was *so wrong* with
   what I stood for?
No tell me.
What was so wrong? I was his sister, he didn't
   have to hate me!
We would call him up at university he'd change
   his voice, pretend he was someone else.
He was a bastard.

DANNY Get lost.

ANNIE (*To* RUKHSANA.)
You got a right little Mogul here, don'tcha?

Simon, he come to see Mum once in fifteen
   years.
He don't even come back for the funeral.
Oh he was a triffic son, he was a wonderful son
   f'r 'er.
Still, Mum gives him the house.
'He was better than us,' that's what she said
'He went off to make the world a better place.'
If you was better than us, why the fuck should
   you wanna come back?
What can we offer you?

You gonna be claiming?
Is that why?

	I would, in your position. Coz I bet he didn't leave you much. Did he? What did he leave ya?
	Still you gotta look after your own, don't you?
	She tosses RUKHSANA *the key.*
	I contacted a school. Well somebody had to. In this country it's the law to go to school. It's not too rough.
DANNY	We won't be here long.
ANNIE	Oh won'tcha?
RUKHSANA	No, we won't be here long at all.
DANNY	We know where we're not welcome.
ANNIE	I didn't say that. Did I?
	ANNIE *points to a plastic shopping bag.*
	I got some groceries. Happy Shopper It's round the corner. Patel's. (*Defensively.*) Nice people, you know? I didn't have a problem. I try to help you. Do my duty. Would you say I haven't tried to help you here?
RUKHSANA	He's dead.
	Beat. ANNIE *picks up her helmet, gently.*
ANNIE	Yeah. Yeah, I know.
	Goodbye, Danny. You got my number.
	You give me a call, yeah? If she can't hack it.
	DANNY *is silent.* ANNIE *exits.*

DANNY	I should have smacked her the way she spoke to you.
RUKHSANA	Yes!
DANNY	A right hook.
RUKHSANA	In the teeth.
DANNY	Put your dukes up, lady!
RUKHSANA	Ha!

Something shifts in RUKHSANA. *A downturn.*

Oh God.

DANNY	Sit down. It's okay. Go on. I'll make us a cup of tea.
RUKHSANA	No.
DANNY	Oh Mum.
RUKHSANA	No tea.
DANNY	Mum.
RUKHSANA	It's nothing.
DANNY	You were doing really well today. (*Imitating* ANNIE.) 'I'll tell ya something for naffing'
RUKHSANA	Ha!
DANNY	'Do you speak Indian then, Danny?'
RUKHSANA	No comedy show!
DANNY	'I'll tell you something for nothing.'
RUKHSANA	Your voices!
DANNY	'I'm telling ya, he was a bastard.'
RUKHSANA	Language.
DANNY	Dad wasn't a bit like her, was he?
RUKHSANA	No.

DANNY   When you first met him?

RUKHSANA   No.

DANNY   Why did we not hear about her?

RUKHSANA   She made her views plain.

DANNY   And your parents?
                 Why did we come back?

RUKHSANA   You always wanted to come back!
                 You remember in India
                 The hassling dirty boys
                 Running alongside you, asking you

DANNY   (*In an Indian accent.*) 'What country?'

RUKHSANA   'What country?'

DANNY   England!

RUKHSANA   'Englan!'

DANNY   Englan!

RUKHSANA   Manchester United!

DANNY   *West Ham* United!

RUKHSANA   Gary Lineker!

DANNY   Why *did* we come here?

                 Beat.

RUKHSANA   Because you educate your children in England.
                 To do otherwise would sabotage your future.
                 Everyone knows that in the end you head to
                    England.

DANNY   I don't think this is what they meant.

RUKHSANA   You remember that time in Bombay.
                 That awful hotel.
                 Before we found our apartment.
                 You turned the tap and it ran red.

DANNY   The pipes were rusty.

RUKHSANA   You thought it was blood.

DANNY	I know now. The pipes were rusty.
RUKHSANA	Remember how scared you were. But this is England.
	Here we don't have to worry about anything. Things not working or malaria pills or power cuts.
DANNY	Or roads.
RUKHSANA	*Danny please!*
DANNY	There aren't any roads in England.
RUKHSANA	*Please.*
DANNY	This isn't what he said it was like.
RUKHSANA	I KNOW THIS ISN'T WHAT HE SAID.
	Beat.
DANNY	All this stuff. Here. There must be something interesting.
RUKHSANA	Don't.
DANNY	Years and years old.
RUKHSANA	Don't open it.
DANNY	And not just… Grandma's
RUKHSANA	Danny!
	DANNY *opens up the trunk.*
	You don't know what you'll find. Please.
	DANNY *pulls out, slowly, a motorcyclist's helmet. A motorcyclist's jacket.*
	RUKHSANA *is sick in the basin.* DANNY *is forced to hold her.*
DANNY	I'll clean you up.
RUKHSANA	Don't creep / around me, Danny!
	She moves to the motorcyclist's suit. She holds it. She barely listens to DANNY.

DANNY   Tomorrow.
            We'll start looking for somewhere else.
            We'll sell this place.
            Move further in.
            Mum?
            It's going to be great.
            Tomorrow, we'll get the newspapers.
            The *London Times*.
            The *Manchester Guardian*.
            Start looking for a job.
            We'll make up your CV:
            University of Sheffield, BA.

            Mum?

            Marketing manager.
            High-level.
            International.
            A big glass office.
            When India went international.

            Tomorrow. Do you promise me?

            You've been like this for weeks
            But we're here now.
            No more waiting.
            You promised everything would be
                transformed.
            As soon as we got here.
            Are you listening to me?

            Beat.

RUKHSANA   Will you leave me for a little bit?

            Please. Go out. Explore the territory.

DANNY   You promised you were going to try.

RUKHSANA   Yes. Tomorrow. Yes.

            She doesn't kiss him.

            DANNY *exits.* RUKHSANA *watches him leave, goes over to the bike helmet and stares it in the eye. She holds the suit.*

PRETEND YOU HAVE BIG BUILDINGS 27

It's you, isn't it?
It's you.

You bastard
You won't even show your face.

You never said you had a motorbike!

There is no reply. She examines the jacket, which has little round subversive badges on it.

These little badges.
Southend. 1977.

You never told me, any of this!

She flings the helmet back into the trunk.

Did I ever know you?

She flings the suit back in the trunk. Shuts it.

She tries to exit, but the dimmer switch is at her eyeline. She stops. She lovingly reduces the light. Until it's all off.

Scene Four

The Pink Room

Later that evening. A master bedroom full of soft pink light and sleep. Hanging from the ceiling is an open clothes rack packed to bursting with women's clothes. To one side, a lady's dresser, packed with cosmetics.

LEON *speaks to the audience.*

LEON   Pretend

He smears dark foundation on his face.

There's no harm in this
You like the feel of it.
So let them go out, the old boy, the old gel

Let them patch things up again.
And creep upstairs when the door slams.
Scan the master bedroom.

He did this place up for her
New curtains
Bamboo bedposts
Winnie-the-Pooh footrug.
'When he did that room up,' she says, 'I fell in love wiv him all over again.'

He takes his shirt off.

So just pretend
You've got all your life ahead of you
All of the future.
Choices.
You could fall in love
You could have kids
You could earn a million.
You could work in a car factory all yer life, there's all to play for.

He applies eyeliner in an impressionist style.

There's no harm. There's no trouble. It's alright.

He opens one of his mother's dresser drawers.

The soft of lacies
Just try em on, for size, like, and *don't worry.*

Underwear falls from the sky into this room.

A lace slip descends from the ceiling. LEON *awaits it.*

Blackout. Time briefly passes, then...

LEON *is wearing the slip, and* ROB, *holding* LEON's *collar, has just swept* LEON's *face, smeared in mud pack, across the dresser.* LEON *has also wet himself, although this isn't clear to* ROB *yet, partly because* LEON *disguises it. Both* ROB, *and* LEON's *mum,* KAREN, *are somewhat undressed.* KAREN *was wearing the dress that* ROB *bought for her a few scenes ago.* ROB *has his shirt undone.*

LEON	Aaaahhhh
ROB	Fackin
LEON	(And they think there's nobody home and they go for it)
ROB	Fackin
LEON	(And it just streams out)
ROB	Want me to put yer face to bed, do ya?
LEON	(Warm and I can't control it.)
ROB	Are you a girl?
LEON	No!
ROB	Putting your face on for a night on the town?
KAREN	ROB!
ROB	There are many things my son could have been There are many things *my son*
KAREN	LEEEVE him
LEON	(And I can see your argument, Dad, in all its clarity and you've got some rock-hard good points in there and I respect that I respect that, Dad)
KAREN	LEEEEVE him, Robert.
LEON	(And though my soul is flingin round the tumble-dryer)
ROB	It's not fuckin right, Kazza.
KAREN	It's
ROB	Not bleedin
KAREN	It's alright
ROB	We know he's a prat. We know he's a fuckin disaster zone. And now it turns out

KAREN	It's
ROB	He's a fackin queer.
KAREN	It's alright!
LEON	Not a queer!
ROB	Are you sayin that's alright, Karen?
LEON	No, it's not alright It wouldn't be.
	Mum, it's not fucking alright, is it?
ROB	Looks like an Asian Boy-George poofta.
	This is who we saved up for, Karen This is who we moved out for. This is our facking son. Disrespecting your beautiful things
KAREN	You're angry, Rob. I can see that.
	Yeah, course he is.
	Leave him to me, lover.
ROB	I just don't understand it
KAREN	I don't blame you, precious
ROB	I don't want him going wrong, that's all
KAREN	We're havin a hard time. He needs a woman's touch, Rob.
ROB	I'd say he's already had that!
LEON	No. Dad.
	ROB *notices* LEON*'s wet patch.*
ROB	Oh God, will you look at him?
KAREN	What?
ROB	He's only gone and
	LEON *scrambles to cover himself up.*
	I do not believe it.

KAREN	What?
ROB	He's
KAREN	Oh
	Leave him to me, Rob.
ROB	It was gonna be a good night.
KAREN	It was a good night.
ROB	Yeah?
KAREN	So don't spoil it then. Off you go.
	ROB *exits*.
	Oh it's alright, sweetheart.
	Why you goin putting on my things? Funny bunny. So which one's ya favourite?
LEON	What?
KAREN	Couldn't resist it. (*The joke*.) Ah, you've got it all smudged! (*The make-up*.)
LEON	Ah, shut up, Mum.
KAREN	You look very cosmopolitan.
	Thank God we noticed you in time, ay?
LEON	Fuck this for a laugh.
	He makes to go.
KAREN	No, don't leave me, babe. Come back. I don't know what to do, Lee.
	He comes back.
	Don't leave me.
LEON	I'm not
KAREN	Come here. Give us a cuddle.

He does.

You're alright.
You don't need to worry bout being a bit

She whistles.

These days.
This is 1995
You can be whoever you wanna be.

LEON   I *don't*.

KAREN   I reckon there's nuffin to be ashamed about.

LEON   I ain't.

KAREN   Fings are difficult between yer dad and me, Lee.
Fings ain't right.
Look at this (*The dress.*) he bought for me birthday.
It's nice, ay?

Beat.

LEON   You gonna stay?

KAREN   Course I'll stay, darlin.
I ain't leaving you.

I promise.

Scene Five

Chips

The railings by the Dolphin, overlooking Romford Market.

DANNY *enters.*

DANNY   Hey, Dad
I've caught the smell of it.
Of England in the rain.
The English countryside.

It's distant but it's here.
And when we struck that deal.
For the one holiday we ever had here.
You got nature.
Hills
Chalk formations
Forests
Limestone caves.
And I got football and fish and chips.
So we're on some country road
And stop off at a village
Some place with a green
And have a kickabout.
And do commentaries
In the voice of Kenneth Wolstenholme.
Do stupid voices from black-and-white comedy.

(*In a Pathé news accent.*) 'Put your dukes up, sonny,'
Charge me to the ground.
'You're asking for a bunch of fives,'
And I've ruined my jeans, and you don't care.
But Mum's angry.
So we get sent off to buy our national dish
Fish and chips
Vinegar steaming
Park bench soggy
Used to love that.
So she sends me off now, just like old times.
Fish and chips
Like it'll make it all worth it.
And I know
I'll end up with both portions.

DANNY *exits to obtain chips.*

STEVEN *and* LEON *enter.* STEVEN *is in the middle of some philosophising.*

STEVEN I reckon she can take it or leave it
I mean, granted
There'll always be a small no-go period in any relationship.

LEON   That's right.

STEVEN   But there comes a time
               I mean I told her, 'I *want* to wait.'
               I tell her, 'I love you, Amy
               You know I respect ya.
               Committed to ya.'

               What you looking so miserable, Lee?

LEON   I ain't, mate – pleased for / ya.

STEVEN   Obviously, there are steps on the proverbial ladder.

LEON   What's that then?

STEVEN   I mean there are small vict'ries.
               One day you kiss her.
               One day you accidentally touch her bra.
               And once you're that far –

               (Noticing LEON*'s glumness.)* WHAT?

LEON   Nah fair play to ya.

STEVEN   And one day, once you're that far
               You say
               'Amy – what do *you* think?
               I think it's time we took our relationship to a *deeper* level?'

LEON   'Would you like to make love?'

STEVEN   Fuck off 'make love'.

LEON   You said you loved her!

STEVEN   Yeah?

LEON   Did you mean it?

               STEVEN *remembers something.*

STEVEN   If you ever tell her, I swear.

LEON   What?

STEVEN   If that's what you're getting at.

LEON	Oh no – in the past, mate, in the past. That was We were slaughtered and that was nothing anyway and anyway it was an accident. And anyway you gotta try everything once.
STEVEN	(*Breaking in.*) You what?
LEON	Nah, not everything! Point taken. I'm gonna do Jenny Tyler, aren't I?
STEVEN	Oh yeah?
LEON	Yeah.
STEVEN	You reckon?
LEON	If she'll have me.
	LEON *spots a car to change the subject.* Look at that That's criminal. Fuckin Datsun Datsun Sunny. Fuckin crap.
STEVEN	That's a Skoda
LEON	It's a Datsun. I know my cars.
STEVEN	You ain't got a fuckin clue, mate. You ain't got much of a clue bout nothing, actually.
LEON	Genus 2.1, you can tell by the hubcaps
STEVEN	Hubcaps my arse, it's a fuckin Skoda. *End of.* I can't wait till I get me motor. Here y'are – have a look at these *He takes out a bunch of keys.* Spare keys to the Cortina. Me dad's getting the Mondeo, innee? Metallic paint. Power steering Well, that's if it all don't fall apart. Things are touch and go, they say.

LEON	Oh no. It's sorted. I swear.
STEVEN	They won't get rid of the Asians. That's what my dad says.
LEON	They ain't laying nobody off.
STEVEN	Political correctness.
LEON	What's that then?
STEVEN	Speed humps in the brain.
LEON	My dad *told em.* Them upstairs. He fuckin He fuckin kicked them up the arse, mate.
STEVEN	The Cortina's mine when I pass me test. Pass me test first time, I will. Me dad's taking me down Rainham at Christmas. It's really quiet down there. He's gonna show me how to get the bite. I reckon I'll be alright at driving. I'll do the circuit. Steve-mobile bombing it round Romford Amy givin it (*He mimes fellatio.*)
LEON	You're fifteen
STEVEN	So?
LEON	You got two years, mate.
STEVEN	Yeah?
LEON	I might get a moped next birthday…
STEVEN	Yeah?
	LEON *has forgotten that he is richer.*
LEON	You coming out tonight?
STEVEN	Nah, mate. Amy.
	LEON*'s glum again.*
	WHAT IS IT?

LEON	What did I do?
STEVEN	Moping around.
LEON	Well, there's fuck all to do on me own, int there?
STEVEN	You should get a girl then. Or boy.
LEON	Fuck off.
STEVEN	Stay in then. Watch TV like normal people. Course – you're not allowed to stay in, are ya? You'll start putting ya fingers in plug sockets.
LEON	No.
STEVEN	Havin little accidents, burnin teatowels, pourin boilin water on yer arms.
LEON	Fuck off.
STEVEN	Pissing on the floor.
LEON	I did not piss on the floor.
STEVEN	What was goin through your mind as all your piss pissed over that carpet?
LEON	Shut up.
STEVEN	I couldn't believe it.
LEON	Someone spiked my drink.
STEVEN	Oh yeah?
LEON	Wish I'd never told ya. Thought you'd find it funny.
STEVEN	I did find it funny.
	Beat. LEON *kicks the air.*
LEON	If my dad asks you where I was, say I was with you, yeah?
	Beat.
STEVEN	I'll say we was at the pictures. Braveheart.

LEON	Yeah… say that…
	Thunder.
STEVEN	Ar, bollocks It don't never stop raining
LEON	That's Romford, though. Old, this market. Smell of it. It's old. Cobbles. It's good. Do you ever get that, Steve? This wacko fuckin feeling something's gone on here? In this marketplace, you know? You know Like the Battle of Agincourt?
STEVEN	What?
LEON	The Battle of Hastings Some big fuck-off historical The Battle of Waterloo. Could of done. Just sayin.
STEVEN	You're such a bender, Leon.
LEON	Leave it fuckin out, Steve.
	Thunder and lightning. DANNY *enters with a bags of chips, defiant at the sky.*
	LEON *spots* DANNY.
	Oi!
	DANNY *faces them.*
	Is it alright if I ponce a chip, mate?
	Is it alright if I ponce a chip, mate?
	What you so scared of? I only want a fuckin chip.
STEVEN	(*An 'Indian' accent.*) 'You speak English?'
DANNY	Have one.
	He unravels the packet. LEON *takes a chip.*

LEON	Did you think I was gonna hit you?
DANNY	No.
LEON	Yeah, well I might have done.
STEVEN	Where you from, then?
	Pause.
DANNY	London.
STEVEN	Where?
DANNY	Here.
LEON	London ain't here.
DANNY	(*To* STEVEN, *of a chip.*) You can have one too if you want.
STEVEN	Don't want a chip, mate.
DANNY	Sorry?
STEVEN	What you saying sorry for?
DANNY	What, mate?
STEVEN	What you saying 'mate' for, I ain't your mate? And I don't like Paki smelly Arab curry shit on top of chips. Greasy stink, like.
DANNY	Just salt and vinegar.
STEVEN	What's wrong with you? *A glance at* DANNY*'s outfit.* Hi-Tecs, trousers with creases, where did you get this shit? And you're posh
LEON	He ain't half posh.
STEVEN	He is marbles-in-his-mouth posh. Still (*In a posh voice.*) 'Pleased to meet you.'
DANNY	Yeah, pleased to meet you.

STEVEN	(*In a posh voice.*) 'I'd like to shake you by the hand'
	LEON *creases up.*
DANNY	Yeah?
STEVEN	Yeah.
	STEVEN *reaches out his hand to shake* DANNY's *hand.* DANNY *moves to reciprocate, but at the moment of contact* STEVEN *flashes it up instead, smoothing his hair.*
	Aaaaaaaaah.
	Beat.
LEON	Where are you from then?
DANNY	England.
	STEVEN *semi-lunges, not making or intending to make contact.* DANNY *is frightened.*
STEVEN	You ought to watch yourself. England! Who d'you think you are? I mean – take it from me
LEON	Go on, mate Say something posh.
DANNY	Get lost.
LEON	Ha ha! 'Get lost' Go on, say something else! I like that, y'know? Posh voices.
STEVEN	What?
DANNY	What do you want me to say?
LEON	Anything, mate.
STEVEN	Nonce.
DANNY	I can do, er
LEON	Don't matter what, mate.
STEVEN	He's winding me up now.

DANNY	'Put your dukes up, sonny'
STEVEN	What?
DANNY	'You're asking for a bunch of fives.'
	'Haven't you ever heard, never hit a man with spectacles.'
	STEVEN *wallops* DANNY *in the stomach, then himself doubles up in pain.*
STEVEN	Owwww
DANNY	What was that for?
STEVEN	Owww. Fuck. Fuckin hurt me hand.
DANNY	What did you bloody do that for?
STEVEN	Hit him, Lee. Go on. Hit 'im.
	LEON *thinks, then gets* DANNY, *even harder, in the face, knocking him to the floor.* DANNY's *been really hurt. His eye is kind of bleeding.*
	Come on, Lee.
	STEVEN *exits.*
	LEON *bends down.*
LEON	I didn't mean to do that. I didn't mean to hit so hard and Jesus you're bleeding.
	He touches DANNY's *cheek, but* DANNY *whips it away.*
	Sorry!
	Poor fucking thing with shit clothes!
	Listen Mate You wanna come over to mine?
DANNY	What? No!

LEON	Get it cleared up? It's close.

Beat. STEVEN *reappears.*

STEVEN	Leon, you bender!
LEON	I just needed to hit something. That's all.

DANNY *gets up, faces* LEON, *and exits.*
STEVEN *exits in the opposite direction.* LEON *speaks to* DANNY's *disappearing figure.*

So listen, the bruises don't last long.
And the cuts close up.
I should know coz I've had em.
I'm really sorry
But you don't wanna walk around with an eye like that.
So now it's done
This is what you have to do:
Sweep indoors without no one seeing
Lock yourself in the loo
And what you need is some foundation.
Your mum should have some.
Match it to the colour of your skin.
You should cake it on, too
And if you can't find that
Then Clearasil will do.

Scene Six

The Motorcyclist

RUKHSANA's *house.* RUKHSANA, *by the trunk. Out of which she pulls the motorcyclist's leathers, and hangs them, man-shaped, on a rack. She finds the helmet, placing it on top, for a head. She gazes at it. This is 'the motorcyclist'.*

She continues to search in the trunk. She pulls out a little tin of tobacco. She registers it.

RUKHSANA For your roll-ups

> *She opens it. Some ancient rolling papers and the rest – she blows – is dust.*

Gone to dust
But I could smell it on your breath when you
    took it up again
The shock of not knowing you
The smell on your breath
And when you bought that bike
It was me who felt betrayed.

I can explain everything. As you rode across the
    city I was prepared to
Tell you everything.
But how can I now?

The phone rings. She freezes. It continues to ring.

I won't pick up the phone till
Till we
Get this straight…

The phone stops ringing. It goes to answerphone.

DANNY *comes out of his bedroom, wearing a white school shirt, blazer and trousers. He is listening to his Walkman.*

DANNY You didn't pick up the phone?

He checks the machine.

There's a message

RUKHSANA What's on the Walkman?

DANNY Tapes.

RUKHSANA What's on them?

DANNY Hindi language.

44   BRUNTWOOD AT 20

RUKHSANA   In Bombay you could have had lessons.

DANNY   You didn't seem fussed.

RUKHSANA   I could have taught you.

DANNY   You were busy.

> DANNY *plays the message. It is, coincidentally,* KAREN.

KAREN   Y'hello, Mrs Parrish? My name's Karen. I'm calling from Anderson Leigh – you applied for a position with us, the Marketing Officer? Yeah, I'm just calling to say we'd like to meet you to talk about the position and any questions you might have? Congratulations! I'm Mr Leigh's PA, so

> RUKHSANA *turns the tape off.*

RUKHSANA   I haven't applied for any jobs

DANNY   No you haven't.

RUKHSANA   Did / you

DANNY   You did a job like this in India.

RUKHSANA   In *India*, / yes

DANNY   You didn't stop going on about it, drove us all crazy.
Everything you said though

RUKHSANA   Did you *make an application*?

DANNY   I made you out really good!
I said you were in the thick of it.
When India went international.
When all the phones started ringing.
All those words.
Glass offices. Corporate functions.
    Conferences. Solutions.
The twenty-first century.

RUKHSANA   What if I had picked up the phone?

DANNY   I would have done your voice.

RUKHSANA	You can't do my voice.
DANNY	I fooled your secretary.
RUKHSANA	Since then your voice has broken fast.

Beat.

DANNY	You promised you were going to try.
RUKHSANA	You tried on your school uniform.
DANNY	So you change the subject?
RUKHSANA	Let's have a look.

She tries to arrange the school tie around his neck.

I'll show you how to do the knot.

DANNY	I can do the knot.
RUKHSANA	I think it's a good school.
DANNY	You haven't seen it.
RUKHSANA	I read the booklet.
DANNY	I've seen it. It's a giant piece of concrete. All the boys have their heads shaved. Like the whole school's been infected with lice. You said I had to come back here for my *education*. It's no good, Mum – all this stuff – all these curtains closed – how's that gonna help?
RUKHSANA	You'll make friends.
DANNY	It's not about friends
RUKHSANA	And all the girls will be after you.
DANNY	Fuck off
RUKHSANA	Language
DANNY	Fuck off
RUKHSANA	Just look at you.
DANNY	I mean it.

RUKHSANA So handsome.

She spots something.

What's on your face?

DANNY Nothing.

RUKHSANA Make-up?

DANNY No.

RUKHSANA It looks like foundation.

DANNY No!

RUKHSANA What is it?

DANNY It's nothing.

RUKHSANA Let's see.

DANNY It's for spots.

RUKHSANA It'll give you spots.
Let me

She tries to wipe DANNY*'s face.*

DANNY Get off.

RUKHSANA Daniel.

DANNY Don't touch me!

She tries to wipe his face harder.

Aaahwwwh!

The bruising is revealed. Pause.

RUKHSANA What happened?

DANNY Fell over.

RUKHSANA No.

DANNY Tripped on my laces.

RUKHSANA Someone hit you.

DANNY No.

RUKHSANA Why didn't you tell me?

DANNY	What could you have done? Don't touch me No, seriously.
	I don't even know you care. So what, it's all his old stuff, (*On the* floor.) so what? You were getting divorced, anyway.
RUKHSANA	Not divorced
DANNY	Separated, whatever. I know why, as well. Your disappearances. Did you have an affair?
RUKHSANA	I'm going out
DANNY	Did you?
RUKHSANA	No.
DANNY	Go out then. If you're going to go out.
RUKHSANA	I'll sort it out
DANNY	Don't come back until you do.
RUKHSANA	Don't say that.
DANNY	Don't come back until you do.

DANNY angrily collects the things on the floor and puts them back in the trunk. But he spots something in there. A shoebox. He opens it. A shoebox full of tapes. He looks at them. Picks one out. Puts it in his Walkman. It is a language-instruction tape. The instructor is from India.

INSTRUCTOR	Repeat after me, and try to make your pronunciation sound like mine. The phrase meaning 'Do you understand English?' – '*Kyaa aap Angrezee samazhteehey?*'
DANNY	*Kyaa aap Angrezee samazhteehey?*

INSTRUCTOR   '*Angrezee*'

DANNY   *Angrezee*

INSTRUCTOR   Excellent!
             '*Samazhteehey*'

DANNY   *Samazhteehey*

Scene Seven

Strip of Green

The strip of green, sunset.

ANNIE *enters in clothes for farming. Wellingtons. She is planting a rose bush.*

RUKHSANA *enters.* ANNIE *doesn't recognise her.*

ANNIE   Oi
             Can't you read?
             This is private property

             Do you understand English?

RUKHSANA   Yes.
             I can understand English.

ANNIE   Oh…

RUKHSANA   You said I could find you here.

ANNIE   I don't own it.
             The farmer employs me.

             We're trying to get the planting done before the frost gets bad.
             He's started a sideline in roses.
             You
             You gotta give em time to take root
             Before they're under pressure to flower.

RUKHSANA   What's the fire over there?

ANNIE	Dead wood.
RUKHSANA	I like it here. It's like countryside.
ANNIE	Horses down there.
RUKHSANA	The concrete starts again soon enough.

Beat.

ANNIE	You left Danny on his own, did you?
RUKHSANA	Yes.
ANNIE	Well, you can't stay here long.

The farmer will come and get you with his gun!

Beat. That was a joke. RUKHSANA *stares at* ANNIE.

You doing anything nice for Christmas?

RUKHSANA	No. You?

Beat. ANNIE *shrugs.*

You not spending it with your…

ANNIE	Bill? Hah! No, I ain't spending it with Bill.

Pause.

He fucked off, didn't he? Years ago.
That's an old story.

I wanted to have kids and he didn't.
Then coupla years ago he goes all daft –
   some mid-life crisis and all of a sudden he
   thinks he wants to procreate.
But after all that it turns out I can't have em
   anyway and so he fucks off.
I think, suit yerself, but by then I'm forty.
Wouldn't want him as a father anyway.

Nah, you're better off without them, aren't you?
You're better off.

RUKHSANA   What was he like? Simon. When you knew him?

ANNIE   Oh no.

RUKHSANA   What was he like?

ANNIE   I ain't doing this.

RUKHSANA   In that house there are
All these things
In boxes.

ANNIE   You looked?

RUKHSANA   Can't help it.

ANNIE   Stupid

RUKHSANA   Clothes. Things. A tin of tobacco.

ANNIE   Should have burned it all years ago.

RUKHSANA   But you left it.

ANNIE   Stuffed in boxes, never opened them!
It wasn't worth opening to get to burning.
I don't think he could make anyone happy in the long term, Simon.
All his *ideas* he dragged you into, the way he got you so enthusiastic, then he just turns his back and fucks off.
At least you got Danny. Be grateful for that.

Pause. RUKHSANA *produces the tin of tobacco dust.* ANNIE *takes it.*

We used to go down London on the bikes.
Down the East End. And sometimes we went out into Essex.
Used to go to these amazing pubs.
He used to smoke these dirty little roll-ups.
We used to go to gigs.
Some bands we saw become famous.
It was the happiest time of my life.
And he was *funny.*

RUKHSANA   Yeah?

ANNIE	Really funny. He cracked me up.
RUKHSANA	He *was* funny. I had forgot that.
ANNIE	But when he fucked off to university it was like he became a different person. Everything changed. Tried to chuck all his old gear out.

ANNIE *gives the tin back.*

RUKHSANA	You know… he was on a motorbike… when he died?
ANNIE	No. No I didn't know that.
RUKHSANA	He'd just bought it
ANNIE	I didn't know that. Listen. Christmas Day. You and Danny could come round. I could cook.

Beat.

RUKHSANA	Do you ever have blue sky in this country?

Beat.

ANNIE	Well, fuck off then.
RUKHSANA	I'm sorry.
ANNIE	No, if you're gonna be like that you can fuck off.

RUKHSANA *turns and heads off.*

You're a disgrace, you know?
Your poor son.
Snap out of it.
Forget about Simon.
Forget about him.
Before it's too late or you'll end up like me.
Your mind will spin round and round
You'll end up useless

Working on a fucking farm.
You'll age fifty years.
You'll die.

Did you hear me?

Beat.

Scene Eight

Canary Wharf

Outside his house, ROB *is polishing the hubcaps of his car.*

LEON *appears.*

ROB   Can you see that, Leon?

LEON *sees it.*

LEON   Yeah.

ROB   I've been watchin it.
Coz when night falls, they're gonna turn on all the lights.
They couldn't afford it until today – too much office space empty.

The funny thing is, *we* can see *it*, but from up there they can't see *us*.
Just a mess of houses. From up top Canary Wharf, you can't see where London ends and Romford begins.

I told em.
I said, 'Granted, we're still in recession. But you can't chuck half of us just because the Deutschmark's falling and the boys in Frankfurt are willing to do something for nothing.' That took em by surprise. I said, 'I read the financial pages. I tape *The Money Programme.*'

LEON	They don't expect you to have something up there.
ROB	That's right. They don't expect that. Them upstairs. I told em, 'They're switching the lights on again aren't they? What does that tell ya? We're on the upturn.' I showed them the article I cut out.
LEON	What did they say?
ROB	They said, 'Thanks, we'll have a look at that.' They're gonna build more of em – these skyscrapers. There'll be a whole skyline. The greatest financial centre in the world. It'll beat New York. It'll beat Tokyo. And it'll *cane* fucking Frankfurt. I was born two minutes walk away from that. Your nan and grandad moved me away coz it wasn't a nice area… now it's gonna be the greatest business centre in the whole world. And they laugh at me at reception. They're all Essex. But they try and make that they're something better. I dint mean to shout so loud, Leon.
LEON	No – you were right.
ROB	It was The surprise of it, you know? Walkin in on ya.
LEON	You was right to be angry.
ROB	It's just
LEON	You were right, mate.
ROB	I er The motor was makin funny noises. I bet it's the carburettor. You seen how the carburettor works?

| | I could show you.
It's a tricky little thing. |
| --- | --- |
| LEON | You showed me before. |
| ROB | Oh, right / sorry |
| LEON | Nah you could show / me again |
| ROB | Don't be daft |
| LEON | It's a lovely motor. |
| ROB | I might have to sell it. |
| LEON | You won't |
| ROB | Sell the hubcaps, anyway.
Jesus you didn't half look different with that gunk on…
You are just messin around, intcha? |
| LEON | Course I'm
I'm toughening myself up, Dad. I do press-ups. |
| ROB | I wondered what the creaking was |

Pause.

I mean, it's a free country and all but
I wanna make sure you turn out right.
If you turned out… a bit
(*He whistles.*)
D'you understand me?
You are just messin around?

LEON	Course.
ROB	Yeah?
LEON	There are girls at school I like.
ROB	Yeah?
LEON	Yeah.
ROB	(*An assessment.*) Well, you're not too bad.

Pause.

PRETEND YOU HAVE BIG BUILDINGS 55

	You could invite one of them out for a date, couldn't you?
LEON	Dad!
ROB	Here y'are.

He gets out his wallet and gives LEON *a fiver.*

LEON *takes it, forlornly.*

Christmas coming.

Scene Nine

Speaking to Gravestones

That evening. RUKHSANA, *in the Docklands, staring at the Canary Wharf Tower. Which is still mainly in darkness. She holds the tobacco tin as if it were a tiny urn.*

RUKHSANA Hey
You.
So people speak to gravestones, don't they?
And I've been having trouble getting through.
And I think you'd have loved this.
You'd have loved to wire this whole building.
And I remember you took me here in 1977.
When all this was just mud and rusting metal.
You waved your arms about. Talked about the
 future
I can see you
Right here, waving your arms about.
Lamenting its darkness
Gazing at it
Like you'd invented veins.
You bastard, you never said a word about
 anything east of here.

But I will
Release you

If you believe me.
I loved you. I was faithful. I will explain everything.
Do you believe me?

Beat. Then the lights of Canary Wharf flicker on, slowly, magically. She gazes, amazed.

Good.
Danny's waiting at home for me.
But he's going to have to wait

The tip of the tower flashes.

We have a lot to talk about.
Before I leave you.

Scene Ten

Unit One

Morning. DANNY *is in the kitchen, wearing his school uniform. He is listening to the tape.*

INSTRUCTOR

Repeat after me, and try to make your pronunciation sound like mine.

DANNY Mum!

DANNY *rips off his headphones furiously.*

Where are you? You can't just not be here. *Mum.*

Then, a piece of magic. Something happens inside the helmet of the motorcyclist. DANNY *nearly misses it, but he doesn't miss it.* DANNY *investigates.*

Nothing.

Mum!

PRETEND YOU HAVE BIG BUILDINGS 57

Another burst of magic. Spooked, DANNY *puts the headphones on again.*

INSTRUCTOR Repeat after me, and try and make your pronunciation sound like mine…

And then DANNY*'s father is magically on the tape.*

HIS DAD'S VOICE
Hello, Danny

DANNY *rips off his headphones, spooked as hell.*

He puts them on again. The tape has moved on a little bit…

I dint touch nuffing

Beat.

DANNY I dint touch nuffing

HIS DAD'S VOICE
Nuffing

DANNY Nuffing

HIS DAD'S VOICE
Come on, Sunshine

DANNY Come on, Sunshine

HIS DAD'S VOICE
We all got inta the Fiesta

DANNY We all got inta the Fiesta

HIS DAD'S VOICE
And went Nan's for tea

DANNY And went Nan's for tea

HIS DAD'S VOICE
Tea

DANNY Tea

HIS DAD'S VOICE
Oh Danny

DANNY   Yeah?

HIS DAD'S VOICE
               At the end of the day

DANNY   At the end of the day

HIS DAD'S VOICE
               We'll go back to Essex.
               Return to the land of my birth
               It's not what you think, it's different
               But I missed it. So much.
               I missed the yellows in the summer
               The burnt grasses
               The hubcaps in the scrapyard
               The hubcaps in the rosebeds.

               There is sudden and intense snowfall, like a swoon.

Scene Eleven

Snowfall

RUKHSANA *and* DANNY*'s house. Afternoon.* RUKHSANA *is wearing a business suit, looking outside.* DANNY *enters, in school uniform.*

RUKHSANA   Hello
               Have you seen the snow?
               It's astonishing!

               You look cold.

               We'll have to get you a proper coat!

               DANNY *puts his bag down.*

               So how was school?

               How were the other kids?

               Danny, come on, speak to me

	Was it rough?
	Was it racist?
	Because, listen, we can find you another one. That's no problem.
	I'm sorry I wasn't here last night.
DANNY	Really I don't care what you do.
RUKHSANA	There was something I had to do.
DANNY	Did he follow you over here?

Beat.

RUKHSANA There was never anyone other than your father.

Beat.

DANNY School
School was great.

Better than looking after you.

They were friendly

RUKHSANA What did you say?

DANNY 'Alright.'

RUKHSANA What did they say?

DANNY 'Alright.'

Why are you wearing that? (*The suit.*)

RUKHSANA I called that woman back.
About the interview.

DANNY Did you?

RUKHSANA I can do that job

DANNY Can you?

RUKHSANA They're going to fit me in at the end of the day
Will you come with me?
You can help me.
Mock interview.

	You can decide whether they're good enough. And afterwards We'll go into London. Have dinner. See some sights. We can decide where we want to move to.
DANNY	It's too late.
RUKHSANA	What?
DANNY	I mean I already have plans. Some people from school. Invited me out
RUKHSANA	Some friends?
DANNY	I don't know.
RUKHSANA	What are they called?
DANNY	Lewis. Tom. Amy.
RUKHSANA	Amy?
DANNY	Shut up.
RUKHSANA	Will there be alcohol?
DANNY	Shut up.
RUKHSANA	Please. Come with me. You can go out tomorrow Please.
DANNY	It's too late.
RUKHSANA	I forbid you
DANNY	You can't. It's too late.
	Pause.
RUKHSANA	I'll never disappear again, Danny. I'll be here when you get home. Danny.

Well will you wish me luck?
Please.

Pause.

Scene Twelve

We're Going Out Tonight

ROB*'s house, a little later that afternoon.* STEVEN *and* LEON *are still in school uniform, their ties at quarter-length.*

STEVEN	Just take some.
LEON	No.
STEVEN	I'll ask him, he likes me. He's sound, your dad.
LEON	He only lets me drink if he's around. He don't think we're old enough.
STEVEN	I'm old enough. I can hold my drink.
LEON	(*Affirmatively.*) Oh yeah.
STEVEN	We goin down the ditch tonight?
LEON	I thought you was going out with Amy?
STEVEN	Yeah, she was comin.
LEON	Too good for us, is she?
STEVEN	Oh fuck off, Leon. We're taking a break, int we?
LEON	Why?
STEVEN	I told her first! I say: 'It's not working Amy.' You know what I mean?

LEON	Plenny more fish in the sea, though.
	Beat.
STEVEN	More fun with the boys anyway.
LEON	Eh?
STEVEN	Nah. (*He doesn't mean anything by that.*)
LEON	It's good to have you back, mate.
STEVEN	We'll take some beers, like.
LEON	Get mashed up. Find some girls!
STEVEN	(*Explodes.*) I'll fucking do him if I see him.
LEON	Who?
STEVEN	Fuckin
LEON	Who?
STEVEN	It don't matter who, Leon.
	Beat.
LEON	So where we gonna get the beers from?
STEVEN	Your dad
LEON	I told you
STEVEN	Off-licence, then.
LEON	We won't get served
STEVEN	I'll get served. 'Ere y'are – got some fags yesterday.
LEON	You'll get cancer.
STEVEN	I don't get cancer.
	LEON *gasps in admiration.*
	Enter ROB, *hassled.* STEVEN *frantically hides the cigarettes.*
	Alright, Rob

ROB	Steven.
LEON	We're going out, Dad
ROB	Yeah?
LEON	With the lads like.
ROB	In the snow?
LEON	Not too cold.
ROB	Making snowmen, are you?
LEON	Is that alright, Dad?

Beat.

ROB	Yeah.
STEVEN	Rob, yeah?
ROB	Listen, boys
STEVEN	How old would you say I was, Rob?
ROB	I know how old you are, Steven. You're in my son's class at school.
STEVEN	Yeah, but if you didn't know that, how old would you say I was? Fifteen, seventeen, eighteen?
ROB	Thirteen, I'd say
STEVEN	No, seriously
ROB	Your balls have barely dropped Steven. It's not so long I remember you in here bawling your eyes out coz you grazed your knee on the patio. You said your dad was gonna come round and beat me up.

STEVEN *clicks his neck.*

STEVEN	How's work, Rob? You was in London today weren'tcha?
LEON	Can me and Steve have a Heineken?

STEVEN   What's wrong, Rob?

ROB   You got the head for it, Steve?

STEVEN   What?

ROB   For a Heineken.

STEVEN   Course.

ROB   Yeah, you can have a Heineken.

LEON   Ah, it's beautiful, Heineken.

ROB   We'll see if you have the head for it.

LEON   Can we take a couple down the ditch and all?

ROB   Oh yeah?

STEVEN   Leon reckons he's in tonight.

ROB   Is that right, Lee?
You takin a beer for a lady too, are ya?

LEON   Well, we'll see how it goes.

ROB   Good man.

LEON   If she'll have me.

LEON moves into the kitchen.

ROB   Should be int'restin, anyway.
You can get me one an all, Lee.
(*Clarifying.*) A beer, not a little girl.

LEON goes out to get a beer.

Can fackin do with one…

STEVEN   Why's that?

ROB   You look after him, Steve.

STEVEN   Yeah, alright.

ROB   He's alright, isn't he?

STEVEN   My old boy said there were more meetings today.

ROB   I'm not in the mood.

STEVEN	Have you heard anything, though? I hear they're not going to lay off any of the Pakistanis Any of the blacks.
ROB	I wouldn't know.
STEVEN	He reckons you upstairs
ROB	I'm not upstairs.
STEVEN	The talk is that you upstairs wouldn't be sorry to take the package.
ROB	What does he know?
	ROB *remembers that he is, relatively, a little bit upstairs.*
	Sorry
STEVEN	He's got repayments to make, Rob. Christmas coming up
	LEON *shouts, from off.*
LEON	Oh shit
ROB	What you done now?
LEON	Oh shit oh shit oh shit
ROB	What?
LEON	I'm sorry, Dad.
	LEON *appears with the beers. He has spilt them all down him.*
	I'm really sorry.
ROB	What?
LEON	I've spilt it all down me.
ROB	You wally.
STEVEN	Seriously, Rob
ROB	(*To both, or either of them.*) I'm not going to hang you out to dry.

He looks at both, separately. He walks off.

The boys drink their beer. STEVEN *clicks his neck.*

STEVEN You got any deodorant, Lee?

LEON Yes, mate

STEVEN Give us some? I left mine at home.

LEON Lynx Africa?

STEVEN Goo on then.

LEON *tosses* STEVEN *the can. It looks like Lynx Africa, but it isn't.*

What's this?
'Menzone'.
'Menzone Musk'?
What the fuck is Menzone?

LEON I got it down the market.

STEVEN It's fake.

LEON Try it, it's alright.

STEVEN *thinks. He opens his shirt up.*

He sprays his armpit. Cautiously – as if dipping his toe in the sea.

STEVEN Don't look, then.

LEON Not looking.

STEVEN *sprays his armpit long enough to make some difference to the burgeoning rupture in the ozone layer.*

Yeah, easy on with it.

STEVEN *pointedly sprays for another five seconds, then gives the other armpit a deluge.*

Oh come on, Steve

STEVEN FUCK OFF, YOU QUEER

	STEVEN *sprays it down his pants, then tosses* LEON *the can.*
LEON	What's got into you?
STEVEN	Let me borrow your Ralph Lauren jumper, yeah?
	Beat.
	Do you want to go out or what?
LEON	Yeah, alright.
	STEVEN *gets* LEON *in a headlock and sprays deodorant at him… and they play-fight…*
	…as DANNY *becomes part of the scene.* DANNY *stands on his bed, listening to the tapes.*
HIS DAD'S VOICE	Stand with your legs apart, with a pint in one hand, and make your point with the other. Your elbows at right angles You should never change that angle.
	DANNY *plays with his new kinaesthetic.*
	You drink at that angle
	DANNY *drinks at that angle.*
	You fight at that angle
	DANNY *slings a punch.*
	Click your neck and make conversation
	DANNY *clicks his neck, and:*
DANNY	You Alright, mate?
HIS DAD'S VOICE	Not so bad, yerself?
DANNY	Not so bad, yerself?

HIS DAD'S VOICE
> Not so bad... how ya keeping?
>
> *Pause.*

DANNY Goin down the Hammers soon.

HIS DAD'S VOICE
> Oh yeah?

DANNY Taking little Jason.

HIS DAD'S VOICE
> Oh yeah?
> Well take care of yerself, mate.

DANNY Yeah, take care of yerself...
Be good.

> DANNY *applies deodorant, excessively. He puts on the motorcyclist's leather jacket. It looks good.*

Scene Thirteen

The Docklands

RUKHSANA *is waiting in a glassy office, in her suit. A PA's desk, a phone. A sofa. On a table rests an architect's model. A vision of the Docklands in the future.* RUKHSANA *holds a glass of water.* KAREN *emerges from another room – Mr Leigh's office.*

KAREN He won't be long
Are you sure you just want water?
We just got ourselves a cappuccino machine.

RUKHSANA I'm fine. Thank you.

KAREN Seems a shame to just have water. Mr Leigh, he loves his coffee.
And there's all sorts of variations.
All sorts of things to sprinkle on top.

	He's always popping in just to try a new one – I don't get no work done! No need to be nervous. You'll be fine.
RUKHSANA	I like this. This model.
KAREN	That's how it's all gonna look. When it's finished. And it's where we're moving. Only a few more weeks here. We're moving to the Docklands. I'm being made office manager. I'll show you where we're going.

She points to the place.

	There. A converted warehouse. It'll make the commute easier, anyway. You're Romford, aren't ya?
RUKHSANA	Yes.
KAREN	I remember from the letter! I put you on the top of the pile. I'm Romford, too, y'see. It's not too bad, is it?
RUKHSANA	No.
KAREN	It could be worse. Mr Leigh commutes from Surrey. He's got this massive house but it takes for ever. Your husband English, is he?
RUKHSANA	Yes.
KAREN	That's where you get the Parrish from?
RUKHSANA	Yes.
KAREN	I was gonna say Coz that's not an Indian name, is it? What's he do, then?
RUKHSANA	He's in construction.

KAREN	It's a good field to be in.
RUKHSANA	He plans the electrics. The wiring. For these big buildings. In big cities. He gets very taken up with it
KAREN	It's that kind of work.
RUKHSANA	And you wouldn't think you could Talk for so long about So many light bulbs.
KAREN	Boys and their toys, ay?
RUKHSANA	You get dragged in.
KAREN	You do.
RUKHSANA	If you're not careful.
KAREN	If you're not careful. That's right. They don't understand you working, do they? That's the thing. My husband he basically thinks I'm a typist but I'm so much more! 'How was your day,' he goes, and before I can answer he goes: 'Boring was it?' 'No… Beg yer pardon but I love my job.' And if he doesn't appreciate that… Did you ever get that?
RUKHSANA	Yes
KAREN	Is that wrong? *Beat.*
RUKHSANA	Sometimes I thought it would be better just to take off. Forget him. Leave my son in his care and just take off. KAREN *thinks.* When you no longer reward each other. KAREN *thinks.*

I left my husband. At last. Yesterday.

It was the right thing to do.

Pause. A buzzer on KAREN's *desk goes off.*

KAREN That's you.

RUKHSANA Right.

KAREN Mr Leigh, he's a nice man.

RUKHSANA Thank you.

KAREN I hope you get it.

RUKHSANA Thank you.

> KAREN *leads* RUKHSANA *into Mr Leigh's office. She returns. She thinks. She looks at her model, which glows, in the darkness, just like the real thing.*

Scene Fourteen

All the Dinner Parties

The master bedroom. KAREN *is updating her make-up.* ROB, *tired, enters, in his socks.* KAREN *notices. Outside there is a neon reindeer.*

KAREN You scared me.

ROB Got no shoes on.

KAREN What you creeping up for?

ROB Admiring ya.

KAREN Well, don't, I'm not fit to be seen.

ROB Oh, you are.
You see Leon and Steve getting ready?
They're keeping Brut in business I can tell ya!

The fumes!

KAREN	Ssshhhh.
ROB	I wouldn't light a fag in there!
KAREN	They might hear ya.
ROB	I wouldn't light a fag in there, it might set the house on fire!
	You putting that stuff on or off? (*The make-up.*)
KAREN	You still want to come out?
ROB	Yeah! Let's go out.
KAREN	Coz if you like we can stay in. I'm not fussed.
	Pause.
ROB	When did you get back?
KAREN	You were in the garden.
ROB	You came straight upstairs?
KAREN	Long day.
ROB	Boring was it?
KAREN	Why should it be boring?
	Beat.
ROB	Leon reckons he's gonna pull tonight.
KAREN	Leave him alone.
ROB	What if he did drag some poor girl back here?
KAREN	You know how he is.
ROB	There's something about him It's not right.
KAREN	He'll work it out for himself.
ROB	That's what I'm worried about.
	Long pause. KAREN *has finished her make-up. She turns to* ROB, *to have a Conversation.*
KAREN	What d'you reckon about getting another car?

ROB	What kind of car?
KAREN	For when I move office
ROB	A city runner?
KAREN	So's you don't have to drop me off all the time
ROB	A nice little two-door runaround you're after?
KAREN	We can afford it. My wages are going up. My wages are for luxuries. Why should I rely on you to pick me up? I want to go places on my own.
ROB	What kinda places? We'll see
KAREN	We'll see, will we?
ROB	Yeah.
KAREN	We'll see, will we?
	ROB *sits down next to her.*
ROB	We'll see
	He starts kissing her.
KAREN	Don't. Rob.
	He withdraws.
ROB	We can't buy another car
KAREN	No?
ROB	I can't buy you a car
KAREN	Why not?
	Beat.
ROB	Because we're all gonna go on strike
KAREN	You are going on a *what*?
ROB	We're going on strike.

KAREN   You promised me. Rob.
               We discussed this over glasses of wine,
                   expensive wine… at dinner parties.
               You were very loud.
               You were loud about your admiration for the
                   Iron Lady, how she was the best thing that
                   ever happened to this country. You wore your
                   politics on your sleeve, Rob.
               'I look after my own, that's my first priority.'

ROB   This is my own!

KAREN   You are not a coalminer, Rob.

ROB   They *are* my own.

KAREN   With coal on your fucking face.

ROB   Mickey, Trevor

KAREN   You wear a tie, now.

ROB   We're in it together. Dave, Jock, Alan. I can't
                   shit on them!
               We gave an inch and the bastards took a mile.
               And it's not just the blokes on the floor.
               It's all joined up, that's what I've been
                   realising.

               LEON *and* STEVEN *enter, all done up for the evening.*

KAREN   Oh, you look nice.

LEON   We're off.

KAREN   Have you got Leon's Lauren jumper on, Steve?

STEVEN   No.

LEON   He's got the same one as me.

KAREN   Well, have fun, boys

STEVEN   Thanks

KAREN   Be good.

LEON   (*To* ROB.) See ya, mate.

ROB flinches.

ROB Yeah.

LEON and STEVEN exit.

They called us in today.
All the supervisors.
Offered us… a five-figure sum
If we took redundancy now.

KAREN What kind of five-figure sum?

ROB It don't matter what kind

KAREN Ten grand?
Fifty grand?… Well?

ROB Twenty grand.

KAREN You turned that down?

ROB I'm not going to shit on my boys.

KAREN You could start up with that.
That's what you've always wanted.
To go out on your own.

The factory is *closing.* Maybe not this year.
But it's the *way* things are *going*.
They'll give you fuck all when that happens.

I ain't gonna provide for you, Rob.

ROB I love you.

KAREN You've always wanted to start up something.
   Go into business. You'd be good at that. You
   won't get many chances.

ROB They reckon the markets are changing, Karen.
   We're coming out of the slump. The lights
   are coming on.
In India, people will be buying. They reckon
   hundreds of millions of Indians with enough
   money to buy a car.
It's gonna be incredible.

>   KAREN *begins to put her make-up on, then*
>   *grabs her make-up bag and gets up.*

KAREN   Actually I was putting my make-up on, Rob

ROB   Just a couple more years.

KAREN   I'm going out.

ROB   Where?

KAREN   Some people at work are having a Christmas party.

ROB   You already had that.

KAREN   It's been a good year.
                 They're having another one.

>   *She exits.* ROB *takes stock. He thinks some*
>   *more. He sits down and looks at himself in*
>   KAREN*'s mirror.*
>
>   *He goes to pick up the phone, and puts a little*
>   *pair of spectacles on to read his address book.*
>   *He finds a number. He dials a number.*

ROB   Terry
                 It's Rob, mate.
                 You alright?
                 Yeah not so bad, yerself?
                 Yeah, not so bad, yerself
                 Yeah
                 Yeah, sorry to call you at home.
                 No no, I'm fine.
                 No, all it is…

                 Are you sitting down mate?
                 Can I speak to you in confidence?

Scene Fifteen

Braveheart

LEON *at the strip of green, by a ditch. It is snowing. Winter coats. Cans of beer.*

LEON   So we go to the border
The strip of green
Where the London Road meets Whalebone Lane.
The border, the end of London.
A farm
Some scrubland.
A ditch that cuts across it.

You gather in clumps along the bank
Drinkin just to keep warm
And when you run out, Steve goes on a mission to the offie.
I bet he'll get served!

And on this night anything could happen
You could fall in love
You could get pregnant
You could smoke till your lungs are like caviar.

And over there
They're playing Top Trumps for beats on the arm.

And over there
Tim and Jenny Tyler have gone into the bushes.

He breathes deeply. He closes his eyes.

And way over there, as the ditch curves by the bridge.
Amy's just arrived with three blokes in tow.
Two blokes and the new kid.
And then it becomes clear to you what Steve was talking about.

He sees STEVEN *approach with great determination, carrying a blue polythene bag full of booze.*

	D'you get em then? I bet he didn't even ask you.
STEVEN	He didn't even ask me.
	STEVEN *tosses the booze onto the* floor.
LEON	You always get served.
STEVEN	Yeah, me and Mr Patel.
LEON	You're like 'that'.
STEVEN	We were chatting.
LEON	Were ya?
STEVEN	You little fucking shit you've been quiet haven't ya?
LEON	What?
STEVEN	Your old man
LEON	What?
STEVEN	It's all over the fucking town, mate.
LEON	What?
STEVEN	You don't know?
LEON	No.
STEVEN	He took redundancy.
	Pause.
LEON	That's a lie.
STEVEN	You sayin I'm lying, Lee?
LEON	He wouldn't do that.
STEVEN	He always thought he was better.
LEON	I swear, Steve.
STEVEN	Lordin it round in a fucking suit, course he's the first to take the money.
LEON	He don't

PRETEND YOU HAVE BIG BUILDINGS   79

STEVEN   How else is he gonna get you a moped?

LEON   Steve

STEVEN   Don't speak to me

LEON   Mate

STEVEN   Fuck off

LEON   Please, Steve.

STEVEN   Fuck off back to Daddy. Spoilt little
Go on, run back home
You look like you're gonna cry.

LEON   Not gonna cry.

STEVEN   Or piss yourself.

Pause. LEON *suddenly realigns his loyalties.*

LEON   Have a look over there, Steve.
Over by the bridge.

STEVEN *suddenly realigns his emotions.*

STEVEN   What's she doing?

LEON   I dunno, can't make it out.

STEVEN   Is he talking to her?

LEON   I dunno, looks like it.

STEVEN   Looks like she's talking to him.

LEON   It's probably only talking.

STEVEN   Probably?

Beat. STEVEN *breathes deeply, trying not to crumble.*

She's

LEON   Nah

STEVEN   I knew there was someone.

LEON   It probably don't mean nothing.

STEVEN	I'll kick his Paki head in.
	Beat.
LEON	What?
STEVEN	I'll fuckin kill him.
	STEVEN *tries to run off.* LEON *restrains him.*
LEON	What are you doing? It's not worth it, Steve. It's not worth it.

STEVEN *shrugs* LEON *off, propelling him into the ditch, and charges off.* LEON *is wet through and freezing. But something is changing in the atmosphere.*

Oi! Steve!
Steve.

LEON *notices what's going on, off.*

Oh fucking hell.
Whatchoo doing, mate? You can't take on Steve!

LEON *picks up a bottle of clear white cider from the bag, twists it, and has a swig. He follows the fight, as something weird is happening, a build-up to something. He puts the bottle down.*

That's it, mate, hit him!
Fuckin hell
Fuckin hell

STEVEN *is walloped onstage by an extraordinary source of propulsion – causing him to be almost – if not entirely – in flight.*

DANNY *calmly follows him, and socks him again, forcing him another three or four metres and onto the floor, near the blue polythene bag.* DANNY *seems to have developed an Essex accent since the afternoon.*

DANNY	Come on! Come on, you yellow bastard, putcha fists up.
	Come on, Sunshine!
STEVEN	Go on, Lee, hit him. Go on.
LEON	Fuck off, Steve
STEVEN	(*To* DANNY, *of* LEON.) I don't know what he's getting all funny for, he was the one who set me onto you.

STEVEN *gathers the cider bottle, and swigs from it like he's a Viking. He replaces the cap. Now he has a weapon.*

He stands. He raises the bottle above his head, like a Viking club. Something charges inside it. Like it contains lightning.

Thunder.

LEON	No
STEVEN	Come on then!
LEON	It's not worth it, Steve!
STEVEN	Fuck off, Leon
LEON	Play fair!

LEON *approaches* STEVEN, *and* STEVEN *swings at* LEON, *at precisely the moment when there is lightning.* LEON *backs off.*

DANNY	Come on then!

STEVEN *charges at* DANNY. *There is even stronger lightning as* STEVEN *smashes the bottle down between* DANNY's *eyes.*

DANNY *is propelled into the ditch.* STEVEN *follows* DANNY *into the ditch, grabs* DANNY's *hair, pulls his head up then plunges it down.*

STEVEN *holds* DANNY*'s head down. Then, job done, he gets out of the ditch.* DANNY *does not move.*

LEON   What the fuck have you done?

STEVEN *isn't sure.*

Call an ambulance
Call an ambulance
Well GO, THEN!
Run
Run!

STEVEN *runs.* LEON *assesses the job at hand.*

Come on, Leon.
Come on, mate

He sprints into the ditch like a number one action hero.

He pulls DANNY *up. Both of them are soaking wet and freezing.* DANNY *is in pain.*

Alright alright alright, mate.

I'm not gonna hit you!
I'm not gonna touch you.

An ambulance is on its way.

And LEON *is right on top of* DANNY.

I just wanna know that you're breathing.
I thought you'd drowned.

Beat.

I don't think you need mouth to mouth

A moment. DANNY *drifts away.*

Oh shit.

Don't take this the wrong way.

LEON *tries CPR. A moment.*

Listen
New Kid on the Block
What's your name?

LEON *fumbles in* DANNY*'s jacket. Finds his wallet. Finds a name.*

No, I just want your name. Danny. Can you hear me, Danny?

DANNY *can, groggily.*

Yeah?
Say 'Yes mate.'

DANNY　　Yes mate

LEON　　You put up a good fight but he played dirty.

The sound and light of an ambulance.

Can you hear that? You'll be alright soon.

(*To the paramedics.*) Oi!
Here y'are!

(*To* DANNY.) You sank, mate
Right down.

I pulled you up.

I pulled you up, mate.

The lights and siren of an ambulance grow near.

End of Act One.

ACT TWO: The Dolphin

Scene Sixteen

Hospital

A waiting room, Oldchurch Hospital, Romford, about 10.30 p.m. DANNY *lies on a hospital bed, unconscious. He is strapped to the kind of backboard used to treat concussion. On a chair hangs the motorcyclist's jacket.* ANNIE, *in a thick coat, keeps watch.*

ANNIE   You know… you look so like your dad.

Those (*The jacket.*) were his leathers. I reckon you knew that.

He used to be ever-so-into his bikes.

When he turned seventeen he wanted one. So he and Bill they went out and found an Old Enfield. Used to talk about it all the time, that's what got me into it.

ANNIE *gets a photograph out of her purse.*

I always keep this. Look, there he is. And me
It all still fits.
I still wear those.
I can't stop thinking about him.

LEON *enters, with a blanket round his shoulders.*

LEON   There's still nobody answering.

ANNIE   Fuckssake

LEON   It's bad, that.

ANNIE   Where is she? What a fucking night.
Never thought I'd spend it making your acquaintance.

LEON	I didn't have to stay.
ANNIE	You ain't shown any signs of going though, have ya?
LEON	I could have walked off
ANNIE	So why didn't ya? What kind of guilt compels you? Did you start it? I weren't born yesterday, I know what you lot are like. Causing trouble.
LEON	I don't cause trouble.
ANNIE	And you have to pick on this one, don't you? The poor little thing, he couldn't have had a worse year.
LEON	You said. I didn't know that. He kept all that quiet though God knows it's nothing to be ashamed of. It don't matter where he's from, I wouldn't hurt him.
ANNIE	I want to know who's responsible. Why I get a phone call *from the police*. 'There's been an assault. The mother's not answering so we're giving you a try.' How'd they even get my number?
LEON	It was in his wallet.
ANNIE	Was it?
LEON	Yeah.

Beat.

ANNIE	Yeah, well, I want to know who's responsible. Draggin me out in the cold. I want you to tell me what happened.
LEON	Ah 'S a long story.
ANNIE	Were you drunk?

LEON	No.
ANNIE	How comes I can smell it on ya? Lookin a state, I've seen ya. Tennants Super.
LEON	Heineken
ANNIE	Silly prat, all it takes is a fuckin Bailey's and you boys are on the floor being sick and singin fuckin sea shanties. Was he drunk?
LEON	No He wasn't drunk The problem was, was this bloke.
ANNIE	I'll want his name.
LEON	He shall remain nameless.
ANNIE	Oh, shall he?
LEON	He's havin an hard time of it: love life, family
ANNIE	Don't excuse it.
LEON	I'm not excusing it.
ANNIE	Friend of yours, is he?
LEON	I don't know any more.
ANNIE	Well, I'll want his name.

DANNY *wakes up.*

DANNY	Whooaahh.
ANNIE	You're alright, love. There's been no damage. You ain't woke up in a different universe.
DANNY	Feels like it.
ANNIE	You were thumped, hard, apparently. Concussed and knocked into a bit of water. This is Oldchurch Hospital, and you can thank your lucky stars to be in a bed. The nurse

	outside is itching to get you out coz some boy needs his stomach pumped but I told her. There could be complications. I told her you're gonna stay here as long as you want. They ain't gonna touch my nephew.
DANNY	I was winning.
ANNIE	Were ya?
LEON	You were.
DANNY	Where's my mum?
ANNIE	Your mum.

Beat.

	Think of me as your fairy godmother. Here y'are, let me prop you up. That's right.
	I like your jacket. It's durable, that.
LEON	It suits ya.
ANNIE	We tried calling your mum. We left messages. Nobody picked up. Time and time again. Where she is at this hour I don't know, or who she's with, it's a scandal. So when you're ready – there's no rush. I can take you to mine tonight. There's a spare bedroom. Would you like that? And tomorra. I could take you out on the bike. A trip out to Essex or something?
DANNY	What are you doing here?
ANNIE	You had my number in your wallet! You can stay with me tonight.
DANNY	No
ANNIE	You need observing.
DANNY	What do you care?

ANNIE   We always cared about you – your nan and me.
                   We always cared.
                   We sent cards at birthdays. We sent Advent
                       calendars.

                   Beat.

                   I better find a nurse – tell her you're back in this
                       world.
                   Can I get anyone a cup a tea?
                   No?
                   I tell you you've got a friend here in Leon,
                       Danny

                   She exits.

LEON   That stupid wanker Steve, I can't believe it.
                   Bang out of order
                   I never seen him like that

DANNY   It's alright.

LEON   It's not alright

DANNY   Coz at the end of the day

LEON   At the end of the day he faces criminal charges.

                   Beat.

                   You said you was from central London, didn't
                       you? The inner city, I s'pose.
                   My grandad. He was from central London.
                       Well, East End really.
                   It's more or less in the middle.
                   He ended up doing six months hard labour.
                   He was a salesman. He sold housewives
                       ditchweed – told them it was Japanese roses.

                   It's a bit shit innit, here?
                   Well, it's alright.

                   No, it's shit. I look at it, my heart goes grey.
                   What was it like, in the centre?

                   He goes over to the window.

                   You wanna sweet?

DANNY	Yeah, alright. What kind?
LEON	Lovehearts.
DANNY	Go on then.

DANNY takes one. LEON goes over to the window.

LEON	There used to be a swimming pool. The Dolphin. I used to like going. Wave-splash, everything. But they closed it. The building's still there – this dirty glass pyramid wiv an hole in the roof. No one goes in it now. I used to think it might be haunted or full a pharaohs. Wish we had something proper like that here though. Something really ancient. You know, a proper pyramid. A castle or something. I get a bit carried away sometimes. I let my imagination run away with me. I mean – you might think this is stupid. But just think, right, if one day a castle grew up out the Dolphin. And suddenly we had a castle. It would be wicked. Coz then we have a bit of history. I mean people would come here, if we had a castle. Is that stupid?
DANNY	No.
LEON	It's a bit.
DANNY	No. It's not.
LEON	It's a bit gay. Nah it ain't not proper gay. Once we went on an exchange trip to this town in France. And it was mostly taking the piss and trying to pull the girls and get fags and stuff.

	And most of the town was a shithole to be fair. But in the middle of the town they had this fuck-off massive property; turrets; lovely. A 'Chateau'. And Michael Pott nearly set the fuckin thing on fire. Point was: I'd have been sorry to see that burn down if I lived there. But here
DANNY	You just have to pretend, don't you? Pretend you have big buildings. Pretend that tomorrow there'll… there'll
LEON	Be a coachload of French tourists coming to
DANNY	Take the piss
LEON	Set everything on fire!
DANNY	That's right.
LEON	Listen, could I hold your hand? I've always wanted to hold someone's hand in a hospital…
	Sorry, forget it.
	Listen… you don't need to worry any more.
	I'll look after you if you like
DANNY	I'm fine
LEON	You sure?
DANNY	It's weird, I'm feeling blinding. Can you get this thing off? (*The backboard, the neck restraint.*)
LEON	You sure?
DANNY	Yeah
LEON	There could be complications.
DANNY	It's not complicated.
	Beat.

LEON	They did all sortsa tests
DANNY	What kind?
LEON	Your vital signs.
DANNY	Let's get out of here.
LEON	What about your aunt?
DANNY	She'll work it out.
LEON	You can come round mine
	It's close! Nah, it won't be no trouble. My dad'll be out late. Pictures then dancing. We can get some dry clothes on you. You can borrow some of mine. Have a few beers and play Championship Manager. You're West Ham incha? Lewis said. I'm West Ham. Me dad's West Ham. I promised my dad I'd bring a friend home.
DANNY	My dad's West Ham
LEON	Yeah?
DANNY	Yeah
LEON	You sure?
DANNY	Course.
	Beat.
LEON	Your auntie told me, mate. My heart goes out to you.
	DANNY *gets up.*
	No, it's alright. I understand.
DANNY	Come on then.
LEON	What about your auntie?
DANNY	She'll survive, won't she?

Scene Seventeen

Passport

Later that night. ROB*'s house. He has been slumped on his sofa, in his socks and with a heavy night of cans and fags behind him.* LEON *has just awoken him.*

LEON	I thought you was going out.
ROB	So I didn't
LEON	You've been smoking
ROB	Yeah, well
LEON	You're only allowed one a year, Dad. You're allowed one cigarette a year. At Christmas.
ROB	Yeah, well, things are gonna change, Leon.
LEON	I heard about that and all.
ROB	Eh?
LEON	People have been talking about you. What's all this about you taking redundancy?
ROB	Who said that?
LEON	Steve said
ROB	That's bollocks though
LEON	Yeah?
ROB	What does he know, it's just rumours.
LEON	That's what I told him.
ROB	I wouldn't do that, Lee.
LEON	That's what I told him! Do you promise?
ROB	What you coming out with this horseshit for, Leon? Don't talk to me like this.

>   DANNY *enters. He is wearing some of* LEON*'s clothes.* ROB *is shocked.*

DANNY   What do you think?

LEON   They're smart.

DANNY   Yeah?

ROB   Er

LEON   Suits ya.

ROB   (*To* DANNY.) Alright, mate

DANNY   Alright.

ROB   Er, Leon.
            Can I have a word?

>   *They draw aside.*

            What do you bring him for?

LEON   What you got against him?

ROB   He's a bit

LEON   He ain't

ROB   He's a bit

LEON   What?

ROB   You said you was bringing your girlfriend.

LEON   I didn't know you was gonna be here!

ROB   You what!

LEON   I thought you was on the razz with Mum.
            So why aren'tcha?

>   *Beat.* LEON *gets the picture.*

            He got hit on the head, Dad – he had to go to hospital. His mum weren't picking up so I stayed with him.

ROB   She what?

LEON	She couldn't be found
ROB	Fucking hell, why not?
LEON	I don't know
ROB	Fuckin hell.
	Aside over, as ROB *addresses* DANNY.
	I'm sorry I appear a little strange, mate. My plans for the evening fell through. Leon told me he was bringing his girlfriend home. But you're not Leon's girlfriend, are you?
	Pause.
LEON	We thought we'd go Upton Park on Saturday.
ROB	Upton Park?
LEON	Gainst QPR.
ROB	You got your passport, have ya?
LEON	What?
ROB	I heard they'd set up customs at Seven Kings these days.
DANNY	Yeah!
ROB	It's little India, Forest Gate, Upton Park, now, innit?
DANNY	That's right.
LEON	Mate
ROB	It was a joke.
LEON	You'll need to take your passport, that was the joke.
ROB	It weren't a very good joke.
DANNY	No, it was alright.
ROB	I don't mean any offence.
DANNY	None taken.

ROB	It's just I've seen that road change, that's what I mean.
Spent me whole life around it.
It's a Roman road – did you know that?
An ancient road
Into London.
It starts in the East End and makes its way right out into Essex.
And my whole life I've lived on this road.

Me and
My
Wife
We lived in Forest Gate when we were married, until Leon was born. Karen didn't like it – she's from Chigwell, she don't like close quarters.
And to be fair it was no place to raise a kid and it was changing, anyway, and we wanted to get right out of it.
Some breathing space.
So we moved to Romford.
But my parents. They were proper cockneys – they lived in Poplar until I was ten. And they moved out to Forest Gate coz it was nicer!
And all the time London was creeping further and further east.
But it hasn't got here yet. Not to Romford. |
| LEON | It has.
London buses we're on now. |
| ROB | ROMFORD IS NOT A PART OF LONDON YOU DIPSTICK!
What are you like, Leon? What's your problem?
What is it in your brain that doesn't make the connection? Bringing people back here.

(*To* DANNY.) It's alright, mate.

Not London. Not 'Greater London'. We're the only town in 'Greater London' with its own ring road. That says something. |

| | This place was a Royal Liberty.
Do you know what that means?
It means that people were free.
Out of the city bounds.
By order of the crown.
Edward the Confessor used to come here.
For hunting.
Did you know that? |
|---|---|
| LEON | No. |
| ROB | He had a palace
This fantastic property.
Do you know what they used to say?
That when he was praying, the nightingales would fall silent.
Leon… this place once had *nightingales.*
Did you know that?

So now your dad's brought you to Romford, has he?

And when DANNY *speaks, he sounds like he's from Essex.* |
LEON	Dad
DANNY	He grew up here.
ROB	Did he?
DANNY	Yeah, my dad grew up here.
ROB	What's he do then, your dad?
LEON	Can I have a word, mate?
DANNY	No, it's alright, mate.
LEON	You sure?
DANNY	He's in property, my dad.
ROB	Oh yeah?
DANNY	Yeah
ROB	There's money in that.

DANNY	He's got this idea, right? That Basically There are all these places in the East End. In Hackney, Mile End, Bethnal Green, Spitalfields. And basically at the moment they're shitholes.
ROB	We know why that is
LEON	Dad!
ROB	No, I ain't being funny.
DANNY	Yeah, but the point is that the housing stock is very good.
ROB	I tell you what Some of it… is excellent. *Beat.*
DANNY	So one day A lot of people Who need to work in the city Or who want a bit of excitement Are going to renovate these places And they're going to be worth a lot of money. So my dad He's going to buy as many of these up as he can. And do em up.
ROB	You're joking.
DANNY	I'm not.
ROB	You're having a laugh.
DANNY	God's honest truth.
ROB	It's a thought, though, innit? Your mum… She's Indian, is she?
DANNY	Yes. She's Indian.

ROB	Nah, I'm just thinking…
	It's unusual, isn't it – your kind of arrangement?
	Mixing and matching.
	What does Mum do when yer dad come home?
	Does she have to cover herself up?
	Urrrgh! Urrrgh!
	White man, white man!
DANNY	Not quite!
ROB	She doesn't think we're all rapists!
DANNY	Probably!
ROB	You're alright, you!
	Does she cook, then?
DANNY	Sometimes.
ROB	She cook curry, does she?
DANNY	Yeah.
ROB	She eat it with her hands, does she?
DANNY	Yeah
ROB	I like a curry. Hot though.
DANNY	Too hot for me
ROB	Yeah?
DANNY	Too hot for me.
LEON	What, don't you never have chips or anything?
DANNY	Not when she's in the house.
ROB	Women. Who the fuck needs them, yeah?
	Fuck em.
	The moment you love em then they fuck you around.
	KAREN *appears, unseen.*
	They take off for days
	And nothing is said.
	Of course nothing is said

	The worst thing you can do, Leon. Is love a woman. I don't care what you do You can do men up the spout for all I care. But don't ever fall in love with a woman
	KAREN *makes herself seen.*
KAREN	Hello, Robert
	Pause.
ROB	Like this one.
KAREN	I go out for an evening and come back to find my husband has turned philosopher.
ROB	They'll kill you, Leon! You listen to me! No matter how beautiful
KAREN	Leon.
ROB	Ain't she lovely, Danny?
LEON	Dad
ROB	I asked Danny
KAREN	Rob, shut up.
ROB	Danny?
DANNY	Yes.
ROB	Yes you are. That's the answer. But I tell you something, Lee She's a fucking nightmare, she humiliates me every day of the week. Has she told you about Mr Leigh, Leon? With his mansion in Surrey? But he won't leave his wife
KAREN	That's not true, Lee.
LEON	No?
KAREN	I think you should let your friend call his mum, Leon.

LEON	It's through there, mate.
KAREN	You go and show him, Lee.
	DANNY *and* LEON *go off to make the phone call.*
ROB	Well, I did it.
KAREN	What?
ROB	I did what you wanted. I did what you asked. You can have your car whenever you want. I hope you're happy.
KAREN	What am I supposed to say?
ROB	Say you're happy.
KAREN	Course I'm not happy. This doesn't make me happy.
ROB	It's what you wanted.
KAREN	I didn't want this. Have you told Leon?
ROB	No
KAREN	Well, you're gonna have to.
ROB	I can't
KAREN	You're gonna have to. Coz I got my own things I need to tell him.
	LEON *enters.*
ROB	Is she answering?
LEON	Yes
ROB	Where has she been?
LEON	I don't know.
ROB	Was she sorry?
LEON	How am I supposed to know?

DANNY enters.

ROB What did she say?

DANNY She said
She was cooking.

ROB Cooking!

Beat.

LEON I reckon I better walk you home, mate.

KAREN Rob'll walk you

ROB I'll drive him.

KAREN Don't be a fuckin moron, Rob. In your state.

LEON It's *alright*, I'll take him

KAREN Leon. I want you to stay here.

LEON Why?

KAREN Because I want to speak to you.

LEON Yeah?

KAREN Yeah.
There's something important I want to talk about.

Pause.

Please?

Pause.

LEON Come on, Danny.

KAREN Leon.

ROB Come on, boys

KAREN Lee.

LEON Let's go.

He exits. DANNY *follows.* ROB *follows.*

Scene Eighteen

Family Recipe

RUKHSANA *over a hob. Cooking khichiri. There are two pots.*

RUKHSANA My mother's khichiri
An ancient recipe.
The thing she made
The day I left home.
The last time I saw her, 1977.

Poor bruised son

A key in the door. She hears. Dread.

Ach…
How could I have known this would happen?

ROB (*Off.*) So where is she?

RUKHSANA I used to be a good mother.

ROB *storms in.*

Where is she?

ROB Did you not listen to any of those messages?

RUKHSANA Where is he? Danny.

DANNY *enters. They don't hug.*

I thought they'd have put you in some kind of support.

DANNY They called you over and over.

RUKHSANA It's good you're up and walking.

ROB No remorse.

LEON Dad.

ROB And you've just been calmly cookin this stinking what do you call this?

RUKHSANA Khichiri

DANNY (*Imitating the accent.*) 'Khichiri'

ROB	Ha!
DANNY	Velly nice!
ROB	Ha!
LEON	It smells quite nice to me.
ROB	Oh fuck off, Leon, no one asked you to come along. Eh Danny? *To* RUKHSANA. Your son could have been killed and you seem completely unconcerned. Are you even listening to me?
RUKHSANA	Sit down.
ROB	No, I'll stand.
RUKHSANA	What could I possibly have done? If I had been at home?
DANNY	You would have been there. So who was it?
RUKHSANA	What?
DANNY	Who was you with?
RUKHSANA	Who 'was' you with, why are you speaking like this?
DANNY	What you taking the piss for?
ROB	He could have been killed.
DANNY	What are you taking the piss for, Mum? *Beat.*
LEON	I can't listen to this.
ROB	What?
DANNY	What's wrong?
LEON	Can we find somewhere quiet?
DANNY	Why?

LEON	I don't have the head for it.
	Beat.
DANNY	If you want, you can go in my bedroom.
LEON	Yeah?
DANNY	If you want.
LEON	Will you come with?
ROB	Just fuck off out of it, Leon.
	Pause. LEON *goes into* DANNY*'s bedroom.*
	So where were you?
	Beat.
RUKHSANA	It's no secret. I got offered the job, Danny.
	It's not a bad job, good terms, a good company. Small but ambitious.
	They're going to target their product At the Indian middle classes Because you don't get markets like that here.
	And I was trying to think about whether I want to take it. Whether I want to live in this country at all. Or whether we'd be happier where the real opportunities are.
DANNY	What?
RUKHSANA	I've been thinking about moving back to Bombay.
ROB	That's ridiculous.
RUKHSANA	Is it?
ROB	It's ridiculous you're even discussing this. Most people from where you're from would give their front teeth to have what you've got here.

PRETEND YOU HAVE BIG BUILDINGS 105

RUKHSANA	Why do you assume I am privileged to live in a place I do not love? I want to go back to my home. I want to know my family. Danny… has never met his grandparents. We're going to visit them. What about that, Danny?
DANNY	I'm not going.
RUKHSANA	You want to stay in a place like this?
DANNY	Yes.
RUKHSANA	Why?
DANNY	Because this is where I'm from.
ROB	Tell me, what does your husband think about this?
RUKHSANA	What he *thought* was the *problem*.
ROB	Well, that's it, isn't it – that's what it's like with the lot of you!
RUKHSANA	The lot of who?
ROB	He's a local man, isn't he?
DANNY	Rob
RUKHSANA	He was local.
ROB	He's got ideas about the world.
DANNY	I'm going.
RUKHSANA	He did have ideas about the world.

DANNY *tries to move off quickly to his bedroom.*

Danny!

RUKHSANA *catches him but he flings her off and makes for the bedroom.*

What has he said to you? About my husband? What has he said?

Danny!

ROB	He's in property, isn't he? Development.

Pause.

RUKHSANA	He's dead.

He was killed. A few months ago. An accident. And for some reason coming to this country seemed to be the right thing to do.

Why would Danny make that up?

ROB	I'm so sorry. I'm I'm not normally like this. I think my wife's about to leave me.
RUKHSANA	Then perhaps you should go and make sure?

Can you fetch your son? I'm not sure I can face them.

ROB gets up.

It's first on the right. (DANNY's *bedroom*.)

He disappears in the direction of DANNY's *room.*

RUKHSANA *takes stock.*

ROB *reappears. Smiling, almost.*

ROB	You'll never believe this.
RUKHSANA	What is it?
ROB	They've done a runner. The two of em? The window's open, they must have climbed out…

I don't blame them.

RUKHSANA	No!

They laugh. Relief, somehow.

Are you hungry?

ROB	Starving.

RUKHSANA   I could put some chips in.

ROB   You got chips?

RUKHSANA   Yes

ROB   No, I want what smells so nice.
Khichiri.
Is it hot?
I mean spicy hot.

RUKHSANA   No. It's… well I suppose you could say it's quite bland.

ROB   I love my wife so much.

RUKHSANA takes the ginger out of the pot. She places a serving of khichiri on ROB's place.

Pause.

Danny said you, er
You, er
Ate with your hands

RUKHSANA   Did he?
Some people do

ROB   Well if it's no trouble / I'll

RUKHSANA   Have a go

ROB   Oh?

RUKHSANA   Just once. Have a go with your hands, there's nothing wrong with it

Beat.

ROB   Won't kill me, will it?

RUKHSANA   That's right
(*She mimes.*) You sweep up like this.
Use your thumb
Push the rice upwards into your mouth.

She demonstrates, without rice. ROB sweeps up the khichiri with his left hand.

ROB	Okay.
RUKHSANA	Use your right hand.
ROB	Why?
RUKHSANA	The left hand is for wiping your bottom.
	Me, I prefer a knife and fork.
	She gets up.
ROB	You!
	They laugh. ROB *eats.* RUKHSANA *serves herself some. They eat hungrily.*
	This is alright, this.
RUKHSANA	(*Her mouth full.*) Mmm.
ROB	Really tasty. A recipe passed down the generations?
RUKHSANA	Yes.
ROB	Somebody's gonna be a lucky man one day.
	Funny… eating with your hands. Like Did you ever go barefoot in the mud? Squishing about?
RUKHSANA	Yes.
ROB	Some fantastic places when I was a kid.
	ROB *is suffering from some strange inaction. And it is to do with* RUKHSANA.
	Am I going to have to go in a minute?
RUKHSANA	No.
ROB	And what should we do about Our children? If they don't come back? If they're not back by morning.

RUKHSANA	We'll leave no stone unturned.
	But let's just eat, for a minute…
ROB	That's right.
RUKHSANA	'That's right.' You sound just like my husband.

Beat. They eat.

Scene Nineteen

The Sky at Night

DANNY *and* LEON. *The strip of green, a few hours later that evening.*

LEON	(So you go to the border
	The strip of green
	The place by the burnt-out house
	The site of the old tollgate
	Where the London Road meets Whalebone Lane
	The border, the end of London.)

DANNY points at Canary Wharf.

DANNY	I didn't know you could see it from here.
LEON	It looks better at night, dunnit?
	Beautiful.
DANNY	All the light in it.
	At four in the morning, still all lit.
	Come on. We could walk there.
	We could.
LEON	No mate.
DANNY	We could.
LEON	I'm not going any further.

DANNY	Why?
	Pause.
	You cold?
LEON	It's not that.
DANNY	You can have my coat.
LEON	It's alright.
DANNY	I don't mind.
	I fancy another fight. I could have beat him.
LEON	You could
DANNY	You punched me in the stomach.
LEON	I had to.
DANNY	Why?
LEON	I was absolutely terrified.
	I can't stop thinking about my mum.
DANNY	Not worth thinking about.
LEON	It is.
DANNY	You still got your dad.
LEON	Yeah.
DANNY	He'll look after ya.
LEON	Will he?
DANNY	Yeah.
LEON	D'you wanna ciggie, Dan?
DANNY	You'll get cancer.
LEON	I don't get cancer.
	DANNY *gasps in admiration. They light up. They blow streams of smoke that collide like a nuclear explosion.*

DANNY	Look at that.
LEON	Like an atom bomb
DANNY	Tell us a secret.
LEON	What kind?
DANNY	Any kind you like.
LEON	Can I trust you?
DANNY	Yeah.

Beat.

LEON	I used to piss myself.
DANNY	You're joking!
LEON	I'm not joking. No. I get so confused I can't control it. Panicked. I thought it'd stop when I grew up, but now I'm nearly there. Are you becoming unsure about me?
DANNY	No.
LEON	Sure?
DANNY	Yeah, I'm sure.

Scene Twenty

Search Party

The Dolphin/marketplace. ROB *and* RUKHSANA *enter. The clubbers have gone home. The market place is quiet.*

ROB	Not a soul
RUKHSANA	Should have seen it a few hours ago.
ROB	Tell me about it.

RUKHSANA	I don't think we're going to find them.
ROB	They'll be alright.
RUKHSANA	It's so cold.
ROB	At least it's stopped snowing.
RUKHSANA	He's weak.
ROB	Don't worry about that.
RUKHSANA	No?
ROB	Leon'll look after him.
RUKHSANA	Are you sure?
ROB	I'm sure. He's a good boy I'm sure. I've already lost My wife today. And I chucked in my job. So it'd be fucking carelessness to lose anyone else.
RUKHSANA	I don't know what to do.
ROB	No
RUKHSANA	This fear that's growing.
ROB	I know.
RUKHSANA	Cold.
ROB	Come here, then.

They hug. ROB *considers a cheeky swooping snog but thinks better of it.*

RUKHSANA	I want to call my mother. I want to say I'm going to take her grandson to see her
ROB	You really leaving?
RUKHSANA	I think so
ROB	I mean I'm even a bit sad You know what I mean?

RUKHSANA	You've given me the whole tour!
ROB	Here y'are. You see that? That pyramid behind the roundabout? That's called the Dolphin. Our contribution to the architecture of the world. A derelict swimming pool. It won awards. It was alright when it was working. It had a wave-splash. Blinding. I used to take Leon when he was this high. Then the roof started fallin to pieces. The council wouldn't pay to keep it going. Tories. I voted Conservative the last four times and I reckon I've been made a mug.

Pause.

RUKHSANA	You know what it reminds me of? It reminds me of the top of the Canary Wharf tower. The pyramid on top. It's like when they built Canary Wharf they copied this. You know what they should do? Someone should light it up. And keep the lights on all night.
ROB	That's an idea
RUKHSANA	At least for Christmas.
ROB	What did you think of me when I stormed in? Bet you thought I was a caveman?
RUKHSANA	I married a man from here.

Beat.

ROB	I'm not like him, am I?
RUKHSANA	No.

ROB	It crossed my mind.
RUKHSANA	Not when I knew him, no.
ROB	Good. Listen Don't get me wrong I mean given my circumstances it might seem a bit funny, but If you wanted I could take you right out into Essex, in the car. Tomorrow maybe Show you the country. Listen, would you like a fag?
RUKHSANA	Yeah, okay.
ROB	I've started going out in the garden late at night and hope she doesn't notice

They spark up.

RUKHSANA	She'll know
ROB	Yeah?
RUKHSANA	Well, you won't need to hide any more.
ROB	Small mercies, ay?
RUKHSANA	There aren't many nights like this, are there?

She exhales, he exhales – two streams of smoke that collide like an atom bomb.

Scene Twenty-One

The Pink Room 2

The Pink Room, the same evening. From somewhere outside a fluorescent Christmas reindeer buzzes. Hanging from the ceiling is KAREN's *birthday dress. She has left it behind. There are still assorted cosmetics on the dresser.* LEON *and* DANNY *enter.*

LEON	This is it. This is where they sleep.
	He examines the dresser.
	She never goes out without make-up. Look there's still some here! She wouldn't leave her make-up behind would she?
	The bedstead, they got last year in the sale And she loves it. He sleeps on the right and she's on the left. She's the one who snores. When I was little I used to crawl in Make a gap between them.
	This rack. It used to be bursting with clothes.
	That dress. He gave her that for her birthday.
	She must have left it on purpose.
	How could she, you know? He was alright, wasn't he?
	She's definitely gone, hasn't she?
	Listen, Danny, can I trust you? And if I can't that's fine, it don't make no difference.
DANNY	You can trust me.
LEON	It's a bit weird. No it's not, it's not weird. It's okay.
DANNY	Go on.
LEON	You sure?
DANNY	Yeah.
LEON	Okay
	LEON *picks up some make-up.*

                        Can you put this on me? Seriously.

DANNY   What, this?

LEON   There's no harm in it.

DANNY   No, I know.

LEON   Cosmetics.

DANNY   Yeah.

LEON   Changes things.

                You take that sponge there.

DANNY   What if somebody comes?

LEON   It don't matter.
                That's important.
                It doesn't matter.

                DANNY takes up a sponge. It's the sponge you use for foundation.

                And you can do it slowly.

                DANNY applies it, slowly. Quite a pale colour. He holds LEON's face.

                There's no rush.

                DANNY continues applying it.

                The thing with this is

                You have to hold your nerve.

                Because if you don't

                And you cave in

                You'll die.

                DANNY holds LEON's face. He kisses LEON, awkwardly, rigidly. For a time nothing moves, but then LEON nudges DANNY away.

DANNY   What?

LEON   No, it's alright.

DANNY	Sorry
LEON	It's just I'm not
DANNY	No, I'm not!
LEON	It's alright.
DANNY	Something about tonight.
LEON	There's no problem. You gotta try everything once, don't ya? And it works or it doesn't. Well? Did it work?
DANNY	I don't think so.
LEON	You'll work it out. Here y'are. Eyeliner. You sure you're up for this?
DANNY	How do I do it, then?
LEON	Hold my stare.

DANNY *applies the eyeliner. The doorbell rings.*

DANNY	Oh shit.
LEON	It's alright.
DANNY	Oh fuck.
LEON	Whoever it is. It don't matter There's no shame in this. You go and get the door. And don't try and divert them. If they wanna see me, I'll see them.

DANNY *exits.* LEON *breathes deeply.*

You're *alright*, mate.

STEVEN *enters, with* DANNY.

STEVEN	Jesus
LEON	What you looking at?

STEVEN	Nothing.
	LEON *stands up.*
LEON	No, whatchoo looking at?
STEVEN	I just didn't know you still did all that.
LEON	(*To* DANNY.) Steve used to love all this We used to dress up all the time, didn't we? Steve? He grew out of it. So he says. *Beat.* You were bang out of order.
STEVEN	I know
LEON	Danny had nothing to do with it.
STEVEN	Yeah, I know.
LEON	He could press charges
STEVEN	I know. I was bang out of order. I wouldn't blame ya. You'd be within your rights if you wanted to take this further. You don't though, do you?
DANNY	No, mate. Shake?
STEVEN	Yeah.

STEVEN *reaches out his hand to shake* DANNY*'s hand.* DANNY *moves to reciprocate, but at the moment of contact he flashes it up instead, smoothing his hair.*

LEON *laughs.* DANNY *laughs.* STEVEN *laughs.*

DANNY	No, seriously.

DANNY *shakes* STEVEN*'s hand.*

STEVEN	Cheers.
	Pause.
LEON	I'm not finished yet.
STEVEN	Mate.
LEON	I'm not finished. Wait. Just wait
	Reverentially, LEON *takes the dress off the rack, and takes the necessary clothes off in order to change into the dress.*
	Pause. They watch LEON. STEVEN *takes* DANNY *aside.*
STEVEN	I mean I mean, fair play to him Each to his own But…
	I mean, his mum wore that. That can't be right.
	And he's making us feel like we're the queer ones. He didn't use to be like this.
	Pause.
	I was wrong about you. You're alright.
DANNY	Thanks.
	LEON *has now completed his task.*
LEON	Well?
STEVEN	Leon.
LEON	Do you like it?
	Pause.
	What?

STEVEN	Leon
LEON	What d'ya reckon?
STEVEN	Mate.
	Pause.
LEON	Well, don't just stand there
STEVEN	Leon… I've been a dickhead to you, too…
	Pause. Relief.
LEON	About my dad?
STEVEN	Yeah
LEON	That slander.
STEVEN	I shouldn't have taken it out on you.
LEON	No
STEVEN	Coz it's your dad who's the guilty one.
	Elsewhere a key turns in a lock.
DANNY	What's that?
LEON	What?
DANNY	Someone's come in
LEON	Nah
ROB'S VOICE	This is it.
RUKHSANA'S VOICE	It's nice.
ROB'S VOICE	Home. It's not much.
RUKHSANA'S VOICE	It's perfect.
LEON	Oh, fucking hell.

ROB'S VOICE   Let me take your coat

RUKHSANA'S VOICE   Thank you.

STEVEN   Turn the light off!

LEON pauses, then turns the light off.

ROB'S VOICE   You wanna go upstairs?

Pause.

The boys scurry off to hide.

ROB leads RUKHSANA into the bedroom. They are barely visible in the light.

They sit on the bed.

ROB   Feel like I'm fifteen years old.

They sit there. And to be fair to them, they're not really shagging. But LEON can't bear it, and begins to wail.

Wuuuuuuaaaaagh

ROB dives for the light switch. The light comes on.

DANNY   Mum

RUKHSANA looks at her son.

What have you done?

Everyone is visible.

ROB   It's alright.
It's all alright.

And then LEON pisses himself. At first, only a little bit, but gradually and improbably growing into a deluge that engulfs the characters and returns the stage to rain.

Scene Twenty-Two

The Present Day

KAREN. *She is wearing a smart suit, and carries her little glowing model of the Docklands in the future.*

KAREN　　And I'll tell you what it'll be like in the future.
Okay.
I got this flat in Bethnal Green.
It's nice.
Top floor.
Rob owns it.
I pay him rent. He knocks a little off, but it's still expensive.
He owns ten houses just around here.

She holds her model aloft.

And on one side of the building.
Is a window.
And from there I can see this amazing picture
At night.
I almost can't believe what's sprung up.

I'm alone.
But that's okay – there's enough people at work to take care of.
And Leon comes over
He's doing well for himself
He always had a brain.
He's got himself someone.
We go out to a bar.
And I don't like it that he's smoking
But he buys the drinks.
He *knows* how to order drinks.
And he's all grown up.

There is a future. It's been proved
Time and time again.

ANNIE *moves off, out.* DANNY *remains, looking at the house.*

Scene Twenty-Three

The Dolphin

LEON *and* DANNY, *standing outside the Dolphin, all dark. They watch it. Suddenly, it lights up, gloriously.*

The End.

WINTERLONG

Andrew Sheridan

For Rebecca

ANDREW SHERIDAN

Andrew trained as an actor at Rose Bruford and has performed extensively in award-winning theatre, TV and film. Andrew's debut play *Winterlong* won the 2008 Bruntwood Prize for Playwriting. In 2011 the play opened at the Royal Exchange Studio, Manchester, directed by Sarah Frankcom, and subsequently transferred to Soho Theatre, London.
Andrew's play *Hope, Light & Nowhere* was produced at the 2013 Edinburgh Festival Fringe, and in 2014 he was the recipient of the Tom Erhardt Award for emerging writers. In 2018 his play *Paulding Light* was shortlisted for the Nick Darke Award. In 2020 Andrew's adaptation of Emily Brontë's classic *Wuthering Heights* opened at the Royal Exchange, Manchester, to both popular and critical acclaim. Andrew is currently in development for an original TV comedy and a new stage musical. His passion is for telling untold, Northern stories.

Introduction
Andrew Sheridan, 2025

When I told my careers teacher that I wanted to be an actor or a writer, he laughed and told me to join the army. I considered it for a bit. Growing up in eighties Manchester, the lofty idea of going into something so alien as theatre or writing felt impossible. No one did it round my way. Those kids who passed their 11-plus and went to the grammar schools, more often than not went on to university. Those of us who failed were herded through secondary modern schools until we were jettisoned out at the age of sixteen. If you were lucky, you got an apprenticeship at British Gas, saved up for a house, got married, had a couple of kids, and went on holiday to Spain once a year. Creative aspirations were encouraged to be hidden.

But Manchester was going through a renaissance when I was a teenager. Manchester had a new religion, other than Manchester United. Music. And a new cathedral had been built. The Hacienda. Suddenly town was a cauldron of working-class kids making stuff, expressing themselves. The Happy Mondays, The Stone Roses, Inspiral Carpets, James, 808 State were the cultural vanguard leading the way for all of us closeted creatives. If they could do it, so could we. We found our voices. We sang. We played guitars. And some of us picked up our pens and began to write. For a time, anything felt possible. We were the makers. The movers and shakers. The top had been taken off the bottle – and we weren't going to be put back in.

I auditioned and got a place at drama school. Left Manchester Piccadilly station at seventeen and moved to London. There I trained to be an actor. Just before the turn of the millennium I graduated and started working solidly as an actor. I was always drawn to new writing rather than the classics – their immediacy seemed to resonate more with me. I could almost touch them. Sarah Kane had just taken her own life. Though I never got to see *Blasted* when it was first staged at the Royal

Court, her work and words always seemed to sit inside me along with those of Edward Bond.

But Manchester always called me home. It was my city; it runs through my DNA. My work brought me back home to Manchester. I was in the first play at the new Royal Exchange Studio. Little did I know then, that would start a creative relationship with the Exchange that has spanned twenty-five years. It was here that I met two writers that would change my life – Simon Stephens and later Robert Holman. They cast me in their plays. Firstly, Billy Keats in Simon's seminal play *Port*. Then Simon introduced me to Robert. Robert became my closest friend, my mentor, my loudest advocate. He encouraged me to write. This is where *Winterlong* came from. If it weren't for either of these giants, I would never have written my first play that won the Bruntwood Prize in 2011. I can still vividly remember the day I won and feeling both their hands on my shoulder. I'm blessed to have had both of them in my life. Sadly, Robert died in 2021. I miss him every day. I miss his voice down the phone. I miss everything about him. I feel him over my shoulder whenever I'm on stage or whenever I'm writing. I owe him everything.

Winterlong follows Oscar across fifteen years – a boy abandoned by his young mother, raised by emotionally distant grandparents in a world of predators and broken adults. Oscar navigates his love-starved life through this landscape of decay until he finds a glimpse of connection with a stranger. It's about recognising that love, however frail and hidden, always exists inside us. Somewhere. Perhaps I wrote about Oscar because I understood his search.

Winning the prize didn't make me a writer. I don't really know what being a writer is. It still feels too lofty, too self-congratulatory, too alien. But I write. The stuff I write gets performed around the world by amazing actors. I'm lucky. Very lucky. And while sometimes I still wonder about that different path – the army would've made a good play, after all – I know I'm more of a person for doing what I do: write and act.

Winterlong was first performed at the Royal Exchange Theatre, Manchester, on 2 February 2011, with the following cast:

OSCAR/BOY	Harry McEntire
HELEN/GIRL	Rebecca Callard
JOHN	Paul Copley
MALCOLM/NEIL/PHILIP	Laurence Mitchell
JEAN	Gabrielle Reidy
Director	Sarah Frankcom
Designer	Amanda Stoodley
Lighting Designer	Richard Owen
Sound Designer	Peter Rice

The production transferred to Soho Theatre, London, on 23 February 2011.

Author's Note

I would like to thank Sarah Frankcom, everyone at the Royal Exchange, as well as Mike Oglesby and Bruntwood.

I would also like to offer heartfelt thanks to Robert Holman, David Eldridge and Simon Stephens, who I will be forever indebted to for their support, belief and inspiration. Three great men. Three great friends.

A.S.

Characters

BOY, *eight*
HELEN, *fifteen to twenty-six*
JOHN, *fifty-five to sixty-seven*
MALCOLM
JEAN, *fifty-six to sixty-five*
NEIL
OSCAR, *six* (*offstage*) *to fifteen*
PHILIP
GIRL, *fifteen*

Setting and Time

The play takes place in and around Manchester, though this isn't strictly important. The action spans fifteen years of Oscar's life. It could take place anywhere and in any time.

The set should be non-naturalistic and should be evoked by space, detail, lighting and sound rather than realism.

Some characters could be played by the same actor with the exception of John, Jean, and Oscar.

Punctuation is used to indicate delivery, not to conform to the rules of grammar.

Scene One

Bonfire Night. A wall by a canal. A broken street lamp.

It is nearly dark.

The odd firework explodes.

Bonfire mist and the smell of sulphur.

The sound of a fire engine in the distance.

Moonlight falls on the hard outline of a pregnant schoolgirl sat on the wall.

It is HELEN *(fifteen). She has two cut knees.*

A plastic carrier bag of shopping lies at her feet.

She strikes a match on the wall.

She lights a cigarette and her face is brightened by the flame.

She lets the whole match burn.

She throws it in the canal.

She smokes the cigarette.

She rubs her stomach.

The street lamp starts to buzz and flicker. It casts intermittent orange light over the canal and falls on the shape of a BOY *standing underneath.*

He is silent and still.

He watches HELEN.

She doesn't see him.

HELEN (*singing*). Two dead dogs sitting on a wall,
 Two dead dogs sitting on a wall,
 And if one dead dog should accidentally fall,
 There'll be one dead dog sitting on a wall.

The street lamp settles.

The BOY *is soaking wet and wearing white underpants and vest.*

He holds a pair of red wellington boots in his hands.

HELEN *becomes aware of his presence. She hardens. She doesn't look at him.*

BOY. You shouldn't smoke. Give your baby cancer. Make it all small and poisoned. Might come out with no head. Might come out with no head no arms no legs. Just a body. Not even nipples. Not even a belly button. Just a pale body like a bag of milk.

He turns the two wellington boots upside down and water pours from them onto the floor. It forms a puddle at his feet.

The BOY *puts the wellington boots on.*

He kicks and stamps the puddle.

Give us a bit of that cig.

HELEN. Too young to smoke.

BOY. You better give us some.

HELEN. Or what?

BOY. Or I'll come over there and punch that rat in your fat ugly stomach so hard it comes out of your mouth and dies in the dirt. That's what.

Pause.

I'll do it. I touched a tramp's hand this morning. She had shit under her fingernails and I still did it. If I can do that I can do anything.

HELEN. Told you.

BOY. Fuck off you slag.

The BOY *picks up a stone from the floor and throws it at* HELEN.

I said fuck off you slag you deaf cunt.

HELEN *spits at the* BOY.

(*Wounded and wiping the spit off himself.*) Fuck off. Mong head.

HELEN. Why do you swear so much?

The BOY *gives her the finger and mouths 'fuck off' silently.*

He looks at the floor.

Pause.

BOY. I saw three dead cats in there today. They just floated past my face when I was swimming. People fling them in there all the time. They just melt and fall to bits. I'd kill all the cats in the world if it was up to me. That's what I'd do if I was fucking God.

Pause.

Please can I have a bit?

HELEN. Give you cancer.

BOY. I'm not scared.

HELEN. You will be when your balls drop off.

BOY. I won't be. I don't believe in cancer. I don't believe in anything me. I want to see the whole world burn down.

Screaming fireworks explode and wail.

HELEN *goes to leave.*

(*Stopping her.*) It's my birthday. That's what it is. Today.

The BOY *sits on the wall.*

HELEN *stops.*

She returns to the wall and gives the BOY *the cigarette.*

HELEN. Happy birthday.

The BOY *goes to smoke the cigarette but stamps on it instead.*

BOY. Shouldn't fucking smoke.

HELEN *slaps the* BOY *hard across the face.*

The BOY *tries to shield himself.*

As the attack escalates the smacks become full-on punches. It is brutal and ugly and painful.

HELEN (*smacking*). You.

(*Smacking.*) Stink.

(*Smacking.*) Of.

(*Smacking.*) Dog.

(*Smacking.*) Shit.

(*Punching.*) You.

(*Punching.*) Skinny.

(*Punching.*) Fucking.

(*Punching.*) Pig.

(*Punching.*) Baby.

What you crying for?

Why you crying?

That was my last one.

Stop it.

Pause.

I hate people crying.

HELEN *gets a loaf of bread and a jar of jam from the carrier bag on the floor.*

She takes a slice of bread and puts it on her knee.

She opens the jam jar and dips her fingers into it and scoops out some jam.

She puts the jam on the slice of bread and folds it in half.

She offers the jam sandwich to the BOY.

Here.

The BOY *wipes his nose on his knee and takes the sandwich.*

He begins to eat it a corner at a time.

HELEN *puts her fingers in her mouth and sucks the jam off them.*

She puts the lid on the jam jar and puts it and the loaf of bread back into the carrier bag.

HELEN *looks at her reflection in the canal.*

It begins to snow.

BOY. See that bike? I'd never throw it in there if it was mine. I'd polish it every day. Been trying to get it out for weeks. Keep running out of breath. Wish I was a fish sometimes. I could stay down there for ever then.

The BOY *shivers.*

HELEN. It's too cold to be swimming in the canal. You'll die you you know. I've seen it happen loads of times. When you're under the water it'll freeze over and you'll be trapped in there for ever. They'll find you in hundreds of years. Defrost you and put you in a museum in a glass case. All brown and shrivelled with a giant head.

HELEN *takes her coat off.*

You should put my coat on.

BOY. I don't feel the cold me.

The BOY *shivers.*

HELEN *throws the coat toward the* BOY.

It lands on the floor between them.

The BOY *hesitates before putting the coat on.*

I'm only putting it on because you want me to.

The BOY *shivers.*

How did you do that? Your knee?

Beat.

HELEN. Don't know.

The BOY *puts his hand in the canal.*

He cleans HELEN*'s knee with the water.*

He takes one plaster from his own knee and puts it on HELEN*'s cut knee.*

HELEN *rubs her pregnant stomach.*

The BOY *watches.*

BOY. Can I have a go?

Beat.

HELEN. Dry your hands off.

The BOY *dries his hands.*

Warm your hands up then. Rub them together.

The BOY *rubs his hands together.*

HELEN *takes his hand and puts it on her stomach.*

Can you feel its foot sticking out?

BOY. Yes.

HELEN. When I'm in the bath you can see it sometimes. Sticking right out. Like a doll inside a balloon.

BOY. Can I listen?

HELEN *hesitates but lets the* BOY *put his ear to her stomach.*

HELEN *puts her hand on the* BOY*'s head and strokes his hair.*

I wish I was him inside your stomach. I don't think I'd ever come out. I think I'd stay in there for ever. Hanging on to your insides. You're going to be the best mum in the world. I think that you should know that.

A firework explodes overhead, showering them both with an incredible illumination that hangs above them as the moment freezes in time.

They both look at each other and don't look away.

You could call him Oscar. That's my name. I think he'd like it.

HELEN. Might not be an him.

BOY. It is.

HELEN. How do you know?

BOY. I know everything me.

HELEN. Can I have my coat back? I'm going to miss my bus. My mum will kill me if I lose that one. Lost about three already. Not even Christmas yet. Always losing everything me.

The BOY takes the coat off and offers it back to HELEN.

She puts it on.

BOY (*singing*). One dead dog sitting on the wall,
One dead dog sitting on the wall,
And if that dead dog should accidentally fall,
There'll be no dead dog sitting on the wall.

HELEN (*as he sings*). I hope my baby's just like you. I think I could love him for ever. I'd hold his hand and never let him go.

Another firework explodes with a deafening bang and a blinding flash.

Darkness.

The BOY disappears.

Moonlight.

HELEN*'s waters have broken. It steams as it hits the floor.*

HELEN *is left in the moonlight giving birth to her son,* OSCAR.

Scene Two

Two years later. February. A secluded part of a bus station.

It is three o'clock in the morning.

Darkness gives way to oppressive fluorescent lighting.

The sound of plastic seats flapping in the wind.

Hard rain batters the metal roof.

The rain drips and collects in small puddles on the floor.

Somewhere in a different part of the station, a woman howls. It echoes through the space and dies suddenly.

JOHN (*fifty-five*) *is perched on a tall plastic waiting seat. Next to him is* OSCAR (*two*) *in a pram.*

He takes out a flask and pours himself a cup of coffee.

He sips it.

MALCOLM *enters carrying a cardboard box.*

He is dressed in a black suit. The trousers of which are hitched up with bicycle clips.

He doesn't have a bike.

MALCOLM. I've been to a funeral.

Pause.

I said I've been to a funeral.

Pause.

That's where I've been. To a funeral. It's been a particularly difficult day. You know. Emotionally.

Pause.

Life. It can be such an anti-climax don't you think? I say funeral. It was a cremation.

Pause.

I don't suppose you would be interested in sharing that flask? I wouldn't normally be so forward. I wouldn't normally request the company of a stranger. But I've had somewhat of a lonely day and beggars can't be choosers. Not thirty-seven minutes past three and eighteen seconds in the morning. I'm not a scrounger. I've got some Bourbon Creams. We could do a swap.

JOHN *pours* MALCOLM *a cup of coffee from the flask.*

He offers MALCOLM *the cup.*

MALCOLM *takes a packet of Bourbon Creams from his coat pocket.*

MALCOLM *offers them to* JOHN.

They both exchange their offerings.

I always carry a fresh packet of biscuits and a clean handkerchief. You never know when they might come in handy.

MALCOLM *whistles a long continuous note until his breath runs out.*

I hope you don't mind me admitting that asking you to share your coffee is the bravest act of connection I've ever attempted in my life.

JOHN *smiles.*

MALCOLM *dunks a Bourbon Cream into his coffee and eats it.*

My name is Malcolm by the way.

JOHN *nods.*

Do you mind me asking who's in the pram?

Pause.

The pram. Who's in the pram?

JOHN *looks at* MALCOLM.

Sorry. I've overstepped the mark haven't I? I should learn to walk before I can run.

JOHN. He has trouble sleeping.

MALCOLM. Really?

JOHN. So do I.

MALCOLM. Really?

JOHN. A walk in the night seems to help.

MALCOLM. Yes.

What's he called?

JOHN *is silent.*

I've had two teeth out. Two molars.

MALCOLM *shows* JOHN.

JOHN *doesn't really want to see.*

JOHN. Yes.

MALCOLM. My gums were bleeding for hours. I had to put toilet paper in the holes where my teeth had been.

MALCOLM *shows* JOHN.

JOHN *doesn't want to see.*

JOHN. It's my grandson. Oscar.

MALCOLM. Oscar. I don't think I've ever met an Oscar. I collect names.

Beat.

Do you think I could sneak a peek?

JOHN *nods.*

MALCOLM *goes over to the pram and looks in.*

He's tiny. Still looks like a proper baby.

JOHN. He's two.

Beat.

He's not disabled.

MALCOLM. That's good.

Pause.

He has a very distinct odour. I have a very astute sense of smell. Always have done. I can smell a fox a mile off. It's a talent I inherited from my mother.

Pause.

He looks like you. Same ears. He must make you feel very happy. Fulfilled even.

JOHN. He does. I am.

MALCOLM. I'd like to be a granddad one day. I'd have to be a father first I suppose. I'm not really a woman sort of man though.

Beat.

JOHN. You might struggle then.

Beat.

MALCOLM. Yes. I might. I suppose.

JOHN *stands up and prepares to leave.*

Robert was attacked by a stray cocker spaniel this morning. The dog didn't cause any physical damage but Robert's very sensitive. I think it's more of a psychological injury. They often take longer to heal. It will probably take him a while to gather enough confidence before he feels comfortable to be out in public on his own again. It's a shame. He's always been such a free spirit. I feel very responsible. If we hadn't of argued. If I hadn't of lost my temper and locked him out of the house then none of this might have happened. Who would have thought a ham salad could cause such anguish.

JOHN. Who's Robert?

MALCOLM. Robert. My pet tortoise.

JOHN. Right.

MALCOLM. He's in that box. I had to take him to the funeral with me. Sat him on a prayer cushion. I tried to find a black box as a mark of respect but they're very hard to come by.

JOHN *drains his cup quickly and puts the flask away.*

What's your name?

JOHN. I don't think I want to tell you my name.

MALCOLM. I'd like to know your name. Like I said I collect them. Store them up here.

JOHN studies MALCOLM.

Okay. Well, see you then. Thank you for the cup.

JOHN. Yes.

MALCOLM. Night.

JOHN. Goodnight.

Beat.

I hope your tortoise gets better.

MALCOLM. So do I.

JOHN goes to leave.

MALCOLM suddenly sings the theme tune to Jim'll Fix It.

JOHN stops.

He watches him.

JOHN (*as MALCOLM sings*). You're singing.

Pause.

Are you singing?

Pause.

Stop singing.

MALCOLM *finishes the theme tune to* Jim'll Fix It.

Right then.

MALCOLM (*the bravest thing he has ever asked in his life*). I haven't quite figured out how all this works. The mechanics of the situation.

Beat.

I give up. (*Holding his hands up.*) I surrender.

Beat.

I think I would like to have sex with you.

JOHN *is silent.*

Has that come as a shock to you?

JOHN. It has a little.

MALCOLM. You look petrified.

JOHN. I am. A little.

MALCOLM. Are you?

JOHN. Yes. I am.

MALCOLM. Don't be.

JOHN. Right.

MALCOLM. There's no need.

JOHN. Isn't there?

MALCOLM. No. There's absolutely no point in being the slightest bit afraid of what I'm going to do to you.

JOHN. Right.

MALCOLM. I'm going to undo my belt.

MALCOLM *undoes his belt.*

I'm going to unzip my flies.

MALCOLM *opens his flies.*

I'm taking my trousers down.

JOHN. I don't think this is right.

MALCOLM. Unfortunately you don't have a choice in the matter any longer.

MALCOLM *drops his trousers down to his ankles.*

MALCOLM *shuffles towards* JOHN.

MALCOLM *stands face to face with* JOHN.

It's as if they might kiss.

MALCOLM *gently strokes* JOHN*'s face.*

JOHN. I think I should get home.

Beat.

I think this is a mistake.

Beat.

I've got money. I've got fifteen pound. You can have it.

Beat.

We can just pretend nothing has happened.

MALCOLM. We can't.

JOHN. I could just go.

MALCOLM. You can't.

JOHN. Please don't.

MALCOLM *pulls his trousers up.*

I'm going. Thank you.

MALCOLM *slaps* JOHN *across the face.*

MALCOLM. Do you drink pints of cum?

JOHN. No.

MALCOLM *slaps* JOHN *across the face.*

MALCOLM. I bet you wanted to drink a pint of mine.

JOHN. I didn't.

MALCOLM *slaps* JOHN *across the face.*

MALCOLM. Are you lying?

JOHN. No.

MALCOLM. Take your trousers down.

JOHN *unzips his trousers.*

You've fucked men ant you?

JOHN. No.

MALCOLM *rips* JOHN*'s trousers down.*

MALCOLM. Did you cum?

JOHN. I haven't…

JOHN is now stood with his trousers round his ankles exposing his underwear.

MALCOLM. Did you orgasm?

JOHN shivers.

Did they wank in your face?

JOHN. No.

MALCOLM. Did they cum in your mouth?

JOHN. No.

MALCOLM. Did you cum in their mouth?

JOHN. No.

MALCOLM. Look at you shaking like a shitting dog.

JOHN pulls up his trousers.

JOHN (*shouting*). I want to go home.

Beat.

Please help me.

Beat.

Can you help me?

Beat.

Somebody.

Beat.

MALCOLM. Go home. Please go home. Take the baby with you. There's no place like home. Is there?

Pause.

JOHN. No.

MALCOLM. Say it.

JOHN. There's no place like home.

MALCOLM. Louder.

JOHN. There's no place like home.

The fluorescent light flickers and dims.

MALCOLM. Louder.

JOHN. There's no place like home.

Darkness.

Scene Three

Two years later. Christmas. The front room of JEAN *and* JOHN*'s house.*

There is a white artificial Christmas tree that has seen better days.

It is overly decorated with an angel, mismatching tinsel, baubles and fairy lights.

The television is on.

The dark of the room is interrupted by the conflicting light from the television and the fairy lights.

The window is open and the fog slowly invades the front room.

JEAN (*fifty-six*) *stands in the middle of the room with an apron on and some rubber washing-up gloves. She has a full milk bottle in her hand.*

JOHN (*fifty-seven*) *stands in the room. He is holding a suitcase.*

JEAN. A horse has just walked past our window. A horse. A big white horse. Must have got lost in the fog. You can't see a thing out there now. It came from nowhere. Just dropped out of the dark. There'll be people falling into rivers. Floating away. Singing. Old people with shopping trolleys stranded on the curbs of street corners. Pissing their pants. Kids stuck up trees. Choking on the fog.

JEAN takes the foil top off the milk bottle and pours the milk onto the floor.

You made me do that.

JEAN leaves JOHN alone in the room.

JEAN comes back in with a red bucket with hot water in it.

JEAN takes a cloth from the bucket and wrings it out.

She scrubs the milk from the floor.

I bought you a present. It's nothing much. Just something small. Just something.

JOHN goes over to the tree and picks up the present. He shakes it.

JOHN. What is it?

JOHN shakes the present again. He sniffs it.

Give me a clue.

JOHN unwraps the present. It is a box. He lifts the lid on the box. He stares in the box.

JEAN. I wish you hadn't opened that. You should have taken it with you. Where you are going. You should have opened it on your own.

JOHN. I didn't get you a thing.

JOHN closes the lid of the box. He opens his suitcase on the floor and puts the box in it. He closes the case.

You do know the window is open?

JEAN. Yes. I opened the window.

JOHN. Why did you open the window?

JEAN. Because I've not opened that window for a long time. I just wanted to see if that window still opened.

JOHN. I think I will close the window.

JOHN goes to the window and closes it.

The fog continues to seep into the room, coating everything in a thin layer of mist.

I had it all sorted out in my head. What I was going to say.

JOHN *stands in the middle of the room.*

He does his coat up and holds the suitcase in his hand.

A loud thud on the window. The sound is so violent it shocks them both.

They both stare at each other for some time.

JOHN *whispers.*

JEAN *doesn't.*

Did you hear that?

JEAN. Yes.

JOHN. The window?

JEAN. Yes.

JOHN. Something hit the window?

JEAN. Yes.

JOHN. Someone hit the window.

JEAN. I don't…

JOHN. Ssh.

JOHN listens.

I can't hear anything.

JOHN goes to the window and looks.

I can't see a thing.

JEAN leaves.

JOHN opens the window. He steps back to safety. The fog seeps in.

Well? Who's there? What do you want? Are you looking at me? In my own garden? Through my own window? I'm sorry if I did anything wrong. Who's there?

JOHN stands shivering.

JEAN comes in carrying a dead bird.

JEAN. It was a bird. Another one. That's three today.

JOHN. I've never thought my front-room window could be guilty of such slaughter.

JEAN. It's the fog. They don't know which way's up or down. I'll pour it down the drain.

JOHN closes the window.

JOHN. I'm sorry I don't love you any more, I'm sorry I won't love you again. I just don't love you. I'm just very sorry.

Beat.

JEAN drops the dead bird in the bucket.

I'm going to try and go now.

The doorbell goes.

They are both still.

We should ignore it.

The doorbell goes again.

They'll go away.

The doorbell goes again but this time it is continuous.

It's probably nothing.

JEAN looks out of the window. Recognising who it is, she goes to the front door.

JOHN is left in the room alone. He straightens the angel on the Christmas tree.

JEAN enters followed by NEIL and HELEN (eighteen).

NEIL is carrying what looks like something dead in a black bin bag in his arms.

JOHN stares at NEIL and the bundle in his arms.

NEIL is doing his best to not cry uncontrollably. There is no hiding the raw grief he is feeling.

HELEN is barefoot, carrying a torch.

NEIL. What?

JOHN looks away.

What you looking at?

JOHN looks at NEIL.

What you looking at you?

Beat.

My dog got run over today, John. It was a bit messy. One of its eyes was hanging out. Gunk coming out of its arse. I found Oscar and a fat little girl poking it with lolly sticks. I gave them both a crack. He was crying his eyes out. Poor fucker. I didn't want it in the first place. I knew it would end up like this. I never wanted a dog, John. But no it was always

Can we have a dog

can we have a dog

can we have a dog

can we have a dog

can we have a dog

can we have a dog

can we have a dog

Fucking stunk.

NEIL *drops the dead dog on the floor.*

Used to shit everywhere. There were always worms in it. I could have killed it myself the noise it made. I thought dogs were meant to bark. Not this fucker. It was more of a yap than a bark. I wanted to slam the car door on its head myself sometimes. I did love it though. Didn't I? Hello, John.

It's fucking shit out there. It's fucking quiet. Just the sound of hundreds of people shuffling about. Banging into phone boxes and stuff. Could we find your house? Could we fuck. Had to knock on loads of doors. No one answered except for a spastic girl eating cereal. She gave us a torch.

HELEN (*sniffing*). What's that smell?

JEAN. I can't smell anything.

HELEN (*sniffing*). Stinks.

JOHN. We had peppered mackerel for tea.

HELEN. Yes. Peppered mackerel. Stinks.

JOHN. We had it on toast. With grilled tomatoes. We always have mackerel on a Monday. You should remember that. It was your favourite.

HELEN. Yes. I do now.

NEIL. Were you going out, John?

Beat.

Were you going somewhere special? It's just you've got your coat on and you've got a suitcase in your hand. Where are you going on a night like this? What journey can be so important?

JOHN *puts the suitcase on the floor.*

You've had your hair done, Jean. Hasn't she, John? You have haven't you?

JEAN. I have. This morning.

NEIL. I knew it. I knew it, John. I can always tell with Jean. You look incredibly beautiful by the way.

JEAN. Thank you.

Beat.

We haven't seen you both for a few weeks. We've tried phoning but there was no answer. Your dad's popped round with a Christmas card but you were never in. No one.

NEIL. We've been around and about. Haven't we?

HELEN. Yes.

JOHN (*to* HELEN). You alright, love?

NEIL. What do you mean by that?

JOHN. Just asking if she's alright.

HELEN. He was just asking.

JOHN. I was just asking.

JEAN. He was just asking.

Beat.

JOHN. It's just you haven't got any shoes on your feet.

Beat.

Why haven't you got any shoes on?

HELEN. I hadn't noticed. I must have lost them. Or somebody stole them. Just disappeared in the fog. One minute they were there on my feet the next. Gone.

JOHN *picks up a pair of slippers and offers them to* HELEN.

JOHN. Here. You can have my slippers. Put them on. They might be a bit big. But you can't walk round in this weather with nothing on your feet. You don't know what you might be treading on.

HELEN *puts the slippers on.*

NEIL. Right. She's good. Has her bad days, you know. Don't you?

HELEN. Yes.

Pause.

NEIL (*remembering*). Fuck. A. Duck. We've left that thing in the car. You know what I mean. That thing we got for them. Go and get it. Go on. Tie this string round your wrist so you can find your way back. Use the spastic's torch.

NEIL *gets a ball of string out of his pocket.*

NEIL *ties one end of the string to* HELEN*'s wrist.*

HELEN *switches on the torch and exits. The string unravels.*

NEIL, JOHN *and* JEAN *are left in the front room.*

Now you two. I want you both to close your eyes and not open them till I tell you to. Promise me you won't peep?

JEAN *and* JOHN *both nod.*

No. No, I want you to actually promise.

JEAN *and* JOHN. Promise.

NEIL. Thank you. Go on then. Close your eyes.

JEAN *and* JOHN *close their eyes.*

No peeping, John, you little tinker. I can see you you know.

HELEN *returns with a massively oversized Christmas card in its envelope.*

NEIL *pulls on the string, drawing her next to him.*

HELEN *remains bound at the wrist.*

You can open your eyes.

JEAN *and* JOHN *open their eyes.*

Surprise.

It's a Christmas card. We got it on the market. Are you not going to open it?

HELEN *opens the card and it begins to play a Christmas song.*

JEAN. Thank you. We'll have to find somewhere special to put it.

JEAN *takes the Christmas card and gives it to* JOHN.

NEIL. You know what I could murder now? I could murder a glass of wine. I might have a wine. Have you got any wine?

JEAN. Not open, no.

NEIL. Open us a bottle of wine, Jean. Go on. A nice bottle of Lambruscot or something. It is Christmas.

(*To* HELEN.) What do you reckon?

Helen?

HELEN. Have what you want don't you. At Christmas.

NEIL *gets lost in his own head for a few seconds.*

It's as though his brain has been switched off and back on again.

It's like a computer rebooting after a fault.

JOHN, JEAN *and* HELEN *stand silently.*

NEIL *is like a bomb waiting to explode.*

NEIL. Wine? What on its own?

HELEN. Yeah, I think so.

NEIL. Right. Can I have a glass of wine? Please. Jean.

JEAN *looks at* JOHN.

JOHN *nods.*

JEAN *goes to get the wine leaving* JOHN, HELEN *and* NEIL *in the front room.*

Silence.

NEIL *looks at the TV.*

He smiles.

'*Cold Outside*' *is being performed by Dean Martin. A Christmas special or something.*

I love this song. Turn it up.

JOHN *turns the volume up on the TV.*

NEIL *grabs hold of* HELEN.

He begins to dance.

He sings.

JOHN *watches awkwardly.*

JEAN *returns with a glass of wine.*

She stands in the doorway watching NEIL *and* HELEN *dance.*

When NEIL *notices* JEAN *and the glass of wine he dances* HELEN *over to* JOHN.

He gives his daughter to him.

He makes them dance.

NEIL *goes to* JEAN *and takes the glass of wine and downs it. He takes hold of* JEAN *and the two begin to dance.*

The four of them dance around the dead dog on the floor.

The string on HELEN*'s wrist creates a web that surrounds them as they dance.*

The song ends.

HELEN *kicks the bin bag.*

Nothing lasts for ever. I told Oscar you would help him bury it in the back garden under the tree. Make a cross out of scraps of wood. You've got a smart garden. Vegetable patch. Flowers. Roses. Better than ours. Our dead garden. You should make a swing for him. He'd like that. Make him a sandpit. Fill it with soil. He'd like that. Will you bury him, Dad?

JOHN. Yes.

HELEN. Promise.

JOHN. I promise.

HELEN. We could get him a bucket and spade. Pretend he's on holiday.

NEIL. He'll pretend to be a builder, making houses out of mud. He likes playing doesn't he?

HELEN. Yes.

NEIL. He's like a little creature when he's playing.

HELEN. Like a little worm-boy always digging. Dirty little fingernails.

NEIL. We need you to look after Oscar for a while. Let him live here for a bit.

JOHN. It's not a good time at the moment. It really isn't. Is it?

JEAN *looks down.*

NEIL. It was her idea. Isn't that right?

HELEN *looks down.*

Isn't it?

HELEN. Yes.

JEAN. I'll just go and say hello to him.

NEIL. It's cold out there. Don't want to be poorly for Christmas do you, Jean? Who'd cook John's turkey? Eh? Gobble gobble gobble.

JEAN. I'll put my coat on.

HELEN. He's asleep.

JEAN. I'll go and have a look. Just in case.

NEIL. You can't see a thing out there now.

JEAN. I'll use your torch.

NEIL *stamps on the torch until it breaks.*

HELEN. It's broken.

Pause.

JOHN. I think it's getting out of hand all of this. It is. I think…

NEIL. I'd rather shit in my hands and clap than listen to what you think.

JOHN. You don't intimidate me. You don't scare me. This is my house. I've lived here for a very long time. And I won't have your type trying to do what you're trying to do. I'm no walkover. You need to know that.

NEIL. You should sit down. You're getting overexcited.

JOHN. I'm quite happy where I am thank you.

NEIL. Sit down.

JOHN. No. I think I want to stand.

NEIL. I think you should sit down.

JOHN. I don't care what you think. I'm standing. I'm making a stand.

NEIL. You should tell him.

HELEN. Please sit down, Dad.

JOHN. I have no intention of sitting down. I might even stand for ever.

NEIL. I swear to fucking Jesus Christ if you don't sit down right now I'm going to stick my cock right up your little girl's fanny right here in this front room in front of her mummy and daddy. Sit down.

Beat.

JOHN. You're calling my bluff.

NEIL. Take your knickers off and give them to Mummy to hold.

HELEN *takes her knickers off and gives them to* JEAN.

JEAN. I think it would be best if you just sat down now.

JOHN *defiantly stands.*

NEIL. I fuck your little girl until she screams and begs me to stop.

Beat.

Do you understand?

Beat.

Do you get me?

JEAN. –

NEIL. Don't interrupt, Jean. It will only drag this out. I do things to your daughter, John, that you could only wank about –

JEAN (*whispering*). Get out –

NEIL. Sometimes I let my mates do your daughter one after the other –

JEAN (*quietly*). Get out –

NEIL. She can't open her legs fast enough –

JOHN. Shut your mouth –

NEIL. She'd shag you if I told her to –

JOHN *slowly sits.*

Now stay sat down, John. Don't even think about getting up. I want you to sit in that chair and think about what you just did and when you think you can be a good little boy you can join in the adult conversation with me and Jean.

JEAN. I've got money upstairs.

NEIL. I don't want money.

JEAN. I can get more.

NEIL. How much? What she worth?

JEAN *gets an envelope from her handbag.*

JEAN. There's thirty-five pounds and some coins in there. I want you to take it.

JEAN *passes the envelope to* NEIL.

NEIL *opens the envelope and takes the money out of it.*

NEIL. Right.

NEIL *rips the money in half and throws it in* JEAN*'s face.*

I don't want your money, Jean. Did you not listen to what I said? I will say it very, very slowly.

Beat.

We want. Oscar. Your grandson. To come here. To this house. And live. With you. Two. Happily. Ever. After. We don't want him. (*To* HELEN.) Do we? You don't want him. Do you? Tell them.

(*Murderously.*) Please tell them.

HELEN. I wish he was dead. Why didn't I let him die when he was born? Put him out of all this misery. I should've drowned him in that canal. Cut him up to bits with a knife and fork. Fed him to stray dogs. I should've stabbed him through the head with thin knitting needles. Pierced his brain. Popped his head with bricks. Poured concrete in his nose and mouth. Painted him black and sank him in mud.

He makes me feel dirty that he came from me. That he grew inside me. Feeding off me. Chewing on my insides. Taking me over. Stripping the layers off me from the inside out. Poisoning me. Killing me. Turning me into a ruin. A woman who doesn't know how to love. I remember nothing. Why can't he be dead?

NEIL. The worse it is the more you've got to laugh. Now are we all ready to compromise for a bit of freedom, because I don't want this chaos any more?

Beat.

That's a really nice tree.

HELEN. Go and get Oscar from the car, Dad.

JOHN *gets up, leaves the room.*

JEAN *drops the knickers on the floor.*

JEAN *picks up the suitcase and leaves the room.*

HELEN *picks the knickers and puts them on.*

HELEN *straightens the angel on top of the Christmas tree.*

I love you.

Scene Four

Two years later. The end of August. The sand dunes at Blackpool.

It is late afternoon on a quiet and secluded part of the seafront.

It is muggy and the sun keeps disappearing behind the clouds. There will be a storm later. The faint sound of the amusement arcades and the Pleasure Beach can be heard in the distance.

JEAN *(fifty-eight) is sat on a deckchair.*

She looks through a telescope.

JOHN (*fifty-nine*) *is a few feet away from her. All we can see is his head poking out of the sand. He has been buried up to his neck.*

A bucket and spade are discarded at his feet and two glittery windmills on sticks are stuck in the sand. They are slightly turning in the breeze.

A pair of children's socks and shoes are placed neatly by the bucket.

OSCAR (*six*) *is playing on a part of the beach some way away. We can't see him.*

JEAN. He's kissing that young girl.

JOHN. Who is?

JEAN. That man from the chip shop. The one who shared our table.

JOHN. The one who ate all our bread and butter?

JEAN. Yes. Him. He's got his hands all over that young girl who gives the change out at the amusement arcade. The one with the boy's haircut and the gammy hand.

JOHN. Smarmy bugger. I knew there was something about him. You can always tell a lot about a man from how much salt and vinegar he puts on his chips. Flamboyance with condiments smacks of depravity. That's what my dad used to say.

Pause.

What they doing now?

JEAN. They keep looking round to see if anyone can see them. I don't think she wants to be seen.

JOHN. I don't bloody blame the poor cow. I bet he's diseased with God knows what. Riddled. Did you see the way he was eating. Got more on his face than in his mouth. Bits of batter in his sideburns.

JEAN. They're lying down on the sand. He's using her overall as a pillow.

JOHN. He's a parasite.

JEAN. She's stroking his face.

JOHN. I hope she washes her hands.

JEAN. She's resting her chin on his beer belly.

JOHN. Is she looking him in the eye?

JEAN. She's very beautiful.

JOHN. Is she looking at him in the eye?

JEAN. He's closed his eyes.

JOHN. Scum.

Pause.

What they doing now?

JEAN. Holding.

JOHN. She's teasing him. That's what it will be. She'll have made a bet with the girls she works with in the arcade.

JEAN. She's very attentive. She looks very experienced for such a young girl.

JOHN. What's she doing to him?

Pause.

What's she done?

JEAN. She's watching him sleep.

JOHN. Sleep? Not very likely. He's probably died. That's what it is. That's what it will be. A mortality on the beach. How very embarrassing. They'll have to drag his fat pustulated carcass off the sand. With ropes and a tractor. Like a dead sea creature covered in sewage and seaweed. String him up on the promenade. Cut him open. Like a prized shark. Let all his secrets splatter on the ground. I'll take my bread and butter back thank you very much.

JEAN. He's snoozing. He's not dead. He's just snoozing. I can see him breathing. He's dreaming.

JOHN. Well… we'll see.

Where's Oscar? He's not near them is he?

JEAN. No. He's over there. Stroking donkeys.

JOHN. Good. Out of my sight. He played up like a right bloody lunatic in that toy shop. Out of control he was. Embarrassing. Going mad because I wouldn't buy him a cowboy costume. I wouldn't mind but I'd already bought him a plastic sword. And a gun. Bloody shouting. Swearing. Hitting me with that sword right across my face. Nearly had my sodding eye out. Nearly bloody blinded me. I grabbed hold of his arm. I pulled his pants right down to his ankles and I belted him as hard as I could on his arse. If I say he can't have something he can't have it.

A bird shits on JOHN*'s head.*

A bird has just shit on me.

Beat.

A bird has just shit on my head.

JEAN. Good for you.

JOHN. What?

JEAN. I said it's good for you. It's good luck. That's what they've always said. If a bird… poos on you it's good luck.

JOHN *looks at* JEAN.

JEAN *looks at* JOHN.

It's always been like that. For ever.

JOHN (*incredulous*). What? I don't care if it's good luck or not. I've got birdshit on my head and I want you to wipe it off, Jean. That's if you don't think it's too much trouble.

JEAN. I don't know if I can do that. It might cancel out the luck.

JOHN. What?

JEAN. We could do with some good luck.

JOHN. Just wipe it off my head. Jean. Please.

JEAN *gets up.*

JEAN *switches off her fan and puts it down.*

JEAN *gets a tissue out of her pocket and goes over to* JOHN.

JEAN. It's only a little bit. Must have been a small bird. A baby or something.

JEAN wraps up the tissue and puts it in the bucket.

JEAN *goes back to her chair, picks up the fan, switches it on and sits down.*

JOHN. Thank you.

A distant rumble of thunder is heard in the distance. A dog barks.

JEAN. I love it here. I love the beach. I love the sand between my toes. If I close my eyes I'm a little girl again. I can almost feel my mother next to me. I can hear my dad breathing. I can smell them. I can hear my mum laughing. I really can. I think this is the happiest place in the world. If I close my eyes life doesn't exist any more.

JOHN. We'll have to go soon. It's going to rain. I can smell it.

JEAN. You're always saying it's going to rain. It never does. You're not very good with the weather.

Beat.

JOHN. It's cold.

JEAN. It's not. It's warm. I dripped ice cream onto my dress. It must be hot. I hope the raspberry sauce doesn't stain. I can always try and take it back. I've kept the bag and the receipt.

The windmills stuck in the sand begin to spin faster.

It thunders again.

JOHN. What time is it?

JEAN *ignores* JOHN.

Look at the state of that sky. It's gone black.

Beat.

It feels like we've been here for hours. How long's it been? It must be at least an hour.

JEAN. It isn't.

JOHN. We must have been. My arse has gone numb. And my legs. I can't feel a thing. Nothing. Anything could be going on down there. I haven't got a bloody clue. I feel like one of them paraplegics.

JEAN. We've only been in here for twenty minutes. (*Looking at her watch.*) Thirty-five minutes.

Beat.

Always exaggerating.

JEAN *gets up.*

JEAN *stretches.*

OSCAR *shouts from a different part of the beach.*

OSCAR (*offstage*). Nana. Nana.

JEAN *looks through the telescope.*

Look. I found it.

JEAN. Oscar's found a kite.

JOHN. What colour?

JEAN. Red.

OSCAR (*offstage*). Can I keep it?

JEAN. Be careful.

JEAN *goes back to the deckchair and sits down.*

A rumble of thunder is heard. This time it is closer.

JOHN. Was that thunder?

Beat.

Was that thunder, Jean?

Beat.

JEAN (*not listening to what he said*). What's the matter with you?

JOHN. I didn't want to come to Blackpool in the first place. It's horrible. Grotty. Stinks of egg. Everywhere stinks of egg. The sea doesn't even like coming here.

Beat.

And a bird has shit on my head.

JEAN. You're a right miserable sod.

JOHN. I'm not.

JEAN. You are, John. The only chance we get to get away for a few days and all you do is moan.

JOHN. I don't.

JEAN. You do.

Beat.

A bit of poo never hurt anyone.

Pause.

JOHN. How long do I have to stay like this for? I can't feel my toes any more.

A rumble of thunder is heard. The storm is getting closer.

You should keep an eye on Oscar. He can disappear just like that.

JEAN *looks through the telescope.*

JEAN. I can only just see him. I think that kite's too big for him. It's lifting him off the ground.

JEAN *shouts to* OSCAR *who is now quite far away.*

Oscar.

Beat.

Oscar.

Beat.

Let go of it. You'll get blown away if you're not careful.

Pause.

Can you remember when we brought his mum here when she was little? That red-hot summer. You got sunburnt that bad you had to sleep in a bath full of cold water. Nearly bloody killed yourself, daft sod. You lost her in the arcades.

JOHN. I didn't.

JEAN. You bloody did. I was playing bingo and you said you would take her to play on the two-pence machines that she liked.

JOHN. I can't remember that.

JEAN. You did, John. You lost her.

Beat.

She was gone for a few hours. You must remember.

Beat.

JOHN. She always had a good sense of direction.

JEAN. You wanted to tell the police then we found her in Woolworths. She'd walked up to the manager's office and told him she was lost.

Beat.

I can't believe you don't remember. He'd given her a packet of Rolos to stop her crying. She'd lost her shoes. She wouldn't talk to you for days.

JOHN. That blue pair with dogs on?

JEAN. No, not the ones with the dogs on. The red ones. The red ones with the gold writing on the bottom. You spent a whole day going all over trying to find a pair. She never forgot that.

JOHN. Didn't she?

Beat.

JEAN. No. She never forgot that.

It starts to spit with rain.

The storm is on top of them now.

It's incredibly still.

It is black.

It's spitting.

Pause.

JOHN. How do you lose your shoes? I don't understand. A shoe in the road. On a wall. Floating in the canal. Where do they all come from? I don't understand it. Do you?

Beat.

That dead girl I found. She had no shoes on. Funny what you forget. How you remember.

JEAN *gets a small hand-held umbrella out and raises it.*

JEAN *looks for* OSCAR.

JEAN. I can hardly see him. He's just a dot on the horizon.

JOHN. She had no arms. I thought it was her. I was convinced it was our Helen. On a dirty mattress with ants everywhere.

JEAN (*shouting*). Oscar, come on now it's starting to rain.

JOHN. I wanted to touch her.

JEAN (*picking up his shoes and socks*). Your socks will get all wet.

JOHN. I wanted to protect her. I wanted to wrap her up in a blanket and tell her she was alright, that everything would be okay. I wanted to stroke her hair and sing her to sleep. What she must have gone through.

JEAN. Come on, Oscar, I'm not messing now. Your shoes are getting wet.

JOHN. I just stood there being sick through my hands at a dead girl with hair but no face.

It flashes with lightning and a loud rumble of thunder briefly follows.

JEAN. Oscar. Hurry up.

JEAN *takes off her sunhat and sunglasses and puts them in her bag.*

JOHN. She'd started to rot.

JEAN. You'll get struck by lightning, Oscar, and that will really hurt.

JOHN. She'd started to melt. She was disappearing into death. It became her. Life was giving her back. She was more than the thing she was.

JEAN. I'm going to leave your bucket and spade here.

JOHN. And in that moment I spent with the dead girl I felt a closeness and love that I've never had with my own daughter.

JEAN. Come on, Oscar, don't ruin a good day.

JOHN. I will always remember everything about that girl in death. Why can't I remember my own daughter in life?

JEAN. I'm not joking, Oscar, you'll catch your death.

JEAN goes off to get OSCAR.

JOHN is left alone.

It thunders really loud.

JOHN. A father should remember he lost his little girl. He should remember what colour her shoes were.

The sky darkens.

Scene Five

Two years later. The final day of autumn. A wood on the edge of a graveyard.

Late afternoon. Dusk approaches.

Mottled sunshine dances through the treetops casting rippling puddles of light on the ground.

The chatter of leaves and shy birdsong fills the clearing.

OSCAR (*eight*) *is looking at the tops of the trees through a small telescope.*

He is wearing a pair of red wellington boots.

His bike leans against an old forgotten bench.

PHILIP *is sat on the bench.*

He watches OSCAR *silently.*

After some time.

PHILIP. I don't know much about birds.

>OSCAR *is still.*

>Is that terrible?

>OSCAR *is still.*

>I wish I did.

>OSCAR *is still.*

>I wish I'd paid them more attention.

>OSCAR *is still.*

>Do you mind me sitting here?

>OSCAR *is still.*

I've never had a telescope. I always wanted one. When I was a boy I really wanted a telescope. My insides used to ache I wanted one so much. I remember that feeling. Its taste in my mouth. The things I imagined I could've seen if only I'd had a telescope. The faces I might have captured. Eyes glistening. Upturned smiles. Arms outstretched and wanting. Touching me from a distance I couldn't quite reach. I never had a telescope. Hello. Can you hear me? I'm sorry.

OSCAR *is still.*

PHILIP *takes a small bird whistle from his bag.*

He plays it quietly.

OSCAR *watches* PHILIP.

PHILIP *is embarrassed.*

He stops playing the whistle.

He wipes the corners of his mouth.

He smiles.

He offers the whistle to OSCAR.

OSCAR *hesitates.*

He looks back to the tops of the trees through his telescope.

PHILIP *places the whistle on the bench next to him.*

He looks up into the trees.

He shields his eyes from the sun.

OSCAR. That's a chiffchaff.

Beat.

Where you're looking. It's a chiffchaff. It lives in that tree.

Beat.

It looks like a willow warbler but not as yellow.

PHILIP. They all look the same to me.

PHILIP *opens his bag and takes out a plastic sandwich box.*

He opens it and takes out a sandwich.

He offers the sandwich to OSCAR.

Would you like a cheese sandwich?

Beat.

OSCAR. I don't like cheese.

PHILIP. Everyone likes cheese.

OSCAR *looks at* PHILIP.

OSCAR. I don't. It's yellow. Stinks of cow tits.

OSCAR *turns away and looks back up into the trees.*

PHILIP. Do you mind if I have one?

OSCAR *shakes his head.*

PHILIP *eats the sandwich.*

He brushes the crumbs from his clothes.

OSCAR. Would you like to look through my telescope?

OSCAR *offers the telescope to* PHILIP.

There aren't many birds here today. The rooks have scared most of them away. I hate rooks.

Beat.

PHILIP. Thank you.

PHILIP *takes the telescope and looks into the trees.*

OSCAR *takes a small book from one of his wellington boots.*

OSCAR. My nana bought me this book at a jumble sale. It was only five pence. When I see a bird I tick it off. There were already a lot of ticks in it when I got it but I just rubbed them out. Started again. Bargain.

Beat.

PHILIP. Do you spend a lot of time here?

OSCAR. Sometimes.

PHILIP. Me too.

PHILIP *lowers the telescope and offers it back to* OSCAR.

I think I've seen you here before. You haven't seen me but I think I've seen you.

Beat.

You're always alone.

Beat.

Do your friends not like looking at birds?

OSCAR. I have got friends. Loads of friends.

PHILIP. I'm sure you have.

OSCAR. About one hundred.

PHILIP. Good.

Pause.

Can I see your book?

OSCAR. Do you like birds?

PHILIP. I think so yes.

OSCAR *isn't sure if he should let* PHILIP *see the book.*

I do. I don't know much about them but I do like them.

OSCAR. Spell albatross.

PHILIP (*struggling*). A.L.B.A.T.R.O.S.S.

OSCAR *passes the book to the man.*

(*Reading the title.*) 'A Pocket Guide to Birds.'

PHILIP *flicks through the book.*

You've seen a lot of birds. There are a lot of ticks.

OSCAR. My granddad has seen most of them. He's ticked off most of them. I've ticked off quite a few though.

PHILIP. Your granddad comes birdwatching with you?

OSCAR. Sometimes.

PHILIP. Does he?

Beat.

Is he here today?

OSCAR. No, he's at home.

PHILIP *sits on the bench.*

He plays the bird whistle quietly.

OSCAR *watches him.*

He looks back to the tops of the trees through his telescope.

Do you know what my name is?

PHILIP *stops playing the whistle.*

PHILIP. No. I don't. Would you like me to know your name?

Beat.

I think I'd like to know your name.

Beat.

What's your name?

OSCAR *looks at* PHILIP.

OSCAR. You'll never guess.

PHILIP. I might.

OSCAR. You won't. It's too hard.

Beat.

PHILIP. I bet you a go of my bird whistle I do.

PHILIP *stands.*

OSCAR *hesitates.*

OSCAR *looks at his bike.*

OSCAR. I bet you a go of my bike you don't.

They stand opposite each other.

Three guesses. That's the rule. Agreed?

PHILIP. Agreed.

OSCAR *holds out three fingers as markers.*

OSCAR. Go on then.

Pause.

PHILIP. Robert.

OSCAR. No.

OSCAR *lowers one of his fingers.*

Two chances left.

PHILIP *inhales a large breath.*

PHILIP. Ian?

OSCAR. Wrong.

OSCAR *lowers another finger leaving one remaining.*

Last guess.

PHILIP. Simon.

OSCAR *lowers his final finger.*

OSCAR. No. You lose.

PHILIP *smiles.*

PHILIP *holds out the bird whistle.*

My name is Oscar.

OSCAR *slowly walks over to PHILP.*

They both hold the bird whistle.

They hold each other's stare.

My nana says it's very distinguished.

PHILIP. It is.

PHILIP *lets go of the bird whistle.*

OSCAR *retreats.*

You win, Oscar.

OSCAR *quietly plays the bird whistle.*

He stops.

OSCAR *returns the bird whistle to the bench.*

OSCAR. I don't have one hundred friends. I lied. I don't have any friends.

Beat.

I'm too selfish.

Beat.

That's what my granddad says.

Beat.

PHILIP. I don't think you're selfish.

PHILIP *sits on the bench.*

He takes a bottle of suncream from his bag and begins to apply it to his arms.

You let me look through your telescope. I don't think a selfish person would do that. I think that's kind. That is kindness, Oscar. I appreciate it. Thank you.

Beat.

I come here just to look at the trees like you just come to look at the birds. I'm never disappointed because they are always here. They never go away. They change and grow but they're always here. Constant. I appreciate that.

I sometimes imagine that these are the only trees left in the world and that every single bird has to come here to make its nest. Silly isn't it. But if you think like that then you start to see them differently. It makes you really appreciate them the way I do you and the way your granddad should too.

Beat.

I think your granddad is wrong.

The sun goes behind a cloud.

The sun has gone in.

Everything is grey.

The world has stopped.

They both look up at the sky.

OSCAR. It's like looking at another galaxy. I think it looks beautiful. My granddad says grey clouds are bad.

PHILIP. Does he?

OSCAR. I don't. I think if you really look at them they're never really just grey. The sky seems more important when the sun goes behind a cloud. I don't know why. It's more hopeful.

OSCAR *looks at* PHILIP *who continues looking at the sky.*

We could be friends.

PHILIP. I'm not sure. I don't really know you.

OSCAR. You know my name.

PHILIP *looks at* OSCAR.

PHILIP. What do you think my name is?

OSCAR. I don't know.

PHILIP *laughs quietly.*

PHILIP. If you can guess my name you can keep my bird whistle. But if you don't you've got to give me something in return.

OSCAR. Like what?

PHILIP *shrugs his shoulders.*

You can't have my telescope. It's priceless.

Beat.

PHILIP. I don't want your telescope.

OSCAR. You can't have my bike either.

PHILIP. I don't want your bike.

OSCAR. I haven't got anything else.

Pause.

PHILIP. I know.

OSCAR. What?

PHILIP. No…

OSCAR. What?

PHILIP. It's silly.

OSCAR. What?

Beat.

PHILIP. Promise you won't laugh?

OSCAR. I promise.

PHILIP. If you don't guess my name… If you don't guess my name… you've got to…

Beat.

You've got to take your shorts off and you've got to sit on my knee.

Beat.

OSCAR. I don't think I want to take my shorts off. I don't think I want to sit on your knee.

PHILIP. I don't want you to sit on my knee either. I don't even know you, Oscar. It's just a bet. It's a game. It's what friends do.

If you don't want to win the bird whistle then…

PHILIP *picks up the bird whistle.*

If you don't want to be friends…

PHILIP *picks up his bag.*

If you don't think you can guess…

PHILIP *stands and goes to leave.*

Goodbye, Oscar.

OSCAR. Okay.

PHILIP. Good boy.

PHILIP *returns to the bench and sits down.*

He puts the bird whistle on the bench.

You've got three guesses.

PHILIP *holds out three fingers as markers.*

OSCAR *concentrates.*

OSCAR. Tom.

PHILIP. Wrong. Two more guesses.

PHILIP *lowers one of his fingers.*

OSCAR. Neil?

PHILIP. Wrong. Last guess.

PHILIP *lowers another finger, leaving one remaining.*

OSCAR *closes his eyes.*

The sun comes out.

OSCAR. Philip.

OSCAR *opens his eyes.*

Your name is Philip.

Pause.

PHILIP. Yes.

I am called Philip.

PHILIP *holds the bird whistle out to* OSCAR.

Good guess.

OSCAR. I'm good at guessing things.

PHILIP. You are aren't you?

OSCAR. I always have been.

OSCAR *takes the bird whistle.*

PHILIP. I didn't know I was playing with an expert.

OSCAR. I know your wife's name as well.

PHILIP. What?

OSCAR. I know what your wife's called.

PHILIP. I'm not married.

OSCAR. Yes you are.

PHILIP. No. I'm not.

OSCAR. Your wife is called Carol.

OSCAR *has correctly named* PHILIP's *wife.*

PHILIP. No… Oscar… wrong… You're wrong this time… wrong I'm not married.

OSCAR. And you have a daughter. Called Karen.

Beat.

PHILIP. What?

OSCAR. She's very poorly. She cries a lot. She's dying.

PHILIP (*lying and confused by* OSCAR*'s clairvoyance*). No... No... Not right... No no no, that's wrong no, wrong. Do you know me... Oscar?

OSCAR. No.

PHILIP. Did you guess we'd be friends?

OSCAR *looks at* PHILIP *and smiles.*

OSCAR. Yes.

PHILIP. Good.

PHILIP *offers* OSCAR *his hand.*

OSCAR *doesn't offer his.*

Pleased to meet you, Oscar.

PHILIP *offers his hand for an uncomfortable amount of time.*

OSCAR *looks at the offered hand.*

OSCAR *looks through his telescope into the trees.*

PHILIP *sits on the bench.*

He looks at OSCAR.

PHILIP *takes the bottle of suncream out of his bag.*

He places it on the bench next to him.

He looks up at the sky, shielding his eyes from the sun.

He looks at OSCAR.

He picks up the suncream and squeezes a small amount into his hand.

He rubs the suncream into his legs.

I think I've burnt my neck.

Beat.

Oscar.

OSCAR. Yes.

PHILIP. I think I've burnt my neck.

Beat.

I hope you've got some suntan cream on.

OSCAR. What?

PHILIP. The sun is really strong when it gets through the trees. You don't want to burn.

OSCAR. I won't.

PHILIP. You don't want to die of cancer. Shall I rub some cream in for you?

OSCAR. No thank you.

Pause.

PHILIP. I think my neck is burning.

Beat.

Is it red?

OSCAR *looks at* PHILIP*'s neck.*

OSCAR. No. It's alright.

PHILIP. It feels very burnt.

OSCAR. It's not.

Pause.

PHILIP. Will you rub some cream into my neck?

OSCAR *looks at* PHILIP.

They hold each other's stare.

OSCAR. Would you like me to?

PHILIP. Yes. I think I would like that. It's probably for the best.

OSCAR *goes to* PHILIP.

OSCAR *picks up the bottle of suncream.*

OSCAR *shakes the bottle.*

OSCAR squeezes some of the cream into his hand.

OSCAR puts the bottle on the bench.

OSCAR rubs his hands together.

PHILIP lowers his head exposing his neck.

OSCAR rubs the cream into PHILIP's neck.

OSCAR sits on his bike.

OSCAR starts to leave.

OSCAR stops.

OSCAR gets off his bike and puts the bird whistle back on the bench.

OSCAR gets back on his bike.

OSCAR. I'm sorry.

PHILIP. I know.

OSCAR leaves on his bike.

PHILIP is left alone.

After a very brief time, OSCAR *returns on his bike.*

In his hand is a doll. It has fallen out of a child's pushchair.

OSCAR offers PHILIP *the doll.*

OSCAR. Do you want this?

Beat.

I found it in the leaves.

Beat.

It's not dirty. Someone must have just lost it.

Beat.

I thought you could give it to your little girl.

Beat.

I think she would like it.

Beat.

I think she would appreciate it.

OSCAR *goes to* PHILIP.

OSCAR *offers* PHILIP *the doll.*

PHILIP *looks at* OSCAR.

PHILIP *looks at the doll.*

PHILIP *takes the doll.*

I know you're not a bad person. You're not.

Beat.

Philip?

PHILIP. Yes.

OSCAR. I hope your little girl gets better. I really do. I hope she stops crying soon.

PHILIP. Thank you, Oscar. Goodbye.

OSCAR. Goodbye, Philip.

PHILIP *stands.*

PHILIP *wipes his eyes.*

PHILIP *puts the suncream into his bag.*

PHILIP *picks up the bird whistle.*

PHILIP *leaves.*

OSCAR *circles the clearing on his bike.*

The birdsong gets louder and all the leaves fall from the trees.

OSCAR *leaves the clearing.*

Scene Six

Two years later. The first day of spring. JEAN *and* JOHN*'s back garden.*

The sounds of the first grass-cut of the year.

Lawnmowers and dogs. A semi-distant crying baby.

JOHN (*sixty-three*) *is in the middle of the garden.*

He is in the process of building something that resembles a bird stand.

OSCAR (*ten*) *is helping construct the bird stand.*

OSCAR *is wearing a World War II tin helmet and carrying a hammer.*

A radio is playing in the background.

OSCAR *listens to the music.*

OSCAR *begins to dance.*

JOHN *tries not to watch.*

OSCAR. I can't believe we had a bloody earthquake, Granddad.

JOHN. What've I told you about swearing?

OSCAR. Bloody isn't a swear word, Granddad.

JOHN. It is.

Beat.

It wasn't an earthquake anyway. Just a bloody big tremor.

OSCAR. Everything in my classroom started to shake. Even my fat teacher. You could see her big fat face wobbling. I thought the roof was going to fall on my head and smash my brains in. All the windows explode in people's faces. People fall down holes of fire in the floor. Legs squashed flat like toilet paper. The ground might just swallow us all up. I hope it does. I can't decide now whether the world is going to end with a massive earthquake or a big nuclear war. I don't know which one's best.

Beat.

I'm going to wear this hat now forever just in case.

OSCAR *hits himself on the head repeatedly with the hammer.*

It makes a tune and he dances.

You know the first thing that happens when a nuclear bomb explodes. There's a massive flash and it can melt your eyes if you look at it. Your skin can set on fire and start to bubble up. Most people are dead straight away. But some people are left without anyone to look after them because everyone they know is dead and they start being sick and bits of their stomach start coming out of their mouths. Your head starts to die and all your hair falls out and you go bald like a granddad. You can't eat anything because it's all poisoned so you start to turn into a skeleton and your gums and your mouth and throat start to bleed. Then you get the runs all the time and you can't stop pooing your pants and when you've run out of poo your insides start to fall out of your bum. Then you die.

JOHN (*concentrating on the bird stand*). Who told you that?

OSCAR. My dad. He said it's going to happen soon.

JOHN (*ignoring* OSCAR). Did he?

OSCAR. He said that I would be at school and the air-raid siren would go off and I would only have three minutes left to live.

JOHN (*ignoring* OSCAR). Did he?

OSCAR. If it happened on a Thursday Nana would be shopping in the Co-op so I bet she would die. You'd be alright cos you could just hide in next door's old air-raid shelter.

JOHN. Oscar.

OSCAR. You'd have to stay in there for ages. I think you will still die though.

JOHN. Oscar, will you shut your face for a bit. You don't know what you're talking about. We need to finish your bird stand.

OSCAR *goes to his bird stand and starts to work on it.*

OSCAR. I do know what I'm talking about you know. My dad tells me all about it when I go to see him.

JOHN. Give me that hammer.

OSCAR. Granddad, do you think about the day you will die?

JOHN. Only when I spend a lot of time with you.

OSCAR opens the tin of paint. He dips his brush in and starts to paint the bird stand.

OSCAR. I think about the day I'm going to die and I think about that day all the time. You're an old man which means you must think about the day you're going to die a lot more than I do.

JOHN. You don't know the day you're going to die, Oscar, nobody does, not even your nana and she knows everything. If we all knew the day we were going to die then the world would stop. Nobody would do anything.

Pause.

Did you get the bus to see Dad?

OSCAR. Yeah.

JOHN. Did you have to wait again to see him?

OSCAR. We always do but the man Nana talks to gets me a hot chocolate from the machine in the waiting room.

JOHN. Does he?

OSCAR. He's always there when we're there. We always see the same people in that room.

JOHN. Do you?

OSCAR. The man sits next to me. He talks to Nana but he sits next to me.

JOHN. Your nana speaks to all the strange people. It's the same when we go to the dentist. She attracts them. She's like a magnet for weirdos.

OSCAR. I don't think he's weird I just think he's lonely.

Pause.

JOHN. So what do they talk about your nana and this man?

OSCAR. I don't think I'm meant to listen.

JOHN. I bet you do.

Beat.

It's human nature to do things we're not meant to do.

Beat.

Like picking your nose.

OSCAR. I pick my nose all the time, Granddad. Does that mean that I'm allowed to do anything I want even though it might be wrong?

JOHN. No, Oscar, I'm just saying that sometimes we have to choose. You're not meant to pick your nose because other people don't like seeing you pick your nose. But if you pick your nose when no one is looking it doesn't really matter.

OSCAR. I think I understand, Granddad.

JOHN. So what do they talk about?

OSCAR. They talk quite quietly. He cries sometimes.

JOHN. Your nana never mentioned she spoke to a man at the hospital. Not a man that cried anyway.

OSCAR. They all do in that room. One starts and then they all start.

JOHN. There's a lot of brokenness in the world, Oscar. A lot of people find themselves drawn together without knowing it and end up sharing things they wouldn't normally dream of doing. That room is like a Hoover sucking them all together.

OSCAR. All you can hear is the whispers. I think it's a bit rude. I get told off by my big fat teacher for whispering. You don't get children whispering like that, Granddad.

JOHN. If I was you, Oscar, next time I was there I would turn round to this man and say – 'Excuse me, my teacher said it is rude to whisper.'

OSCAR. I don't think Nana would be very happy if I said that to her friend. It might make him cry and then Nana would have to hold his hand again.

Beat.

Nana never holds my hand. When I cry Nana never holds my hand.

Beat.

Does Nana ever hold your hand, Granddad? When you cry does she hold your hand?

JOHN. No she never holds my hand.

OSCAR. Why does she hold hands with a man she doesn't know?

Beat.

Why can't she hold hands with me or you?

Beat.

She knows me and you better than that crying man in the hospital waiting room.

JOHN. I think your nana would love to hold your hand.

OSCAR. I don't think she does.

JOHN. I think that is what she most wants in the whole world.

OSCAR. I think you know that isn't true, Granddad.

JOHN. Sometimes we can't touch the people we care and love the most because we just don't know how to do it. It just feels wrong.

OSCAR. I'm ten. I think I know how to hold hands.

JOHN. You're lucky. It's been taken from us. We've lost it.

Pause.

So how is your dad?

OSCAR. I was enjoying talking to you about life, Granddad.

JOHN. He's a very sick man your dad, Oscar.

Beat.

Does he still stink of shit?

Beat.

Does he still try and touch himself when you talk to him?

Beat.

Does he still not know who you are?

Have you ever wondered why he doesn't recognise you, Oscar? Why he never remembers your name?

OSCAR. He had an accident when I was small.

JOHN. He didn't have an accident, Oscar.

OSCAR. He fell off a crane.

JOHN. He didn't fall off a crane, Oscar.

OSCAR. He did. He worked on the world's biggest crane. That's how he damaged his brain.

JOHN. He never worked on a crane. He never worked. It was a story we made up to stop you asking stupid questions.

OSCAR. Stop it, Granddad.

JOHN. He jumped off a bridge in front of a train. The thick bastard couldn't even do that properly. He missed the train.

OSCAR. That's not true, Granddad. He's the strongest man in Manchester.

Beat.

JOHN. They never loved you. How could they? They didn't know how to do it.

OSCAR. That's not true, Granddad. They always loved each other and they always loved me.

JOHN. You're making yourself look incredibly ridiculous.

Beat.

When they left you on our doorstep that Christmas you didn't even have your own underpants. You were wearing a pair of your mum's old knickers. They were so full of dried piss they were stiff. They were stuck to your skin. We had to put you in the bath and peel them off you. You screamed the house down. You must have been wearing them for days. They were probably like that when they put them on you.

Beat.

That's how much they loved you.

Beat.

Why have you never seen your mum? Why has she never sent you a birthday card or called to see if you're okay? Why did she abandon you with nothing but a dead dog for company?

OSCAR. Because sometimes we do things that we don't really mean and then find it very hard to say we are wrong. It's why you still pretend that you love Nana.

JOHN. I do love your nana.

OSCAR. I don't think you do.

I don't think you can have ever loved anyone in your life, Granddad.

JOHN. I've never loved you, Oscar. No one has. No one ever will.

OSCAR. You don't have the honesty needed to love.

JOHN *goes over to the bird stand.*

JOHN *looks at it.*

JOHN *looks at* OSCAR.

JOHN *picks up the hammer.*

JOHN *starts to smash it up systematically. He is quite controlled at first but as the deconstruction escalates he is almost singing in his ferocity. It is as though he isn't smashing the bird stand but something bigger, maybe himself.*

My dad's brain doesn't work that well any more. It's stuck in another time. He thinks he is the same age as me. He might not have worked on the tallest crane in the world or be the bravest man in Manchester but the blinding blizzards in his head aren't controlled by the same fear that blind the truth in yours, Granddad.

Pause.

I love you.

JOHN *leaves.*

OSCAR *is alone.*

Scene Seven

Two years later. Autumn. A small wall by a canal. A broken street lamp.

Late evening sunshine casts giant shadows.

Three people sit on the wall.

JEAN (*sixty-four*) *is sat at one end of the wall.*

Her handbag is on her knee.

HELEN (*twenty-six*) *is sat on the other end of the wall.*

OSCAR (*twelve*) *is sat in the middle of the wall.*

He is wearing a school uniform. The jumper is pulled up over his head so the shape of his face is stretched through the jumper.

All three are eating ice creams in silence.

OSCAR *is trying to eat his through his jumper.*

HELEN. I watched an old man die this morning. On a disused railway footbridge. I watched his lips turn from red to blue. He had no shoes and socks on. Have you ever watched someone die? Has he? I bet you haven't. I bet you three pounds seventy-eight, a battery, and a peanut which is all I've got in my pocket that you haven't. Are you not going to talk to me?

JEAN. You can't eat your ice cream through your jumper. It's impossible. You're just making a mess.

HELEN. I've been eating grapefruit a lot recently. Grapefruit. It's bloody lovely. Have you ever tried it?

JEAN. He doesn't eat fresh fruit do you, Oscar?

OSCAR *doesn't answer.*

He doesn't. It goes right through him. Comes out like a flock of sparrows.

HELEN. If you eat it it's so refreshing. Pink grapefruit. I've got these white grapefruit now. I bought ten of them so I can have one every day. Five white ones and five pink ones. The pink ones are expensive but the white ones aren't. I don't know why. Must be harder to grow or something. Anyway this man. This old dying man. He was nearly naked. I could see his erect dick peeping through his green dressing gown. Just before he died he asked me to show him my right breast. It was very cold and frosty but I did. He asked to smell my hair. I let him. I touched his hand and he died very, very quickly.

Beat.

When you talk to him does he answer you straight away? He's quite…

JEAN. He can talk. He's very capable. When he wants.

HELEN. I've brought him a biscuit. A chocolate one. I went out especially to get it. It's a treat.

HELEN *takes a chocolate biscuit from her coat pocket and holds it out.*

She talks to him as though he were deaf.

Do you want this chocolate biscuit?

OSCAR *stands with his jumper still over his head and goes over to* JEAN.

OSCAR *whispers in* JEAN*'s ear.*

JEAN. Yes you can. Don't wind him up though.

OSCAR *runs off.*

JEAN *and* HELEN *watch him go.*

They slowly eat their ice creams.

He's gone to speak to the ice-cream man. He knows him very well. He visits our road every evening without fail. Mr Stone is a very nice man. Always smokes a cigar as he serves you. Doesn't charge for crushed nuts if you give him a wink. He's very well-to-do. Got a sunbed in his loft I believe. He's very fond of Oscar. They had a fall-out over the summer though. Oscar squirted the hosepipe through his van window. Most of his ice cream melted. Our road's the start of his round so you can imagine what trouble it caused. A local outcry. He smashed Oscar's head against his counter. Gave him a deep cut on his eyebrow. Bled for hours. I would've gone mad, kicked up a bit of a fuss but he deserved everything he got. Turned out he'd had it coming for a long time. He'd started an ice-cream feud between Mr Stone and another ice-cream man. An Algerian called Black Bruno. Oscar had been going from one to the other telling each the other one had been questioning the quality of their ice cream. That's like a red rag to a bull for an ice-cream man. They ended up fighting in a park full of children one Saturday afternoon. The kids went mad. Showered them with spit. It made the evening paper.

HELEN. I'll leave his biscuit on the wall for him. He might want it when he comes back. I could never resist a chocolate biscuit when I was his age.

HELEN *stands and places the chocolate biscuit on the wall where* OSCAR *has been sitting.*

She returns to her end of the wall and sits.

They both continue to eat their ice creams.

Silence.

You look different.

JEAN. Yes.

Pause.

HELEN. Not how I remember.

JEAN. No.

Pause.

HELEN. You don't know what to say do you?

JEAN. No I don't. You don't make it easy. You really don't. You never have.

HELEN. Words. Difficult sometimes. Aren't they.

Silence.

JEAN. I thought you might have died.

HELEN. No.

HELEN *puts her ice cream on the floor and stamps on it.*

I hate ice cream. Tastes like dirty cocks.

HELEN *sits on the wall.*

She rubs one of her eyes.

She yawns.

She hums loudly.

JEAN. That's what I thought. I've had visions of you dying in so many different ways. A different picture in my head every day. I didn't want them there. Not when they first came. They just scratched through my eyeballs when I wasn't looking. Like beautiful stained-glass windows shining in my brain. I started keeping a diary. To write them down. They were important. A diary of how my daughter died. I've got seven of them now. All in different colours. I keep them in my handbag.

JEAN *gets the diaries out of her handbag and opens one at random dates.*

Tuesday eighth February –

In a dirty toilet gagged on her own sick.

Friday thirteenth May –

Strangled in a muddy field underneath a broken scarecrow.

I kept on thinking I'd see you on the news at teatime or something. Hear about you on a car radio through a wound-down window at some traffic lights. Never alive. Always dead. Always totally destroyed.

HELEN. How is he? How is my son?

JEAN. He's not your son. He stopped being your son the night you dumped him on our doorstep. The same night you stopped being my daughter. He'll never be your son.

Pause.

HELEN. How is he?

JEAN. You can't say his name can you? Your mouth can't shape the word.

Beat.

HELEN. How is... he?

Beat.

JEAN. Oscar. He needs to be loved. People find his shyness very vulgar. It takes a lot of guts to be gentle and kind.

HELEN. Right.

Beat.

Dad. He alright?

JEAN. He still puts his coat on, zips it up and goes out looking for you. Gets on a bus. Goes wherever it takes him. I tell him not to bother. He thought he found you once. Rotting away in a falling-down factory. Dead on a shit-stained mattress. Surrounded by milk bottles full of piss and dried up condoms. It nearly killed him. It wasn't you but that didn't matter. It might as well have been. If you cut a hope in half is the bit that's left really worth it.

HELEN *laughs. She stops herself.*

HELEN. I've been all over the place. I think I walked to Scotland once. I don't know how I did it. I don't know which way I went. The roads I walked down. I can't remember. I just arrived in places. Existed for a bit. Not living. Just ticking over. Everywhere I went was just black.

JEAN. Oscar doesn't see his...

HELEN. His dad?

JEAN. He doesn't see him any more. I don't let him. He's not really a person any more. He's just a shell. I go and see him quite a bit on my own. Just sit in an orange plastic chair. Watch him dribble into a child's bib they put on him. I watch him struggle to control his bowels. His muck squirts up his back. I watch him tug at the catheter that drains his bladder. I feed him biscuits until he's sick and biting chunks out of his own tongue. It makes me smile. Sometimes a little bit of wee comes out. I know it's wrong but it makes me feel all warm inside. I think we all get punished for the bad things we do.

HELEN (*simultaneous*). I'm pregnant.

JEAN (*simultaneous*). I'm dying.

I am. I'm dying. I'm going to be dead very soon. No one knows. Not even your dad. Not even Oscar. I don't even know why I told you because you don't mean anything to me. You're a stranger. It just feels the most important thing in the world that in this tiny moment I tell you I'm going to die. That it hurts. That I'm scared. That I'm very tired. You've got raspberry sauce all over your face.

JEAN *spits on a tissue and wipes* HELEN*'s face clean.*

I've brought you a cigarette.

JEAN *gets a cigarette out of her handbag.*

You do still smoke don't you?

HELEN. When I can.

JEAN. I got it off a teenager. I offered him some money. He wouldn't take it.

HELEN *takes the cigarettes from* JEAN.

She strikes a match on the wall.

She lights a cigarette and her face is brightened by the flame.

She lets the whole match burn.

She throws it in the canal.

She smokes the cigarette.

She rubs her stomach.

The street lamp starts to buzz and flicker. It casts intermittent orange light over the canal and falls on the shape of OSCAR *standing underneath.*

He is silent and still.

He watches HELEN *and* JEAN.

They don't see him.

HELEN. I sent him a birthday card. It had a badge on it.

JEAN. Yes.

HELEN. Did he like it?

JEAN. I didn't give it to him.

HELEN. I understand.

JEAN. No you don't.

HELEN. Tried to phone.

JEAN. Changed the number.

HELEN. I know. Ex-directory. Gone all posh.

JEAN. Had to.

HELEN. Why?

JEAN. Nuisance calls. All the time. Day and night.

HELEN. Did you?

JEAN. I knew it was you. I know how you breathe. I've watched you sleep remember.

HELEN. I only wanted to hear him speak. One small word. I was curious.

Pause.

Sorry to hear about you dying and everything. What is it? Cancer or sommat. It's funny.

HELEN *laughs.*

It's not. Sorry for laughing. It's a nervous thing. It's cos I'm shocked. It's not quite sunk in. I love you.

JEAN. Do you?

HELEN. Mmmm.

JEAN. I don't feel loved.

HELEN. Don't you?

JEAN. No I don't.

HELEN. Can I have some money?

JEAN. I haven't got any.

HELEN. Give us some money.

JEAN. I've told you.

HELEN. You're lying.

JEAN. I'm not.

HELEN. You are.

Beat.

I watched you draw his benefit this morning at the Post Office. I followed you. I hid behind the postcard rack. I pretended to be a foreigner. I saw you put it in your purse. Twenty pounds forty. Two weeks' worth. Two ten-pound notes and two twenty-pence pieces. Am I right? You gave him one twenty pence to get a penny mix. That leaves twenty pounds twenty minus the ice creams you bought. I'm not stupid. Do you think I'm stupid? I'm not stupid. I was always very good at maths.

HELEN *grabs hold of* JEAN*'s handbag.*

They struggle.

Give me your fucking bag you skinny fucking tramp.

HELEN *rips the handbag from* JEAN.

She turns it upside down and empties its contents on the floor.

She scratches around the dirt.

She finds the purse and takes the ten-pound note out.

What's wrong with your face?

JEAN. He needs new underpants. His old ones are all baggy. His balls keep falling out when he does PE. His teachers complained. He's getting teased. I need to buy him some. That's what that's for.

HELEN *throws the purse on the floor.*

HELEN. Who do you think you're talking to, you?

HELEN *blows on the end of the cigarette and it glows red hot.*

She threatens JEAN *with it.*

He grew inside me. Deep down in the arse of your barren stomach you know it's true. That fucking hurts you doesn't it? It fucking burns your insides out like drain cleaner. I can feel the panic from here. I can warm my hands on it. Nothing good ever came from your cunt. Only me. What a crying shame that is. Mother. You're just a dying pig waiting for the soil to fall over your head.

The street lamp settles.

They both become aware of OSCAR*'s presence.*

HELEN *hardens. She doesn't look at him.*

Tears fall from JEAN*'s eyes.*

OSCAR. Granddad's been having a lot of problems with his bottom recently. He had this lump on his right bumcheek. He said it hurt like hell. He went to the doctor but she said it was just an in-growing hair so he left it, but it turned into a pus-filled blister and when he sat down yesterday to eat his boiled potatoes and bacon he forgot to sit on his cushion. It must have burst because it seeped through his pants on to the seat. He said it didn't hurt but it did smell a lot.

OSCAR *goes to the biscuit on the wall.*

He unwraps it and puts the wrapper in his pocket.

He puts the whole biscuit in his mouth and chews it.

He goes to HELEN *and spits the chewed-up biscuit in her face.*

HELEN *is still.*

You could have come back just once. Looked through my window while I was asleep. Watched me play in the school playground through the wire fence. Followed me when I was going to the shops for Nana on my bike. Watched what sweets I bought. Seen me crying when I fell over. Kissed me better. Looked at the first picture I'd painted. Polished my shoes. Made me a birthday cake. Looked after me when I was poorly. Slept on my bed. Holding me in your arms. I might have missed you more then.

Beat.

It's good to be silent sometimes. Close everything down.

Beat.

My name is Oscar. I am twelve. I like animals especially birds. I have size five shoes. I don't like wearing wool because it makes me wheeze. I've never eaten chips. I like watching television but prefer listening to the radio. I support the greatest football team in the world. Manchester United. I hate City. They are scum. I was circumcised by Dr Singh four months, two weeks and five days ago. I still have the disposable stitches from my willy in a clear hospital sample jar. I sometimes put them in my mouth at night. I once had the runs when I was playing out and had to do a poo in a red telephone box. I wiped my bum on a cigarette box. I have also wee'd against a lamp post nine doors away from my house just for fun of it. I've never been in love with a girl. I don't think. I've never even kissed one. I don't think. I never used to like chocolate but I do now. I like Mars Bars the best but only when they are soft. If they are hard or have been in the fridge I put them in my pants to warm them up. I like salt-and-vinegar crisps with extra salt. I love Coca-Cola. I don't have many friends. I don't have any friends. But I don't mind. I know I am a good person. I think I've always told the truth. I don't walk on cracks in the ground. I always salute magpies. I'm very lucky. I think you gave birth to me. That's my history. Who I am. My place in it.

OSCAR *wets himself.*

A puddle forms at his feet.

I didn't think it would be like this. I didn't think I would have to be the one making all the effort.

Beat.

We are all silly aren't we? The silences we can fall in to. Like giant holes in the snow. It must get harder when you're older. When you're an adult. The responsibility to keep the silences away must be deafening. I decide on my quietness. When to use it. When it will achieve the loudest bang. The biggest explosion. Like now.

Silence.

OSCAR *falls silent. Everything stops. Nothing.*

I stopped the world. I stopped it spinning. Did you feel it? The stillness. The noise.

HELEN *covers her face.*

Why do you have to hide all the time? Cover your face like that? You should look at me.

Beat.

Let me know that you want to see me.

HELEN *looks small.*

That's what I used to do when I was young. Try and make myself too small to see.

HELEN. You are young.

OSCAR. I'm not. I've been old for ages me. What do you want?

Beat.

I can remember the day I started to speak. I remember the hour and the minute. I remember the colour of everything. Can you, Nana?

JEAN *nods.*

(*To* HELEN.) Can you?

HELEN *is still.*

I don't know you. Not really. But I can see it. There is something good about you.

Pause.

HELEN. I love you.

OSCAR. You shouldn't. You will only be disappointed. It's a sacrifice. Don't you think. Mum.

Why are you crying?

HELEN. I don't know.

Goodbye, Oscar.

This is goodbye for ever. They will never see each other again. They stand looking at each other.

OSCAR. Goodbye.

HELEN *leaves.*

JEAN *watches her leave.*

JEAN *takes an Extra Strong Mint from her bag and eats it.*

JEAN *offers* OSCAR *a mint and he accepts it. He sits on the wall and eats the mint.*

Scene Eight

A few months later. January. The bathroom at Jean and John's house.

An old white enamel bath.

The taps are running and eventually the water will overflow.

The water steams.

A black suit, white shirt and a black tie hang on a hook. A pair of black shoes and socks sit underneath them on the floor.

JEAN (*sixty-five*) *sits on a wooden chair.*

She sees the bath overflowing and turns off the taps.

OSCAR (*thirteen*) *emerges from underneath the water.*

OSCAR. How long, Nana?

> *Beat.*
>
> Nana?
>
> *Beat.*
>
> Nana, how long?
>
> JEAN *doesn't answer.*
>
> OSCAR *takes another deep breath and disappears underneath the water.*
>
> *After some time,* OSCAR *emerges again, releasing his held breath.*
>
> How long, Nana?

JEAN. About half a minute.

> *Pause.*

OSCAR (*looking at his hands*). My fingers are all wrinkly. Old man's hands.

JEAN. If you stay in there much longer you'll turn into an old man.

> *Beat.*

OSCAR. Nana?

> I keep dreaming the world is ending.

JEAN. It's just a dream.

OSCAR. When will it?

JEAN. What?

OSCAR. End.

JEAN. The world?

OSCAR. Yes.

JEAN. When it's ready.

>JEAN *goes to the bath.*

>OSCAR *gives her a bar of soap.*

>JEAN *rubs the bar of soap onto* OSCAR*'s head and works up a lather.*

>JEAN *washes his hair in silence.*

OSCAR. Do you want to know my dream, Nana?

>That soldiers came.

>they dragged people onto the road

>the women by the hair

>they castrated the men and made them eat it

>shot them through the face.

>Locked all the children in a garage

>poured petrol through the roof

>set it on fire.

>Pissed into the flames.

>I saw the body of a baby

>I think he was my son.

>Dogs eating his body.

>Told the women to bury their dead under the concrete road.

>It took days.

>They buried the men on a Saturday morning.

>I was in the grave.

>Broken. Twisted. Bodies.

>I lay among them.

>Quiet.

>I was pulled out alive.

The soldier said he would kill me tomorrow

I begged him to kill me today.

I begged him to shoot me.

He gave me clothes and water.

They made me watch them kill.

They had sex with dead people.

Animals.

I saw an old woman who looked like you.

Naked.

I waved.

She was walking over the dead.

The soldiers threw bricks at her face.

They burnt her with cigarettes.

They whipped her with sticks.

They made her sing nursery rhymes

as they cut off her breasts

with garden shears.

They ripped her apart and hung her from a street lamp.

One leg one side of the road.

One leg on the other side of the road.

The soldiers left in the morning.

I dreamt that.

That everyone I know dies.

That I'm left alone. Everywhere is empty. No sound.
Nothing.

Just me on a road of dead bodies.

When will I be like everybody else?

JEAN *doesn't answer. She is looking up at the sky.*

What's up there?

JEAN *still doesn't answer.*

OSCAR *disappears under the water again.*

After some time he emerges.

When do you think my willy will grow, Nana?

Beat.

Do you think I will wake up one morning and it will have grown massive? Or do you think that it will stay the same and my body will just get big? I don't know what would be better. The biggest willy I've ever seen was on a donkey. It was weeing on the sand. Making puddles. If my willy grows that big I haven't got a pair of underpants or trousers to put it in. I'd have to walk around with nothing on. I don't think I'd like that. It might get a bit embarrassing. Especially on the bus or in maths when I have to collect the books in. That's when my willy always gets hard for no reason. I don't know why.

JEAN *gets a large white bath towel and holds it open.*

Everyone talks about willies in my school. I don't see what the fuss is all about.

OSCAR *indicates with his finger for her to turn around so she can't see his naked body.*

JEAN *gives the towel to* OSCAR *and turns around.*

OSCAR *gets out of the bath and wraps the towel around his wet body.*

There's a group of boys who show each other theirs. They do it in the toilets at breaktime and dinner. There's six of them. They stand in a cubicle and measure whose is bigger with the straight edge on a protractor. I think they take it very seriously because there's always one of them taking notes. I don't know what about. He might trace the outline of each willy on the pages of his book. Just to keep track of any changes. They all concentrate very hard when they are doing it. Their faces look like this.

JEAN *turns back and begins to dry* OSCAR *with towel.*

There's a tall one with ginger spiky hair and a leg brace called Frogger. He's a prefect. He asked me if I wanted to measure his once. He even offered me the use of his protractor. He said it was brand new. That no one else had ever used it. He was very softly spoken and polite. I felt I'd let him down when I told him thank you but no thank you. I thought he was going to cry. He punched me in the face instead.

JEAN *gets* OSCAR*'s white underpants and he steps into them.*

OSCAR *pulls them up.*

I never go to the toilet at school any more. They're always dirty anyway. Bits of poo and wee and soggy toilet paper everywhere. Even on the ceiling. No one knows how to use the toilet properly at my school.

JEAN *gets* OSCAR*'s white shirt.*

OSCAR *puts his arms into the sleeves and she does the buttons up.*

No I hope my willy doesn't get too big. I wouldn't want it getting in the way.

JEAN *gets* OSCAR*'s black trousers and he steps into them.*

OSCAR *pulls them up. He tucks his shirt in and fastens his trousers.*

Granddad's got a big willy hasn't he, Nana? I've seen it. He was playing with it in front of the mirror. The one on his wardrobe door. He was naked. He didn't have a protractor. He didn't see me watching him. He was crying.

JEAN *gives* OSCAR *the black tie.*

OSCAR *tries to tie it but can't.*

JEAN *ties the tie.*

He wiped the mirror clean with his handkerchief. That's when he saw me. He told me to fuck off and closed the door.

JEAN. I know.

OSCAR. I nearly told him to fuck off back.

JEAN. I know.

OSCAR. I didn't.

JEAN. I know.

> JEAN *gets* OSCAR's *socks from the shoes. She puts them on him.*

OSCAR. I like it when it's just me and you, Nana.

JEAN. I do too.

OSCAR. Granddad can't interrupt us.

> *Beat.*

He's ignoring you.

JEAN. He isn't ignoring me, Oscar. He's just sad at the moment.

OSCAR. I thought he was going to hit me.

JEAN. He didn't.

> JEAN *gets* OSCAR's *shoes. She sets them down and he steps into them. She ties the laces.*

OSCAR. Nana, you look beautiful.

JEAN. Thank you, Oscar.

> JEAN *gets the black suit jacket.*

> OSCAR *puts his arm through the sleeves and* JEAN *eases it on.*

> JEAN *combs* OSCAR's *hair neatly.*

You won't be here soon will you? Why does everyone leave me, Nana? I'm sorry if I did anything wrong.

> JEAN *goes out.*

I…

> OSCAR *is left alone.*

Scene Nine

A year later. July. The hottest day of the year. Jean and John's back garden.

The sun burns.

An old bath stands in the garden acting as an improvised water feature and rainwater butt.

A home-made swing hangs somewhere.

JOHN (*sixty-seven*) *is digging a hole.*

As he digs he empties the soil on the ground.

By the side of him there is a watering can and a rose bush still in its plastic pot.

Nearby on a small wooden table there is a jug of water and an empty glass.

After some time he stops digging.

He pours a glass of water and downs it in one.

He goes to the bath tub.

He takes his shoes off. He takes his socks off and puts them in his shoes.

He rolls his trouser legs up and steps into the paddling pool.

He paddles.

He takes out a handkerchief from his trouser pocket and soaks it in the water.

He wrings it out and drapes it over his head.

He closes his eyes.

He is still.

OSCAR (*fourteen*) *enters.*

He is carrying a goldfish in a clear plastic bag full of water. He holds it out in front of him and examines it.

He quietly creeps up to the paddling pool and splashes water all over JOHN.

JOHN (*shocked, angry, and incoherent*). Absolutely bloody stupid you are.

OSCAR *holds the goldfish out in front of him.*

Bloody stupid.

Beat.

What's that?

OSCAR. I won it. It's a goldfish. I won it at the fair. I won it for you. I thought you'd like it.

JOHN. I'm soaking wet now.

OSCAR. I won it on one of them stalls where you have to hook a rubber duck on to the end of a pole. It took me ages. I did it though. I won. I won it for you.

Beat.

JOHN. You shouldn't have wasted your money. We haven't even got a fish tank. Where you going to keep a fish if you haven't even got a fish tank?

Beat.

Eh? Where you going to keep it?

Beat.

Bloody thick sometimes you.

Beat.

Giving your money to Gyppos.

Beat.

It'll be dead in a day.

JOHN *gets out of the bath tub and leaves.*

OSCAR *takes his shoes off.*

OSCAR *takes his socks off and puts them in his shoes.*

OSCAR *rolls his jeans up and stands in the paddling pool.*

OSCAR *opens the bag and empties the fish in to the bath tub.*

OSCAR *watches it swim around his feet.*

JOHN *enters with a towel.*

He stops and looks at OSCAR.

JOHN *sits on the ground and dries his feet with the towel and then puts his socks on.*

JOHN *puts his shoes on and ties the laces.*

JOHN *rolls his trouser legs down.*

JOHN *continues digging.*

OSCAR *looks at* JOHN.

OSCAR *gets out of the bath tub and leaves.*

JOHN *pulls a makeshift cross out of the ground that he had erected years before for the grave of* OSCAR*'s dog and puts it on the ground.*

JOHN *goes to the goldfish in the bath tub and watches it swim.*

JOHN *spits in the paddling pool.*

JOHN *goes back to his spade and digs.*

OSCAR *returns carrying a massive stuffed toy. It dwarfs him.*

OSCAR. Granddad.

JOHN *doesn't answer.*

Granddad.

JOHN *doesn't answer.*

Granddad.

JOHN *doesn't answer.*

I won this for you too.

JOHN *turns to* OSCAR.

I thought it would make you happy.

JOHN. Where did you get that?

OSCAR. The fair.

JOHN. No you didn't.

OSCAR. I did.

JOHN. I don't believe you.

OSCAR. I did.

JOHN. Where did you pinch it from?

OSCAR. I didn't.

JOHN. Pinch it from some children's home or something?

OSCAR. No.

JOHN. Where did you get it?

OSCAR. I won it. I won it for you, Granddad. I didn't rob it. I won it for you.

Pause.

JOHN. What do I want a teddy bear for? What am I going to do with that? Just mess up the house. Get in the way. Covered in dust.

Beat.

You want to start thinking about growing up a bit. Playing with teddy bears. Very childish, Oscar. You want to start thinking about changing a bit. Being more responsible. Being more mature.

Beat.

Do you hear me?

Beat.

Do you hear me?

Beat.

I won't ask you again. Do you hear me?

OSCAR. Yes.

OSCAR sits the teddy bear on the swing and pushes it.

JOHN *stops digging and pulls out a black-plastic bin bag that is worn and covered in soil. Inside the bag are the remains of* OSCAR's *dog.*

JOHN *throws it on the ground.*

JOHN. Bag of bones now. Nothing left.

OSCAR *stops pushing the teddy bear and looks at* JOHN.

OSCAR. You shouldn't dig up dead things, Granddad. Should just let things be.

JOHN. Who says?

OSCAR. That's what Nana would say. Just let things be.

JOHN *laughs to himself.*

JOHN. Remember the night we buried him?

OSCAR. No.

JOHN. It was three days before Christmas.

OSCAR. I don't remember.

JOHN. You were four.

OSCAR. I don't remember.

JOHN. The night your mum left you.

OSCAR. No, Granddad. I don't remember.

OSCAR *goes to the swing and sits on it.*

JOHN. The ground was frozen solid. All cracked and broken. I should've just thrown him in the canal. Made a hole in the ice and dropped him in. I should have. I didn't. I didn't because I promised your mum.

Beat.

It took me an hour to dig a hole that night.

Beat.

I'm going to plant a rose bush here. Scatter your nana's ashes. It was always her favourite place in the garden. God knows why. Contaminated if you ask me.

OSCAR *pushes the teddy bear on the swing.*

JOHN *turns the rose upside down and takes it out of its plastic pot.*

OSCAR. Why don't you like me?

JOHN *loosens its roots and puts it in the hole in the ground.*

Why don't you like me, Granddad?

JOHN *fills the soil that he has dug out back into the hole and firms the soil around the rose with his foot.*

Why don't you like me?

JOHN *gets the watering can and waters the rose.*

JOHN *leaves.*

OSCAR *stops pushing the teddy bear and goes over to the wheel barrow.*

He looks at the dead dog.

He rips open the black bag and touches the remains of the dog.

He goes to the paddling pool and washes his hands in the water.

JOHN *returns with an urn containing the ashes of his dead wife.*

OSCAR *holds his hands out.*

Can I hold the ashes?

JOHN *goes to the rose bush and kneels.*

I think I should hold them, Granddad.

JOHN *takes the lid off the urn.*

Give me the ashes.

JOHN. What?

OSCAR. Give me the ashes.

JOHN. Wha... What?

OSCAR *goes to* JOHN.

OSCAR (*playfully kicking* JOHN *softly*). Give me the ashes.

JOHN. Stop it –

OSCAR (*playfully kicking* JOHN *a bit harder*). Give me the ashes.

JOHN. Don't –

OSCAR (*playfully kicking* JOHN). Give me the ashes.

JOHN. Will you –

OSCAR (*kicking* JOHN). Give me the ashes.

JOHN. I told –

OSCAR (*kicking* JOHN *harder*). Give me the ashes.

JOHN. I want –

OSCAR (*kicking* JOHN *hard*). Give me the ashes.

JOHN *gives* OSCAR *the ashes.*

OSCAR *goes to the paddling pool and stands in it.*

JOHN. I do like you.

OSCAR. No you don't.

Beat.

I know you don't. If you did you wouldn't always hurt me.

JOHN. I do like you.

OSCAR. I don't mind that you don't like me. Just because I'm your daughter's son doesn't mean that you have to like me. It isn't the law. I don't think you can get sent to prison for not liking me.

OSCAR *puts his hand in the urn and takes out a handful of ashes. They run through his fingers.*

There was this girl in my class called Lisa Felix. I really didn't like her. She really didn't like me. There was something chemical about the way we hated each other.

She got leukaemia. She wasn't in school for ages. Then one day she came back. Mrs Troth my teacher told us that she was going to die. That she was coming back to say goodbye to everyone. We all made cards for her. On the inside of my card I wrote:

To Lisa,

I will always hate you. I don't care that you are dying because I hate you. Just because you have cancer doesn't change the fact that you're a cunt. You were before you had cancer. You still will be after you're dead.

Good luck,

Oscar.

JOHN. You cruel b–

OSCAR. I gave her the card and she read it. She looked at me and started to laugh. She laughed so much that the tube up her nose made it bleed. It dripped over her lips onto her chin and she licked it with her tongue. I was honest with her and she appreciated that. It didn't matter that we didn't like each other because we both accepted that was just the way it was. I never saw Lisa again.

I don't care that you don't like me, Granddad, but I'd like to know why you don't. Is it something I've done or is it just something chemical?

OSCAR *goes to empty the ashes.*

JOHN. Give me the ashes.

OSCAR. No.

JOHN. Give me the ashes.

OSCAR. Tell me why you hate me.

Almost emptying the ashes out.

JOHN. I don't...

JOHN *snatches the ashes from* OSCAR.

I don't like...

JOHN *takes a spoonful of the ashes and holds it to his mouth.*

…like you, Oscar. I really don't like you. I've tried to like you for years but I just can't. I hate myself for hating you and then I hate you more for making me hate myself. I look at you and I feel sick. My stomach feels sick. You make my whole body feel sick.

JOHN *puts the ashes in his mouth. He drinks some water from the glass. He battles to swallow the ashes.*

I hate you because my daughter went.

JOHN *takes another spoonful, eats, drinks and swallows.*

I hate you because she never came back.

JOHN *takes another spoonful, eats, drinks and swallows.*

I hate you because you remind me of everything lost.

JOHN *takes another spoonful, eats, drinks and swallows.*

I hate you because I haven't made your life better.

JOHN *puts the empty urn on the floor.*

OSCAR. I love you, Granddad.

JOHN *walks off.*

OSCAR *sits on the swing.*

He swings.

Scene Ten

A year later. Bonfire Night. Anywhere in Manchester.

Darkness.

Fireworks and revelry can be heard in the distance. The sound is ambiguous. It could be mistaken for a city in a state of panic or unrest. The fireworks could be gunshots and mortar explosions. The shouts and cheers could be something more sinister.

OSCAR *(fifteen) sits alone.*

A torch is by his side.

A GIRL *(fifteen) enters.*

Her lips and mouth are bloodied.

Her clothes are ripped.

She doesn't notice OSCAR.

OSCAR *sees her and shines the torch in her face.*

The GIRL *is still.*

OSCAR *throws a stone at the* GIRL.

The GIRL *is still.*

OSCAR *takes a can out of his backpack.*

OSCAR *opens his can.*

OSCAR *offers the can to the* GIRL.

The GIRL *is still.*

OSCAR *walks halfway towards the* GIRL *and places the can on the ground.*

OSCAR *takes off his coat and offers it to the* GIRL.

The GIRL *looks at* OSCAR.

The GIRL *takes the coat.*

They look at each other.

A firework explodes overhead and the moment freezes in time.

OSCAR. You should put it on. It's freezing. I don't feel the cold.

The GIRL *puts the coat on.*

OSCAR *goes to the can and takes a mouthful.*

OSCAR *looks away.*

OSCAR *goes to his backpack and takes out two sparklers.*

He goes halfway towards the GIRL.

Do you want a sparkler?

The GIRL *looks at* OSCAR.

The GIRL *takes one of the sparklers.*

OSCAR *lights the* GIRL*'s sparkler and then his own.*

They both hold their sparklers in the darkness.

Their sparklers stop sparkling.

OSCAR *takes both of the sparklers and pours some of the drink from the can on them.*

The sparklers hiss and smoke.

OSCAR *and the* GIRL *are apart.*

OSCAR *looks away.*

Who's done that?

Pause.

Who hurt you?

The GIRL *opens her hand to reveal a flower head. She has been holding it for a long time.*

It is crushed but it still resembles what it was.

GIRL. She spat in my mouth.

They laughed.

I swallowed it.

I opened my mouth.

They all spat in it.

I swallowed it all.

I wasn't sick.

I didn't scream.

They held me down.

She tore my tights.

I didn't cry.

I wet my knickers.

It went on her shoe.

She wiped it on my face.

She shoved a beer bottle up me.

She pissed on my face.

They took my mum's flowers.

It was white but now it's red.

OSCAR *goes to his backpack.*

He takes out a bottle of water.

He goes to the GIRL.

He holds his hand out.

The GIRL *gives him the stained flower.*

OSCAR *opens the bottle of water and pours it over the flower.*

OSCAR *rubs the flower petals gently.*

The blood staining the flower runs and washes off returning the flower to its original white colour.

OSCAR *gives the flower back to the* GIRL.

Thank you.

The GIRL *stands and goes to leave.*

OSCAR. Are you going?

GIRL. Yes. I think so.

Beat.

Are you?

OSCAR. No, I'm staying here.

GIRL. On your own?

OSCAR. Yes.

The GIRL *goes to take* OSCAR*'s coat off and give it him back.*

You can keep my coat.

GIRL. Thank you.

Beat.

Goodbye.

OSCAR. Yes. Goodbye.

The GIRL *leaves* OSCAR *alone.*

Silence.

The GIRL *returns.*

They stand looking each other.

The GIRL *holds out her hand and offers the flower.*

OSCAR *looks away.*

GIRL. Do you want this?

Beat.

Do you?

OSCAR *takes the flower.*

He looks at it.

He looks at the GIRL.

He picks at the petals.

He is controlled at first but the intensity of the destruction escalates.

He destroys it. It's as though he's ruining something bigger. Maybe himself.

You're not a bad person.

Beat.

You're absolutely not by the way.

Beat.

OSCAR. Neither are you.

Beat.

GIRL. Are you crying?

OSCAR. A little bit.

GIRL. Can I have a sip of your can?

>OSCAR *picks up the can.*
>
>*He wipes it and gives it to the* GIRL.
>
>*The* GIRL *drinks from the can.*
>
>*She wipes it and passes it to* OSCAR.
>
>OSCAR *drinks from the can.*

Can I have some chocolate?

>OSCAR *smiles.*
>
>*He goes to the backpack and returns with it.*
>
>*He turns the bag upside down and loads of different chocolate bars tumble out.*

OSCAR. I like chocolate.

>*The* GIRL *sifts through the chocolate.*
>
>*As she does,* OSCAR *pulls a Mars Bar out from the seat of his pants.*
>
>*The* GIRL *looks at him.*

(*Embarrassed.*) I have to melt Mars Bars a bit. I can't eat them hard. They have to be a bit soft.

>*The* GIRL *picks up a chocolate bar and starts to eat it.*

It's my birthday.

>*Beat.*

GIRL. Happy birthday.

>*The* GIRL *looks at* OSCAR.

Can I hold your hand?

>OSCAR *looks at the* GIRL.

OSCAR. I don't know how.

>*Beat.*

I don't.

Beat.

No one ever has.

GIRL. I will.

OSCAR. You don't have to.

The GIRL *holds her hand out.*

Beat.

GIRL. Hello.

Beat.

OSCAR. Yes.

OSCAR *holds his hand out.*

Hello.

They hold hands slowly. They look at each other.

Silence.

GIRL. Will everything just go dark?

Beat.

Will it just be a moment?

OSCAR. I think it will be nothing. I think it will be alright.

The ground starts to crack and fracture.

It begins to rain heavily.

They sit in the rain.

OSCAR *closes his eyes.*

The world begins to darken and its presence falls away.

They are the centre of the universe surrounded by stars dancing in the darkness.

The End.

THREE BIRDS

Janice Okoh

JANICE OKOH

Janice Okoh is a multi-award-winning playwright. Her first play *Egusi Soup* was produced in 2012 by Menagerie Theatre and Soho Theatre, London, and went on a national tour in 2014 with Menagerie and Theatre Royal Bury St Edmunds as producers. It won a Channel 4 Playwriting Award in 2017.

Her second play *Three Birds* won the Bruntwood Prize for Playwriting in 2011 and was shortlisted for the Verity Bargate and Alfred Fagon Awards in that same year. It was produced in 2013 at the Royal Exchange Theatre, Manchester, and the Bush Theatre, London. In 2025, she adapted it into the critically acclaimed TV show *Just Act Normal*.

Her third play *The Gift* was jointly produced by Eclipse Theatre, Theatre Royal Stratford East and the Coventry Belgrade and was a finalist for the Susan Smith Blackburn Prize in 2020.

Janice writes for television, is a multi-award-winning radio dramatist, and her debut novel will be published in 2027.

Introduction
Janice Okoh, 2025

When I entered the competition in 2011, I hoped it would help my writing career, and it did in so many ways and still does.

Being a prize winner enabled me to teach at university level without a PhD, and it opened doors in the TV world, which is a really difficult place to be as an older black female writer. Getting to create and show-run a TV show as I did with my Bruntwood-winning play means that I am now among only a handful of black female writers in the UK ever to have done so in the history of British television.

I won the prize fourteen years ago, but the amount of kudos it brings makes me stand out in a writer-saturated industry. Looking back over my career, the Bruntwood Prize is the most prestigious of all my awards, and I am so happy that I won it because I feel that without it, I wouldn't have lasted as long in theatre and TV as I have done.

Three Birds was first performed at the Royal Exchange Theatre, Manchester, on 27 February 2013, with the following cast (in order of appearance):

TIANA	Michaela Coel
TIONNE	Jahvel Hall
TANIKA	Susan Wokoma
DR FEELGOOD	Lee Oakes
MS JENKINS	Claire Brown
Director	Sarah Frankcom
Designer	Louie Whitemore
Lighting Designer	Kay Haynes
Sound Designer	Emma Laxton

The production transferred to the Bush Theatre, London, on 20 March 2013.

Characters

TIANA, *sixteen, female*
TIONNE, *thirteen, male*
TANIKA, *nine, female*
DR FEELGOOD, *thirties, male, white*
MS JENKINS, *twenties, female, white*

Scene One

Sunday.

A ground-floor council flat, Lewisham.

Inside is tidy, the furniture sparse, the only items of real value being a laptop and a large flat-screen television, which used to be hooked up to a DVD player. The DVD player is missing.

There is a kitchen area, a back door with a frosted window. A corridor leads off to the three bedrooms.

To the left is the bathroom, under whose door light filters at night.

The curtains are always drawn.

A whole chicken sits in a baking tray on the table. TIANA *and* TIONNE *stand behind it. They wear mismatching aprons.* TIONNE *wears rubber gloves. Beneath his apron,* TIONNE *wears pyjamas.*

TIONNE *presses a kitchen knife to the bird's neck.* TIANA *looks at the laptop.*

TANIKA *is on the sofa.*

TIANA. Lower.

    TIONNE *moves the knife.*

    Lower.

    TIONNE *moves the knife.*

    Higher.

    A pause.

    It's there.

    TANIKA *gets up from the sofa to take a look.*

    Sit down.

TANIKA *sits back down.*

Higher.

TIONNE. You just said it was there.

TIANA. It is. About there.

A pause.

TIONNE's *hands start to shake. He puts down the knife.*

TIONNE. It ain't fresh, anyway.

TIANA. It is.

A pause.

The halal man swore.

TIONNE. Well, it don't smell it.

TIANA. You know what fresh chicken smells like?

TIONNE. So where's the blood?

TIANA. There ain't none. There ain't none cos when they kill it, when they kill it they slit its throat, hang it upside down and all the blood drains out. It's fresh. It's fresh. It's the freshest I can get.

TIANA *picks up the knife and cuts off the chicken's head. A tiny bit of blood spools out onto the table.*

See?

TIONNE. What d'you do that for? It's got to be whole.

TIANA. It is whole.

TIANA *puts the head back on the table and lines it up with the body.*

We could pretend it is.

A beat.

TIONNE *heads for the bathroom.*

Where you going? T!

TIONNE *exits.*

A pause.

TANIKA. You shouldn't of decapitated it.

A pause.

TIANA. You done your homework?

TANIKA *nods.*

TIANA *picks up* TANIKA*'s exercise book.*

'A week in the life of the god Proteus.' Who's he?

TANIKA. Some god.

TIANA (*reading*). 'Sunday nothing happened. Monday, nothing's gonna happen. Tuesday, not much again.' What's he the god of?

TANIKA. The future.

A beat.

TIANA. Do your homework.

TANIKA. Why? It's so dry. Ms Jenkins is so dry. What's learning about the gods gonna get you? And dressing up. She's making us dress up, you know. For assembly. Really she should be teaching year fours.

TIANA *takes the chicken into the kitchen.*

We eating that one as well?

TIANA. Yeah.

TANIKA. Let's just throw it away.

TIANA. We got to eat it.

TANIKA. I ain't a dustbin.

TIANA. Tanika –

TANIKA. Can't we get something from Iceland?

TIANA. I could mince it. Do a bolognese or something.

TANIKA. Why don't we get something from Iceland? Fish fingers are only a pound and you get hundreds.

A pause.

Why can't you do it on something else?

TIANA. Like what?

TANIKA. A dog or a fox or something.

TIANA. How we gonna catch a fox?

TANIKA. A dog then. Could get that one from number eighteen. I hate that dog. Barks at me all the time.

TIANA. Don't bark at me.

TANIKA. We could get it with a bit of meat or something. Chicken.

A pause.

TIANA. Suppose we could lure it in.

TANIKA. Yeah.

TIANA. And you would grab it.

TANIKA. Why me?

TIANA. Cos I'll be luring it in.

TANIKA. Why you?

TIANA. Cos it don't bark at me.

TANIKA. Then what?

TIANA. You strangle it.

TANIKA. Nah, man.

TIANA. Stab it then.

TANIKA. Why me?

TIANA. Cos I'm luring it in.

TANIKA. But it'll be lured in by then.

TIANA. We can't stab it. It'll be barking and everything.

A beat.

TIANA/TANIKA. Poison.

TANIKA. In the chicken.

TIANA. Poison it then cut it up. Cook it and stuff. Make jerk dog.

TANIKA *stares at her.*

I'll have to make jerk dog if you don't want to eat chicken.

TANIKA. I ain't eating no dog.

TIANA. They eat dog in China.

TANIKA. Lie.

TIANA. They do. So we'll eat dog, yeah?

TANIKA. I ain't eating no dog.

TIANA. Well, we can't just put it out in the bins –

TANIKA. You ain't making me –

TIANA. For the binmen to find.

TANIKA. I ain't gonna eat no jerk dog! And it's gonna be all poisoned up.

A pause.

You're so stupid.

TIANA. You're stupid.

TANIKA. I knew you were joking. I did. Joker.

A pause.

T – ?

TIANA. No.

TANIKA. Please?

TIANA. No.

TANIKA. I could do the –

TIANA. No.

TANIKA. Why does he get to stay?

TIANA. Because he's doing things.

TANIKA. I could do things. Do the bids.

TIANA. No.

TANIKA. But he won't do them.

TIANA. No.

TANIKA. Ms Jenkins hates me. She never picks me when I know the answer and she always picks others when they don't.

TIANA. You got to be normal.

TANIKA. Being off sick is normal!

TIANA. I said no.

TANIKA. But –

TIANA. What part of no don't you understand?

TANIKA bursts out crying.

A pause.

I won't do chicken tomorrow, alright? I'll do whatever you want. What do you want? T?

A pause.

T?

A pause.

TANIKA. Chips.

TIANA. Okay. I'll do chips.

TANIKA. From McDonald's.

TIANA. Okay.

TANIKA. And Strawberry Millions. And Cheestrings.

TIANA. Gonna get you a fridge full of them.

TANIKA. How big?

TIANA. Like this big. And when you open it Akon comes on.

TANIKA. Justin Bieber.

TIANA. Since when?

TANIKA. Since like for time.

TIANA *goes over to* TANIKA *and they lie in spoons on the sofa.*

TIANA. And we're gonna have, we're gonna have a garden and a swimming pool and a bedroom and a toilet each with a shower you walk into.

TANIKA. What's in the attic?

TIANA. The attic? Well, that's the playroom, yeah, where you play table tennis and Wii and watch films.

TANIKA. And where the fridge is.

TIANA. Yeah and all your friends come round like they do on *MTV Teen Cribs* cos you got the best clothes and things.

TANIKA. And Ugg boots.

TIANA. Yeah.

TANIKA. Real ones.

TIANA. Yeah.

TANIKA. Not ones that go all mash-up after like one day.

TIANA. I ain't gonna get you side Uggs and –

TANIKA. I hate side Uggs.

TIANA. Yeah and –

TANIKA. Cos my feet ain't getting wet in the rain.

TIANA. Yeah and you'll wear them to school.

TANIKA. Yeah?

TIANA. Cos there's no school uniform.

TANIKA. No school uniform?

TIANA. Yeah.

TANIKA. Now you're going on extra.

TIANA. I ain't.

A long silence.

TIANA *gets up.*

Tionne!

A pause.

Tionne!

TIONNE *comes out.*

Do we need it? I'll get it. If we need it.

TIONNE *nods.*

Tomorrow.

TIANA *picks up the chicken and lays it out on the table.*

We can still practise.

TANIKA. Where you gonna get it from?

TIANA *looks at her.* TANIKA *gets on with her homework.* TIANA *hands* TIONNE *the knife.*

TIANA. Go on.

A pause.

T –

TIONNE *takes the knife.*

Scene Two

Monday.

TIONNE *carefully unpacks a hand-pump and its accessories from a boxed delivery from Amazon. He lays them out on the floor. He examines them.*

TIONNE. A man goes to the doctor. He says to the doctor, doctor, my life seems so harsh and cruel. I feel all alone in a threatening world. The doctor replies, the circus has come to town. The great Tagalichi's going to be doing his magic tricks. Go see him. That should pick you up. But, doctor, he says, I am the great Tagalichi…

A pause.

I am the great Tagalichi… and… and…

A pause.

I got the Havabi one. Only forty-nine ninety-nine, without postage and packaging. Reduced from seventy-five. (*Reading.*) 'The Havabi Total Seven Multi-Function Sprayer. Can be used for agricultural, industrial and domestic uses.'

TANIKA *enters. She's back from school.*

TANIKA. What's for dinner?

TANIKA *goes to the kitchen, lifts the lids from the pots. She slams the lids back down.*

The liar! I ain't eating it. I ain't. I'd rather eat my own doo-doo in a sandwich. You think I won't? T?

She pulls her knickers down, climbs onto the sink and strains as if doing a shit.

A pause.

It's not ready yet. When it's ready, yeah, and I ain't gonna go to McDonald's.

A pause.

What you doing?

TIONNE *ignores her.* TANIKA *goes over to the laptop. Looks at it.*

Knew you wouldn't do it.

A pause.

They're gonna split us up, T. Do you want them to split us up? They'll split us up and I'll get adopted because I'm young and pretty but you'll stay in the home because you look like you got problems and white people'll touch you up. Is that what you want? To be touched up? T?

A pause.

TANIKA *sits down on the sofa and opens her school bag. She takes out an expensive camera and begins to play with it. She presses a button. Part of it zooms out, surprising her.*

TIONNE *looks up at her.*

Do you think it's expensive? I think it's expensive. Ms Jenkins gave it me. It's my responsibility, she said. I'm responsible. She gave it to me after she tried to speak to me about Disney and Kimone but I wouldn't let her cos she thought, like, that's what I was crying about but it weren't. I hate Disney and Kimone. No, I hate Kimone truly because she only follows Disney cos Disney's mixed-race. Ms Jenkins thinks I'm very mature for my age. That's what she said. She gave it to me and said, I want you to take care of this. Take pictures. Take pictures of what? She said life. Life, life, life, life, life.

TIONNE *goes back to his package.*

She's alright, you know, Ms Jenkins. She's got two nieces. Daphne and Freya. Says I remind her of the oldest one. Daphne. She said it's your manner. You've got an inquisitive manner. But then I was thinking, I don't want to be like her niece cos she's got a stupid name, like who calls someone Daphne? It's like really boring and sounds made up. And anyway, she's, like, five. Ms Jenkins's got this red bike, looks like old but it's new. Got it from a specialist shop. One that makes things in an old way. Anyway, I said I liked it and she asked what bike I had. I said why and she goes why? That was funny. You know, cos she said why like how we say it, you know like, why. Then I said, why ride a bike to school when you got the bus? She laughed. She asked if I knew how to ride a bike I said I did but she knew I was lying. She said she's gonna bring this bike she's got to school for us to ride in after-school club but she's gonna check it with the headmistress cos of health and safety cos it's a bike and we could fall or something and would I like that? I said I don't mind.

A pause.

You can have a go if you want.

He ignores her. She wanders around with the camera, looking through the viewfinder, not sure what to take.

A pause.

A man goes to the doctor's.

TIONNE *looks at her.*

Says he feels alone.

TIONNE. Shut up.

TANIKA. All alone in the world.

TIONNE. I said shut up.

TANIKA. The doctor says to him –

He goes for her and they tussle, land on the floor.

The doctor says – The doctor says to him – The doctor says why don't you join the circus?

TIONNE. You can't tell it right.

TANIKA. Neither can you.

A pause.

He releases her.

TIONNE. And I can tell it right. I just don't want to tell it.

TANIKA *examines her camera.*

TANIKA. If you've broken it you're gonna get killed.

TIONNE *ignores her. She takes a couple of pictures with the camera. She turns towards the kitchen. A figure appears at the kitchen window. She screams.*

TIONNE *runs for the corridor. Remains half-hidden.*

DR FEELGOOD. It's alright, it's just me.

TANIKA. Who's me?

TANIKA *peers through the window.*

Oh, it's you. My heart's, like, boom, boom, boom. Thought you were a ghost.

DR FEELGOOD. With no eyes and skin dripping off his bones?

TANIKA. That ain't a ghost that's a nightwalker.

DR FEELGOOD. My bad.

A pause.

TANIKA. You bring something?

DR FEELGOOD. Depends.

TANIKA. On what?

DR FEELGOOD. On whether I'm gonna be parlaying through this window all night.

A pause.

TANIKA. I got three gold stars for my spelling, you know.

DR FEELGOOD. The commotion promotion one?

TANIKA. Yeah.

DR FEELGOOD. So where's my token of appreciation?

TANIKA. For you?

DR FEELGOOD. Yeah.

TANIKA. You kept chatting to Tiana, asking her about *Glee* and she don't even like *Glee*.

DR FEELGOOD. You got three stars, didn't you?

TANIKA. Could've got four.

A pause.

DR FEELGOOD. So where's she at?

TANIKA. Who? Tiana?

DR FEELGOOD. No, Jackie.

TANIKA. I already said.

DR FEELGOOD. No. No, you didn't.

TANIKA. She's gone out.

A pause.

DR FEELGOOD. Get Tiana, then.

TANIKA. She's not in neither.

DR FEELGOOD. I'll wait for her then.

TANIKA. Who? Tiana?

DR FEELGOOD. No, Jackie.

TANIKA. Can't.

DR FEELGOOD. You gonna let me in?

TIONNE. T!

> TANIKA *looks at* TIONNE.
>
> *A pause.*
>
> *She goes to the living room, pulls back the window curtains and opens the window a crack.*

T!

> DR FEELGOOD *appears in the window.*

DR FEELGOOD. What's this?

> TANIKA *shrugs.*
>
> So I'm like the window cleaner, now, am I?

TANIKA. No.

DR FEELGOOD. That's cool. That's okay.

> *He mimes window cleaning.* TANIKA *laughs, takes a picture of him.*
>
> Nice picture box. Let's have a squiz.

TANIKA. Ain't mine to sell.

DR FEELGOOD. You think I'd – ? I'm hurt, T. I'm deeply wounded.

> DR FEELGOOD *turns away, covering his face. He begins to snivel.*

TANIKA. Stop it. You ain't crying. I know you ain't. You ain't – ?

> DR FEELGOOD *takes his hands away from his face.*

I knew it! Joker.

They laugh.

DR FEELGOOD. Tiana really don't like *Glee*, then?

A pause.

So Jackie in there playing hide-and-seek?

TANIKA. No.

DR FEELGOOD. She tell you to keep lookout? All paranoid and running about?

TANIKA. No.

DR FEELGOOD. If she's out we can chill then. Watch a bit of *Corrie*. Chill, watch a bit *Corrie-Orrie*. Though it's not the same since Blanche died.

TANIKA. That ain't on yet.

DR FEELGOOD. *Hollyoaks* then. *Hollyoaks*. Do a bit of homework. What you got for homework?

TANIKA. We got to do a diary on the gods.

DR FEELGOOD. Yeah?

TANIKA. But it's too hard cos Ms Jenkins gave me a rubbish god. I wanted the one Lucien got. He's like the god of everything, which isn't Lucien cos Lucien's an idiot. You know he calls everyone a battyboy now? Shut up, you battyboy. So I asks him, do you know what one is and he said yes it's a boy that likes putting his thingy up girls' bums so I said he was an idiot. He said that China said that Skye said that Kimone said that Disney said it was true and she got it from me so I must be an idiot, too. But I got it from you.

DR FEELGOOD. That ain't exactly what I said.

TANIKA. What did you say?

DR FEELGOOD. Let me in and I'll tell you.

A pause.

TANIKA *goes to the front door.*

TIONNE. T!

TANIKA. Shush!

TANIKA puts the chain on the door and opens it a crack. DR FEELGOOD appears at the front door. He pushes it. He's blocked by the chain.

DR FEELGOOD. What's this?

A pause.

Okay. Fine. As crystal. This ain't got nothing to do with you. I get it. Bye.

TANIKA. You going?

DR FEELGOOD *produces a Yorkie bar.*

You said you didn't get me nothing!

TANIKA goes to take the bar. DR FEELGOOD grabs her, brings her up against the door.

DR FEELGOOD. Tell me the truth. Will you tell me the truth, Tanika?

TANIKA *nods.*

She in there?

TANIKA *nods.*

She incapable?

TANIKA *nods.*

So why didn't you just say, eh? Cos there ain't no point, there ain't no point if she's incapable, is there? You tell her, tell her, tell her if she ain't picking up her phone tomorrow and talking to me like I'm a civilised human being then Indian Paul's coming for the telly and whatever else you got in there, understand?

TANIKA *nods.*

DR FEELGOOD *releases her.*

See, that's what she's like. Messing up the routine when you got homework to do. *Glee* and shit.

He offers her the Yorkie bar again.

Go on. Have it. Have it after dinner or something. What you having?

TANIKA. Chicken but I don't like it.

DR FEELGOOD. Yeah? And give some to your brother. T, I know you're there. Can see your feet. Oh, and, T?

TANIKA. Yeah?

DR FEELGOOD. Well done with your spelling.

DR FEELGOOD leaves. TANIKA closes the front door.

A long silence.

TANIKA breaks the chocolate in half, offers TIONNE some. TIONNE picks up the equipment and takes it into the bathroom.

TANIKA. T!

He shuts the door. TANIKA goes to the door. Listens. She puts half the Yorkie on the floor outside the door, sits down on the sofa and eats the other half.

Scene Three

Same evening.

TIANA *enters through the front door with a battered Primark carrier bag. She puts it in the fridge. She comes out, checks the laptop, goes into the corridor. She comes out with some of Jackie's clothes. She puts them on the floor by the laptop. She passes the bathroom, picks up the chocolate, throws it in the bin. She goes into the kitchen, removes the plates from the sink, puts a pair of rubber gloves on and starts to clean the kitchen.*

Scene Four

Tuesday.

TIANA *sleeps on the sofa. She still wears the rubber gloves.* TANIKA *enters. She is half-dressed for school. She goes to the kitchen, has a wee in the sink and then fills the sink with water. She begins to wash herself down.*

TIANA. You ain't done your neck.

TANIKA. I have.

TIANA. I been watching.

A pause.

Anyone come round?

TANIKA *shrugs.*

Whose turn was it to do the washing up last night?

TANIKA. Dunno.

TIANA. Tanika –

TANIKA. I didn't even eat.

TIANA. It's a rota. It don't matter if it's a rota.

TANIKA. We were meant to be having McDonald's.

TIANA. No, we –

A beat.

We'll have it tonight, yeah? I promise.

TANIKA *drains the water.*

You done it properly?

TANIKA. Yes!

TIANA *gets up, goes to the kitchen.*

I'm gonna be late.

TIANA. I ain't having no one say I ain't looking after you.

TIANA *smells her armpits, refills the sink.*

TANIKA. Maybe if we all could go to Shanice's for a bath we could all smell nice.

TIANA. A wash-down's just as good.

TANIKA. Then why don't you have one?

TIANA. I have.

TANIKA. When?

TIANA. When you were sleeping.

A pause.

TANIKA. Don't know why you ain't concerned about T when he ain't touched water for time.

TIANA *starts pulling at* TANIKA*'s hair. Tries to comb it.*

I ain't a baby.

TIANA. Babies fight.

TANIKA *stills.*

TANIKA. I'm gonna be on late now.

TIANA. So?

TANIKA. Gonna be on red.

TIANA. You ain't even meant to be on amber.

A pause.

What you done?

TANIKA. Nothing.

TIANA. You been fighting?

TANIKA. No.

TIANA. Cos if you been fighting –

TANIKA. I ain't stupid.

A pause.

Disney, yeah? She said I stole her Shamballa bracelet but I never and then Kimone joined in. Ms Jenkins caught us all talking about it when we were supposed to be listening.

A pause.

TIANA. I'll follow them home.

TANIKA. No.

TIANA. You a thief then?

TANIKA. It's fixed.

TIANA. How?

TANIKA. Ms Jenkins fixed it.

TIANA. By putting you on amber?

TANIKA. Yeah but then she made us sit in a classroom in break and talk about it. Made us address the underlying problem.

TIANA. What underlying problem?

TANIKA. How we were feeling about the change in the dynamics of our relationship.

TIANA. What?

A beat.

Let me follow her home, man!

TANIKA. No! She's fixed it!

TIANA. She ain't –

TANIKA. Leave me! I'm gonna be late!

TIANA. Go on then!

A pause.

TANIKA. I need some money.

TIANA. What for?

TANIKA. Break.

TIANA. You don't need money.

TIANA *brings out an abnormally large quantity of Cheestrings out from the fridge and dumps them on the table.*

TANIKA. Cheestrings? I hate Cheestrings.

TIANA. Since when?

TANIKA. Since Ms Jenkins said we need to be eating five a day.

A pause.

TIANA. Fine. Well, if Ms Jenkins says.

TIANA *hands her some change.*

TANIKA. This ain't enough.

TIANA. You can get two packets of Tangy Toms with that. That's two of your five already.

A beat.

Ain't you gonna be late? T! Get in here! I got you something!

TIANA *gets the Primark bag out of the fridge.*

T!

TIONNE *enters from the bathroom.*

A pause.

You been in there all night?

TIONNE. Yeah.

TIANA. Why?

TIONNE *shrugs.*

TIANA *puts the Primark bag down, goes into the bathroom and has a look. She comes out. She gets a bucket and begins frantically scraping the ice out from the freezer compartment into it.*

You never did the bids.

TANIKA. Told you he wouldn't.

TANIKA *picks up the Primark bag and opens it. She recoils. Drops the bag.*

TIANA (*like Nelson from* The Simpsons). Ha ha.

TANIKA. Where d'you get it from?

TIANA. Surrey Docks Farm.

TANIKA. Surrey Docks?

TIANA. Yeah. Yeah. Me and Shanice, right – You should've seen us. No one was about. Just some kids. So we climbed over the fence. Climbing over the fence like, like –

TANIKA. Jackie Chan?

TIANA. Yeah. Jackie Chan in *Rush Hour 2*! And then I said. I said I dare you to kill that chicken.

TANIKA. Nah, man!

TIANA. Yeah. We watched it all on YouTube before we did it. Running around trying to catch them. Running around like a chicken.

TANIKA *laughs.*

It was like they knew it was coming. Like they could sense it cos they started clucking really loud when before we went in they were like silent. Anyway, I did it cos she couldn't do it and you know how big she is, yeah? How she likes killing things. Remember how she killed that mouse with the boiling water? But she couldn't do it so I did it. Broke its neck but it kept flapping. Flapping even with its neck broken. Could feel its heart stop beating, beating all the way up to my elbow.

A pause.

Then these security guards came. Four, five, like nine of them like from nowhere.

TANIKA. What did they look like?

TIANA. Like ugly.

TANIKA. Like Hulk?

TIANA. Yeah.

TANIKA. With green saliva coming off his teeth?

TIANA. Yeah. So we had to hide.

TANIKA. Where?

TIANA. In the farm. We put, like, hay all over us. Yeah, it was really funny.

A pause.

Go on. It's fresh as a fresh as a fresh.

TIONNE *picks up the bag, gets out the chicken and begins to pluck it.*

I got everything else as well.

She brings out an assortment of bottles of vodka, a box of Saxa salt, a bottle of rose water and cocoa-butter moisturiser.

A pause.

TIANA *goes back to getting the ice.*

After the farm we went back to Shanice's, yeah? Talked about things. And we decided, we decided, yeah –

TANIKA. What?

TIANA. We're gonna have our first premises in the West End.

TANIKA. Nah!

TIANA. That's where you get the best clients. This fridge is shit. I'm gonna get us a new one. A massive one. A new fridge, yeah. One that makes ice for drinks and all that as well as Akon.

TANIKA. Justin Bieber.

TIANA. Yeah, Justin –

There's a noise from outside. TIANA *and* TANIKA *hide behind the sofa. A man peers through the back window.*

T? T?

TIANA *signals for* TIONNE *to get down.* TIONNE *slips down onto the floor. The man tries both of the doors. The man leaves.*

A long silence.

You think that was him?

A pause.

It looked like him, didn't it?

A pause.

You ain't going to school.

TANIKA. What? Why?

TIANA. Why d'you think why?

TANIKA. But we're starting a new Mr Gum book and everything.

TIANA. You can watch *Horrible Histories.*

TANIKA. That ain't the same.

TIANA. You didn't want to go to school in the first place!

TANIKA. Yeah well –

TIANA. You can do the bids with me.

TANIKA. I don't want to do the bids.

TIANA. You wanted to do them so now you got them. You got them, yeah, so just, you know, just do 'em.

TANIKA. You can't tell me what to do!

TIANA. Yes I can. And you're eating those Cheestrings. Cos you can't say you want something and then say you don't so you're eating them.

TANIKA. Make me!

TIANA grabs the Cheestrings.

TIANA. Tionne, get her! T!

TIONNE doesn't move and TANIKA scrambles out of the way.

TANIKA (*like Nelson from* The Simpsons). Ha ha.

TIANA. You still ain't going.

TIANA *gets the bucket, opens the bathroom door and chucks the contents of the bucket into the bath at a distance. She closes the bathroom door.*

(*To* TIONNE.) And you should've done this, T. You should've done this.

TIANA *resumes scraping the ice from the freezer.*

Scene Five

Night.

TIONNE *stands in front of the plucked chicken. He wears rubber gloves and a mask. The bottles of alcohol are open around him. He finishes syringing a concoction into the chicken's neck.*

TANIKA *watches* TIONNE *from the corridor. She is in her nightdress.*

TIONNE. It's done. I did it.

A pause.

Couldn't sew it up so I clipped it.

A pause.

TANIKA. Who you talking to?

TIONNE. No one.

TANIKA *enters.*

TANIKA. Lie.

She goes to touch it.

TIONNE. Don't.

TANIKA *looks into the bowl.*

TANIKA. Is that all its blood?

TIONNE. Yeah.

TANIKA. What you gonna do with it?

TIONNE. Drink it.

TANIKA. Lie.

TIONNE *pretends to drink the blood, fooling* TANIKA.

You're disgusting!

TIONNE. Shhhh.

TIONNE *laughs.*

TANIKA. Joker.

A pause.

You gonna get her?

A pause.

You should get her.

A pause.

You think its ghost is walking around somewhere with a broken neck?

TIONNE. Ain't no thing as ghosts.

TANIKA. Yeah, I know. (*A beat.*) What about nightwalkers?

TIONNE. Yeah, they exist.

TANIKA. I knew that.

TIONNE. The neck's fixed now, anyway.

TANIKA *leans in closer.*

TANIKA. Smells funny.

TIONNE. That's your breath.

TANIKA. Its eyes are funny.

TIONNE *pops the chicken's eyes out.* TANIKA *squeals.*

TIONNE. Shh! You scared?

TANIKA. No.

He chases her around with the chicken's eyes, catches her.

Get off! Get off!

TIONNE. Shut up!

A pause.

Go on. Touch them. It's alright.

TANIKA *touches the chicken's eyes.*

TANIKA. Feels like a jelly gobstopper.

TIONNE *pops the chicken's eyes back in.*

How d'you do that?

TIONNE *demonstrates.*

TIONNE. Out. In. Out. In. See? The sockets stay open.

A pause.

TANIKA. What do you think it's like?

TIONNE. What?

TANIKA. Being dead.

TIONNE. Being dead feels like you're flying.

TANIKA. Yeah?

TIONNE. Flying high and reaching the stars and you're on a magic carpet like Aladdin and you look down on everyone and they look just like rats in a tight sewer.

TANIKA. That ain't dying.

TIONNE. Might as well be.

TANIKA. I'm serious.

TIONNE. Being dead. Being dead is like being nothing. Black. Like when animals die. Like that. You just rot.

A pause.

TANIKA. Ms Jenkins says we go to Heaven. She says the name's different depending on your religion but it's all the same thing.

A pause.

How long will it last like that?

TIONNE. For ever. Have to keep topping it up.

TANIKA. Who's gonna do that for ever?

TIONNE. We all will.

TANIKA. Even when we're old, like twenty?

TIONNE. Course.

A pause.

Knock, knock? Knock, knock?

TANIKA. Who's there?

TIONNE. A ghost.

TANIKA. A ghost who?

TIONNE. A ghost woooooooo! Wooooooo!

TANIKA. Ghosts don't exist.

TIONNE. Maybe they do-ooooo. Maybe they don't.

TANIKA *gets the camera out from underneath the sofa.*

You can't catch them on that.

TANIKA. I know.

She takes photos. Then stops.

Why didn't you say nothing about Dr Feelgood?

TIONNE *shrugs.*

She thinks she knows everything, don't she?

A pause.

TIONNE *gets the bucket and begins to pour the alcohol in, mix it up.*

What you doing?

A beat.

You really doing it?

TIONNE. Go to bed.

He tastes the concoction.

TANIKA. You doing it? What's it like?

TIONNE. Mmmm.

TANIKA. Let's have some.

She tries it. Spits it out. TIONNE *laughs.*

Joker.

TIONNE *drinks his, like a grown-up.*

That ain't how you do it.

TANIKA *goes to the kitchen, comes back with a bottle of Coke. She pours some into her cup and then tries it again.*

Mmm.

TIONNE *adds some Coke to his.*

That's how you're meant to have it.

TIONNE. I know.

They drain their cups. TANIKA *puts her hand out for more.*

That's enough for you.

TANIKA. You too then.

A beat.

TIONNE *pours them out another glass.* TANIKA *adds the Coke.*

Cheers!

TIONNE. Bottoms up!

They drink it.

A long pause.

TANIKA. Knock, knock.

A pause?

Knock, knock?

TIONNE. You can't do it.

TANIKA. Knock, knock? Knock, knock?

TIONNE. Only me and Mum can do it.

TANIKA. Knock, knock? Who's there? Tionne. Tionne who? Tionne… Tionne.

TIONNE *laughs.*

I can. I can!

TIONNE. Knock, knock? Who's there? Tionne. Tionne who? Tionne the light, please. Tionne-ly way is Essex.

TANIKA. I was gonna say that! I was!

A pause.

Do you really like it?

TIONNE. Yeah.

TANIKA. Me too.

TIANA *enters.*

TIANA. What you doing?

She takes in the empty bottles, the concoction.

What you doing, T?

TANIKA. He's done the chicken.

TIANA *goes over to the bucket.*

TIANA. You been drinking it?

TANIKA. It ain't nice.

TIONNE. It's alright.

TANIKA. I'm hot.

TIANA. Is it? Cos with the chicken you were like it ain't right it ain't right and now it's like it's alright.

TANIKA. I'm hot. T, you hot?

TIANA. Get to bed.

TANIKA. You hot?

TIANA. Or don't you want to do it?

TIONNE. Course I want to do it.

TIANA. Cos it don't look like it. It don't look like you want to do it.

TIONNE. Do you want to do it?

A beat.

TIANA. Course I want to do it.

TIONNE. Yeah, well, it was my idea.

A pause.

TIANA. Well, we can't afford any more drink now, can we?

TANIKA. I'm really hot.

TIONNE. We can still use it.

TIANA. So you've measured it all out then?

TIONNE. We don't have the right stuff so it don't matter.

TANIKA *opens the front door and inhales deeply.* DR FEELGOOD *walks in with a trolley for the telly. He goes straight to the kitchen, opens the fridge and gets a cooked piece of chicken and takes a bite.*

DR FEELGOOD. I'm angry. I'm angry cos of something that was meant to be done and it never was. I'm angry cos of something that never existed cos it never was done. I'm angry cos I've had to listen to Indian Paul and his excuses in his fucking English that don't even sound like English. I'm angry cos –

TIANA. What's that for?

DR FEELGOOD *notices* TIANA*'s nightwear.* TIANA *covers herself up. He's embarrassed.*

DR FEELGOOD. Like you don't know.

TIANA. I don't.

DR FEELGOOD. So you don't know that I been texting and texting, coming round and knocking?

TIANA. No.

DR FEELGOOD. Knocking and knocking and getting no response when she's always on my texts like brown on Coco Pops?

TIANA. No. We've been, like, we didn't know.

DR FEELGOOD. What, that she's been pissing up someone else's tree?

A pause.

Yeah, Tanika told me.

TIANA *looks at* TANIKA.

Last night.

TANIKA. I was gonna tell you.

DR FEELGOOD. I don't mind if she's incapable. I don't care. Just like being kept in the sphere of things. (*Re: cooked chicken.*) This is nice. What you do to it?

TIANA. Nothing.

DR FEELGOOD. Tastes different. You jerk it up?

DR FEELGOOD *heads for the corridor.*

TIANA (*to* TANIKA). Why didn't you tell me?

DR FEELGOOD. Jackie, get your skinny black arse out here!

TANIKA. I did! I forgot.

TIANA. Liar.

TANIKA. I'm not!

DR FEELGOOD. You want me to go in there and drag you out?

A pause.

DR FEELGOOD *makes for the corridor.*

TIANA. She ain't in there!

DR FEELGOOD *laughs.*

DR FEELGOOD. Jackie!

TIANA. She's gone. For good. That's all her stuff. We're selling it cos she left – She left us.

DR FEELGOOD. Yeah?

TIANA. Yeah. For a man. A rich man. With nice hands and snakeskin shoes. And a gold tooth and watch.

DR FEELGOOD. A pimp?

TIANA. No, a businessman. A rich man. With a car. A Beemer. She left us for a man with a Beemer.

DR FEELGOOD. When?

TIANA. Last week and she ain't coming back. It's love. She fell in love. Love like that only comes once in a lifetime so she had to go.

DR FEELGOOD. Jackie's abandoned you for a bloke with a second-hand Beemer?

TIANA. No. It was brand new.

DR FEELGOOD. Oh well, well, that's fine if it's brand new.

TIANA. Yeah, so I want to settle. Settle up.

DR FEELGOOD. Clear the board?

TIANA. Yeah.

DR FEELGOOD. Wipe it clean with spit and all that?

TIANA *nods.*

If that's how you want to play it.

A beat.

Why's that chicken on that table?

DR FEELGOOD *inspects the chicken, looks at* TIONNE.

I get it. You're Dr, Dr, whatshisname? Dr Kildare! I used to play this game but with a girl. Each to his own, eh? So where does your todger go, then? In this bit?

He picks up the chicken and thrusts it towards TIONNE*'s groin.*

I'm joking. I'm joking!

A pause.

So what you doing? Really?

A pause.

Cat got your tongue or should I say chicken?

He laughs.

TIANA. So how much to settle up?

DR FEELGOOD. Gizza go.

He picks up the hand-pump. TIONNE *makes for it but* TIANA *stops him.*

What you doing with it?

TIANA. It's for school. It's their project.

DR FEELGOOD. Yeah?

TIANA. They've – they've got to try to find a way to preserve it.

DR FEELGOOD. Well, that's easy. Bung it in the freezer. Bob's your uncle.

TIANA. It's for GCSE.

DR FEELGOOD. I know it's for GSCE but they could be looking to trip you up. They do that, you know. It's called sorting the wheat from the chaff.

A pause.

Okay, okay. What about pickling it? Like pickled eggs? Pickled cucumbers, pickled cabbage, pickled onions. Pickled chicken. Smoked chicken. You smoke chicken, don't you? Smoked haddock and ham. Kipper! Is a kipper called a kipper when it's in the sea or only when it's smoked?

TANIKA. When it's smoked.

DR FEELGOOD. So what is it before?

TIANA. We ain't smoking it!

DR FEELGOOD. Alright! Alright. Keep your weave on. They won't want you to smoke it anyway. Kids playing with fire and all that. Burn their houses down.

TIANA. So how much is it to wipe it?

DR FEELGOOD. What?

TIANA. The board.

DR FEELGOOD. I'm still thinking.

He picks up his piece of cooked chicken and goes to take a bite. He stops. Looks down at it.

You ain't been fiddling with this?

TIANA. No.

TIONNE *smiles*.

DR FEELGOOD. So what's he grinning at?

TIANA. He ain't grinning.

DR FEELGOOD. He fucking is.

TIANA (*to* TIONNE). T!

A pause.

DR FEELGOOD (*to* TIONNE). Have a bit.

TIONNE *doesn't move*. TIANA *nudges him*. TIONNE *takes a bite*.

A pause.

DR FEELGOOD *looks at the chicken, throws it away and washes his hands in the sink*.

It stinks of piss round here.

TIANA. Yeah, toilet's broke.

DR FEELGOOD *recoils*.

DR FEELGOOD. Well, if someone had told me, I could've fixed it. Brought my tools and shit. If someone had returned my texts. So, is it just you doing this or is the whole class gonna bring in chickens? All of you trotting up to the school gates with your own piece of fowl tucked under your arm? Do you get a prize or something? T, do you get a prize for the best-looking bird?

He laughs.

Best-looking bird.

He begins to load the telly onto the trolley.

TIANA. I thought we were settling?

DR FEELGOOD. We are. You lot really need to communicate.

TIANA. She don't even owe that much.

DR FEELGOOD. Yeah, well, she ain't never given me this much inconvenience.

TANIKA. Don't take the telly.

DR FEELGOOD. She brought it all on herself, T.

TANIKA. Please?

A pause.

DR FEELGOOD. The laptop, then. That's worth two hundred.

TIANA. Two hundred? You sold it to us for three.

DR FEELGOOD. Yeah, well, wear and tear.

TIANA. But they need it for school. They need –

DR FEELGOOD. Sympathy? Sympathy? Oh yeah, that's where it is. In the dictionary. Wedged between shit and syphilis.

A pause.

TIANA. Okay. I just need –

DR FEELGOOD. This ain't your business.

TIANA. Give me a couple of weeks.

DR FEELGOOD. Don't do credit. Don't do credit cos people abuse it. Don't return my calls.

TIANA. I need time to sort, to sort things.

TANIKA. Wanna hear my song? Ms Jenkins taught us a song. *Meunier tu dors. Ton moulin –*

TIANA. I told you to get to bed!

TANIKA heads towards the bedrooms but lingers in the corridor. DR FEELGOOD continues to load the telly.

Me and Shanice, yeah, me and Shanice we're setting up a business. Beauty by Tianice.

DR FEELGOOD. Beauty by Tianice?

TIANA. Tianice. It's Tiana and Shanice put together.

DR FEELGOOD. Ain't she got a moustache?

TIANA. Take it, then. Take it. We're leaving here, anyway.

DR FEELGOOD. Yeah?

TIANA. We're all gonna join her.

DR FEELGOOD. Where?

TIANA. In her place. She's got a place with a pool and nice things.

DR FEELGOOD. With this man?

TIANA. Yeah.

DR FEELGOOD. A rich man with a Beemer?

TIANA. Richer than you. That's why she ain't coming back cos she can't. Cos you can't leave her alone. Bringing her down. Holding her down.

DR FEELGOOD. Me hold her down?

TIANA. Hold her face down in the dirt.

A pause.

She was gonna buy me a pony.

DR FEELGOOD. A pony?

TIANA. Yeah.

DR FEELGOOD. A pony round here.

TIANA. No. Not round here. The school I went to. The primary school. They all had one. She promised me. A white one.

DR FEELGOOD. Spare me the house and the garden with grass that dogs don't shit on shit, T. I know all about it.

TIANA. Yeah, well, you don't know about now, do you?

A pause.

DR FEELGOOD. Well, I'll be sorry to see you go, then.

TIANA. Can't stay here, can we?

A pause.

DR FEELGOOD. I feel all, I dunno, teary. Come here.

A pause.

TIANA *goes in close.*

Come on, T. Jackie meeting some rich fella? You do know Pretty Woman was a hooker, don't you?

TIANA. Shut up! Shut up! Shut up!

TIANA *bursts out crying as* TIONNE *goes for him.* DR FEELGOOD *easily holds* TIONNE *off with one hand, leaving* TIONNE *to swim-punch the air.* TANIKA *tries to pull* DR FEELGOOD *off.*

TANIKA. Get off him! Get off him!

DR FEELGOOD. I was joking! I was –

TIONNE *falls limp and* DR FEELGOOD *lets him go.*

TANIKA (*to* TIONNE). You alright?

TIONNE *shrugs her off.*

DR FEELGOOD. Course he's alright. Course he is.

A pause.

What's got into you all? Acting like – We always do this. Winding each other up. Winding – I mean, snakeskin shoes? That's fucking funny.

TIANA. Just take the telly if you're taking it.

A pause.

DR FEELGOOD. Fine.

A pause.

If you want to get all up in her shit.

A pause.

If I'm gone then I'm gone.

A pause.

Puff of smoke.

A pause.

Poof.

DR FEELGOOD *finishes loading the telly onto the trolley.*

You know, I'm the victim here. She's the one been messing me about. Keeping me out in the cold like I'm the bloody matchstick girl on Christmas Eve with no bloody matches. Well, I ain't interested. I ain't interested in where she is or what she's about. I have things to do. Things to – I have matches.

He goes to the corridor.

I have fucking matches, Jackie!

A pause.

You know, you're lucky it's me come round and not some paedo. I should be onto the Social. You kids running riot, fucking about with her all incapable and shit. You're lucky it's me come round. You're fucking lucky.

DR FEELGOOD *heads awkwardly for the door with the telly, trying to keep his cool.*

And you'd better put her clothes back before she kills you.

DR FEELGOOD *exits.*

A long silence.

TIONNE. You let him talk about her like she was nothing.

TIANA. I never.

TIONNE. Like dirt. Like –

TIANA slaps him. They are both shocked.

TIANA. Next time, next time you tell me, yeah? You tell me when someone comes round. You tell me.

A pause.

And clean this up cos when you cleaned it up we start, yeah? We start tomorrow, yeah. After college. With fresh stuff. I'll get us all fresh stuff and we do it when everything's ready and when I say. (*To* TANIKA.) Come on!

TANIKA follows TIANA to the corridor. TIANA exits.

Silence.

TANIKA. Thought he was gonna kill you.

TIONNE. Him and whose dirty army?

A pause.

TANIKA. He's coming back, though, ain't he?

A pause.

He's coming back. I know he is.

TIONNE. Grow up.

TANIKA. I am grown up.

TIANA (*off*). Tanika!

TANIKA exits.

Scene Six

Wednesday.

Late afternoon. An opened box from Amazon on the floor and the sprayer from Scene Two.

TIONNE *examines the basting nozzle.*

TIONNE. Reduced from ten ninety-nine to nine ninety-nine. It includes two stainless-steel injector nozzles, one thin, ideal for liquid marinades and one thick to marinate using herbs, seasoning or sauces. The thick one or the thin one?

TIONNE attaches the thin nozzle onto the hand-pump with brown tape. He stands up and shoots the sprayer.

You're dead, Dr Feelgood. You're dead.

He pretends to die as DR FEELGOOD.

The Havabi Total Seven Multi-Function Sprayer. Can be used for agricultural, industrial and domestic uses.

He laughs.

The Havabi Total Seven Multi-Function Sprayer. The Havabi Total Seven Multi-Function Sprayer. Knock, knock? Who's there? Havabi. Havabi who? Knock, knock? Who's there? Havabi. Havabi who? How long have I been waiting long for my Amazon delivery?

A pause.

A man goes to the doctor.

A pause.

A man goes to the doctor. He says he's depressed. He says life seems so harsh and cruel. Says he feels all alone in a threatening world. The doctor replies, the circus has come to town. The great Tagalichi's going to be doing his magic tricks. Go see him. That should pick you up. The man says, but, doctor, I am the great Tagalichi.

He shoots the sprayer like it's a gun.

The front door opens. TANIKA *and* MS JENKINS *enter.* TIONNE *is speechless.* MS JENKINS *has her cycling helmet on, she's a bit shaky, limps a bit.*

TANIKA. Tell me who the Hound is.

MS JENKINS. No.

TANIKA. Please?

MS JENKINS. You have to read it.

TIONNE *stares at them in shock.*

Tionne, right? Ms Jenkins. Tanika's teacher. I'm afraid we had a little accident. Don't worry. It's not panic stations. Ignore all the blood and gore.

A pause.

Is it okay if I speak with your mother?

TANIKA. Maybe she's not in. I thought she would be in.

MS JENKINS. Oh right. Well, I can wait.

A pause.

I came off my bike. One minute the road was clear. Then next there she was. Standing right in the middle of it.

TANIKA. I thought the road was clear.

MS JENKINS. Anyway, I'm the worse for wear. Swerved right out of the way. Stopped by a car. Parked. Luckily. She's alright. Doesn't have a scratch on her.

TANIKA. What about my knee?

MS JENKINS. It's a scrape.

A pause.

That looks exciting.

TANIKA. Yeah, he's really clever. He's gonna be an inventor.

MS JENKINS. Really?

TIONNE *looks at* TANIKA.

Is it a cyber gun? I am a Martian.

A pause.

You never told me he was shy.

TANIKA. He ain't shy. He's a selective mute.

MS JENKINS. Oh right. Is it grown-ups he doesn't talk to?

TANIKA. No, just people he don't like. No offence. He's been like that for time. Just depends.

MS JENKINS. Oh. Right.

TANIKA. He likes jokes, though, can make them up like out of nothing.

A pause.

MS JENKINS. Well, it looks very good, Tionne. Very clever.

A long silence.

MS JENKINS *gets out her phone.*

(*To* TIONNE.) Just letting them know where I am so they won't worry.

TANIKA. You gonna stay with me till she comes?

MS JENKINS. Yes. She can't be long, can she?

MS JENKINS *sends a text.*

A long silence.

Well, you've got a lovely house, Tanika.

MS JENKINS *notices the clothes.*

And these are just lovely!

TANIKA. Yeah, they're my mum's. You can have something if you want.

TIONNE *looks at* TANIKA.

MS JENKINS. No, I'm sure –

TANIKA. We're selling them all on eBay.

MS JENKINS. Well, if your mum has to sell them, then I don't think she'd like you giving them away no matter how lovely they might be. Remember what we said about other people's possessions?

TANIKA/MS JENKINS. Respect them and other people will respect you.

A pause.

MS JENKINS. Let's wash that knee before it crusts up, shall we?

MS JENKINS *and* TANIKA *go to the sink.* TIONNE *follows, remains at a safe distance.*

MS JENKINS *cleans* TANIKA*'s knee.* TANIKA *rests her hands on* MS JENKINS*' shoulders. She's in heaven.*

Can you ask Tionne how long your mother will be?

TANIKA. Tionne, miss wants to know how long mum will be.

A pause.

He don't know.

MS JENKINS. Well, is she usually out around this time?

TANIKA *shrugs.*

TANIKA. But then my sister comes back.

MS JENKINS. Oh, right.

TANIKA. She's at college, yeah? She's starting a business. Her and Shanice. Beauty by Tianice. It's Tiana and Shanice joined together. She's gonna be bigger than Rihanna and we're gonna live in a house like the ones on *MTV Teen Cribs*.

MS JENKINS *laughs.*

I ain't lying! You can ask her when she comes. That's why we're selling my mum's clothes.

MS JENKINS. Well, they're very nice clothes.

TANIKA. Yeah. My mum used to have this big job in a bank.

MS JENKINS. Oh, right! Well, that's – That's obviously where you get your brains from.

TANIKA. It was when I was really small so I don't remember. He does, though. And my sister.

MS JENKINS. Does anyone else take care of you?

TANIKA. What do you mean?

MS JENKINS. Apart from your mum and sister. An aunt or a boyfriend, maybe?

TANIKA. My boyfriend?

MS JENKINS. No, your mother's boyfriend.

A pause.

TANIKA *shakes her head.*

MS JENKINS *gets a packet of plasters out of her bag and puts one on* TANIKA*'s knee.*

There. Hands.

TANIKA *shows them to her.*

They're not bad at all. How you managed to fall over I don't know.

TANIKA. I don't neither.

MS JENKINS. Either.

TANIKA. Either.

MS JENKINS*'phone rings.*

MS JENKINS. Just a second.

MS JENKINS *speaks in private.*

Hi. No, I'm fine. I'm fine. I had my helmet on.

TANIKA (*to* TIONNE). I didn't bring her on purpose. I didn't. She knocked me over.

MS JENKINS (*into phone*). She was just standing there.

TANIKA. It ain't my fault. She didn't have to walk me home but she did.

MS JENKINS (*into phone*). Of course I'll make that clear.

TIONNE. Make her go.

TANIKA. Do you want to go to a home?

MS JENKINS (*into phone*). I know it's late –

TIONNE. She ain't gonna help us.

TANIKA. Bet she will.

MS JENKINS (*into phone*). I will if it gets dark. I've got to go. Yes, yes, love you.

MS JENKINS *hangs up.*

TANIKA. Who was that?

MS JENKINS. Nosey-nose.

TANIKA. Was it Daphne and Freya?

MS JENKINS. Sorry?

TANIKA. Daphne and Freya. Was it them on the phone? Do they live with you?

MS JENKINS. No, Tanika. My nieces don't live with me.

TANIKA. Who lives with you?

MS JENKINS. No one lives with me, Tanika.

TANIKA. But you would like someone to. You don't like to live on your own, do you?

MS JENKINS. I definitely think Tanika Sutton's a nosey-nose.

TANIKA. How come you're allowed to ask me lots of questions and I can't?

A pause.

MS JENKINS. Well, I don't think anyone likes living on their own.

TANIKA *beams at* TIONNE.

TANIKA. Why won't you tell me who the Hound of Lamonic Bibber is?

MS JENKINS. I've already told you why.

TANIKA. Cos it's Jake the dog.

A pause.

It is Jake!

A pause.

It ain't a dog. It's too obvious. Bet it's a real monster like a werewolf or a nightwalker.

MS JENKINS. What on earth's a nightwalker?

TANIKA. You don't know? A nightwalker's like a zombie but worse cos its skin's coming off and it's got no eyes.

MS JENKINS. Stop it. I'm scared! Lucky we've got your brother here to save us. Will you save us, Tionne, from the nightwalker?

A pause.

Well, we'll just have to save each other, won't we?

TANIKA. From just monsters or everything horrible?

MS JENKINS. Everything horrible, of course.

TANIKA *beams at* TIONNE.

TANIKA. My sister ain't lying, you know.

MS JENKINS. I know.

A pause.

But sometimes when – Sometimes people say things. They say things to – I'm not saying that Tiana will never be able to afford a house as big as you say because that would be limiting a person's aspirations and who is anyone to say what someone can or can't do? It's just I think you will need to do a tiny bit more than sell clothes on eBay even if some of them might look expensive.

TANIKA. Like what?

MS JENKINS. Oh, I don't know. Get a really good job.

TANIKA. Being a beautician is a really good job.

MS JENKINS. Yes, of course it is. You know, if you do something with that great imagination of yours, Tanika, you'll be able to get a lovely house when you're older.

TANIKA. With a pool?

MS JENKINS. If you like.

TANIKA. And a fridge that plays Justin Bieber when you open it.

MS JENKINS. A fridge that plays Justin Bieber!

TANIKA. Yeah. Or One Direction.

MS JENKINS. Are you going to invent that, Tionne? A singing fridge?

TANIKA. No. My sister's gonna buy it.

MS JENKINS. I think your sister's been teasing you.

TANIKA. Why?

MS JENKINS. Why?

A pause.

TANIKA. She ain't.

A pause.

We're gonna have lots of things. A swimming pool, a playroom and real Uggs that don't go to the side.

MS JENKINS *looks out of the window.*

MS JENKINS. Alright, Tanika. Alright.

A pause.

MS JENKINS *goes up to* TIONNE.

Why do the French only make omelettes with one egg?

A pause.

Because one egg is un oeuf.

A pause.

I think it's funny.

A pause.

I know.

TIONNE *looks at* TANIKA.

I save him for very important people.

MS JENKINS *gets out a sock puppet and puts it on.*

(*Rasta-style.*) What's de problem, man? Ise Mr Mistoffelees and Ise 'ere to help. Is it school? Someone in dere bullying you? You can tell me. Big or small. Mr Mistoffelees has 'eard dem all.

TIONNE *laughs at her.*

Is true. (*As herself.*) I think Mr Mistoffelees deserves a hug. Hug.

TIONNE *cautiously hugs Mr Mistoffelees.*

A bit tighter.

TIONNE *hugs it again.*

Feel better?

A pause.

If you like you can –

TANIKA. Do you want to see my pictures?

MS JENKINS. Just a second, Tanika –

TANIKA *gets the camera out from her bag.*

TANIKA. Do you want to see them, miss?

MS JENKINS. Why don't we look at them tomorrow?

TANIKA. I didn't break it. See?

MS JENKINS. Tanika –

TANIKA. I held onto it when you hit me.

MS JENKINS. I didn't hit you, Tanika. I swerved out of the way.

TANIKA. Oh yeah.

MS JENKINS *sees a picture.*

MS JENKINS. Oh my God! Is that me?

TANIKA. Yeah.

MS JENKINS. I look terrible!

TANIKA. I think you look nice.

MS JENKINS. Really? I'm not too sure about my hair.

TANIKA. I love your hair.

They look at the pictures.

I love this camera.

MS JENKINS. Well, you've got a really good eye. Brainwave! I think you should be class photographer tomorrow. Take pictures of everyone in their costumes.

TANIKA. Do I have to do the diary?

MS JENKINS. Yes you have to do your diary.

TANIKA. But Proteus is so boring! You gave Disney a baby with wings.

MS JENKINS. I think you'll be brilliant at telling me all about the future. You can write about your singing fridge.

TANIKA. It don't sing.

MS JENKINS. I bet you'll come up with a magnificent costume. But if you don't want to do it. It's fine. Of course I'll be very disappointed.

A pause.

TANIKA. I can do it.

MS JENKINS. If you're sure?

TANIKA *nods.*

A pause.

I think the best thing to do is to call her, don't you think?

TANIKA. Who?

MS JENKINS. Your mother.

MS JENKINS *looks out the window. A dog barks. She jumps.*

Jesus!

TANIKA. It's just number eighteen's dog, miss! Or is it the Hound?

MS JENKINS. It's getting late. Let's call your mother.

TANIKA. But my sister's going to be here soon.

MS JENKINS. I know but I'd like to speak to her just the same.

A pause.

Do you know her number?

TANIKA *shakes her head.*

If you give me your phone I might be able to find it.

TANIKA *looks at* TIONNE.

TANIKA. It might be off.

MS JENKINS. I'll leave a message.

A pause.

TANIKA *goes to get her phone.* TIONNE *gets his phone and dials a number, hands it to* MS JENKINS.

Thank you, Tionne! That is really thoughtful.

A pause.

She types the number into her phone.

A pause.

It's ringing. (*Into phone.*) Is this Tanika's mother? It's Tanika's teacher here. Ms Jenkins. I'm at your house with Tanika and Tionne. No, nothing to worry about. I brought her home. She fell over in the road. No, no. She's fine. If anything it was me who came out worse for wear. I saw her standing there and swerved out the way. Went clean past her. Like a whistle. She's completely fine. I really just wanted to make sure she got home safely. She's got a small graze on her knee, which I don't know how she got because I didn't touch her. Do you have anything you'd like to ask? You sure? Okay. Great. That's great. Fantastic. Looking forward to seeing you at parents' evening. Thank you. Don't be – It's nothing. It's just – Well, Tanika's really coming along. Bye.

She hangs up.

Well, she's just lovely.

Gets her things together.

She says she'll be home soon most probably before your sister.

A pause.

Make sure you go to bed early. Don't spend too long on your costume. We don't want you sleeping in class or it's –

TANIKA. Amber.

MS JENKINS. Amber.

A pause.

Alright, then. Bye. Bye, Tionne.

TIONNE *nods.* MS JENKINS *smiles, satisfied. She heads for the door. Hesitates.*

TANIKA. I can walk you out the estate.

MS JENKINS. Don't be silly.

TANIKA. That dog don't bite it just barks.

MS JENKINS. It's not the – I'll be fine. And anyway it's dark.

TANIKA. You call that dark?

A beat.

MS JENKINS. I'll be fine.

A pause.

Alright. Bye.

MS JENKINS *exits.*

TANIKA. You need to get your own teacher.

TIONNE *picks up the camera and throws it against the wall.*

What d'you do that for?

She runs over to the camera and picks it up.

You broke it.

TANIKA *starts to cry.* TIONNE *puts on his coat.*

Where you going?

TIONNE *exits.*

T!

Scene Seven

Evening.

TANIKA *tries to fix the camera.* TIANA *enters. She wears a white smock.*

TIANA. What happened?

TANIKA. Nothing.

TIANA. So she didn't say nothing?

TANIKA *shakes her head.*

You sure?

TANIKA *nods.*

So what did she say?

TANIKA. Nothing.

TIANA. She said she knocked you down with her bike, yeah?

TANIKA. Yeah.

TIANA. I told you about crossing the road.

TANIKA *shrugs.*

So she didn't talk about nothing else?

A pause.

T, this is important.

TANIKA *shakes her head.*

You sure?

TANIKA *shakes her head.*

Yes, you're sure or no, you're not? Where's Tionne? Tionne!

TANIKA. He's gone out.

TIANA. What?

A beat.

TIANA *checks the bedrooms. Comes back. She checks the bathroom, comes out.*

Where's he gone?

TANIKA *shrugs.*

She looked around, didn't she?

TANIKA. No.

TIANA. She must've looked around, T, if he's gone out.

TANIKA. She didn't. He just went.

A pause.

TIANA *calls* TIONNE's *phone. It rings on the table.* TIANA *hangs up.*

TIANA. Don't worry. It's gonna be fine. It's gonna be fine. In the real house we'll have everything we want. You can have anything you want, T. A playroom. A swimming pool. Two swimming pools. One on the roof like in *MTV Teen Cribs.* And table tennis and Wii.

A pause.

In the real house… In the real house.

A pause.

TANIKA. I'm gonna have a bike that's new but looks like old.

TIANA. You can ride your bike and I'll ride my white pony. And we'll have all the clothes we want and massive wardrobes from up here to down there with everything in it. And real Shamballas. Magnetic ones with real diamonds.

TANIKA. I'm gonna play with Daphne and Freya.

TIANA. You can't make no one up. We don't know who we're gonna meet till we get there.

TANIKA. You made the man with the gold tooth up.

TIANA. He ain't made up.

TANIKA. He is.

TIANA. He ain't. He lives in South Norwood. Mum told us. Above a pub called The Railway. It's run by a white woman with fake tits she won on the Lottery.

TANIKA. I still don't want him.

TIANA. In the real house…

TANIKA gets up.

Where you going? T –

TANIKA. I don't want him.

TIANA. T –

TANIKA. You can't have fridges that sing.

A pause.

TIANA. Who says?

TANIKA. Ms Jenkins.

TIANA. Ms Jenkins?

TANIKA. She says it's gonna take time to be rich.

TIANA. Is that what she said?

TANIKA. Yeah.

TIANA. Well, she don't know shit cos Ms Jenkins is a stupid primary-school teacher. What does she know about beauty? All she knows is kids and nursery rhymes blowing that stupid whistle.

TANIKA. She don't have a whistle.

TIANA. Once we sell all her clothes I'm gonna expand into the West End. Be between Topshop and Punkyfish.

TANIKA. Ms Jenkins says –

TIANA. Shut up about Ms Jenkins! And stop playing with that stupid camera!

TIANA snatches it from her.

TANIKA. It's mine! It's mine! Give it back!

A pause.

TIANA. Where did you get this from?

TANIKA. She said she wanted me to be class photographer but I can't now cos he broke it.

A pause.

TIANA. Whose is this?

TANIKA. It's mine.

TIANA looks through the pictures.

You can't see nothing now. It's all jagged.

TIANA. Ain't this Disney and Kimone?

A pause.

And your classroom?

A pause.

This Ms Jenkins?

A pause.

Whose camera is this, T?

A pause.

Why did Tionne break it? Why'd he break your camera? Tell me or I'll break it some more.

TANIKA. Because she wants me and he was jealous.

TIANA. Jealous?

TANIKA. Yeah. Cos I'm gonna live with her.

A pause.

TIANA. Thought you said she didn't say nothing?

TANIKA. Well, she said that.

A pause.

TIANA. Teachers can't say stuff like that.

TANIKA. Well, she did.

TIANA. You ain't gonna live with her.

TANIKA. I am.

TIANA. Teachers don't live with their pupils.

TANIKA. What about Matilda?

TIANA. Matilda's made up.

TANIKA. She's gonna adopt me cos I'm young and pretty like her nieces.

TIANA. What nieces?

TANIKA. Daphne and Freya.

TIANA. You ain't nothing like her nieces, T.

TANIKA. It's my manner. I've got an inquisitive manner.

TIANA. Yeah. Well, that's all it is cos they only like black babies and you ain't a baby. All she's gonna do is break us up and put you in a home. It ain't gonna be like Hogwarts, you know? It ain't gonna be fun. The people, the people smiling at you in the day, coming at you like monsters in the fucking night. That's what you've done, T. That's what you've –

TANIKA. I'm gonna live with Ms Jenkins and it's gonna be better than here with your rules and no baths when you can have all the baths you want at Shanice's.

TIANA. I don't have baths at Shanice's.

TANIKA. You do.

TIANA. I don't.

TANIKA. You do.

TIANA. Did you tell her?

A pause.

TANIKA. You told Shanice.

TIANA. What?

TANIKA. If someone asked me to climb over a fence, catch a chicken and break its neck, I'd wanna know what for. I wouldn't just do it.

TIANA. Shanice is a two-face! I wouldn't tell her nothing no more. She ain't part of nothing. She's gone.

TANIKA. Like Dr Feelgood's gone and Mum's gone.

TIONNE *enters with a Tesco carrier bag. He takes off his coat.*

TIANA. What happened, T? What's going on?

TIANA *notices his pyjamas.* TIANA *snatches the bag from him. Looks inside.*

What you doing with these?

A beat.

We agreed no shaving.

TIONNE. You agreed.

TIANA. I don't think we should do it, T.

TIONNE *enters the bathroom and shuts the door.*

Her teacher's sniffing around!

TIANA *knocks.*

We got to stop.

TANIKA *picks up her camera. Heads for the corridor.*

Where you going?

TANIKA. To bed. I got school tomorrow.

TIANA. No you don't.

TANIKA. You can't tell me what to do no more. Only Ms Jenkins.

A knock on the door.

TIANA *and* TANIKA *look at each other.*

A beat.

They both race to the door. TANIKA *opens the door to* DR FEELGOOD. *He has a workman's bag with him, a toga made from bedsheets and bags of food.* TANIKA *jumps on him.*

Dr Feelgood! I knew you would come! I said you would. I said it!

Scene Eight

Later.

TANIKA *stands on a chair in the toga.* DR FEELGOOD *takes up the hem with a needle and thread. He is in deep concentration.* TIANA *hovers.*

DR FEELGOOD *examines his handiwork.*

DR FEELGOOD. What do you think? T?

TIANA. Yeah, it's good.

DR FEELGOOD. Think something's missing.

A pause.

She needs to be holding something.

TANIKA. Like what?

DR FEELGOOD. You see the future, right?

TANIKA. Yeah.

DR FEELGOOD. A crystal ball. You got something like that? Or a ball. You got a ball? Tennis balls?

TANIKA. They could be like my eyes. Like extra eyes.

DR FEELGOOD. Extra eyes. Yeah. That's well dark.

TANIKA climbs down from the chair and exits into the corridor.

A long silence.

What?

A pause.

You should've said.

TIANA. I did.

DR FEELGOOD. I mean, really said.

A pause.

I'm fixing the toilet, ain't I?

TIANA. I said we're fine.

DR FEELGOOD. So Tanika's gonna keep doing dumps in McDonald's? Well nice.

A pause.

I would've brought the telly but it was robbed off Indian Paul by two men dressed as Japanese geishas.

A pause.

Anyway, you should've told me the truth. The truth without all the fiction.

A pause.

She'll come back. When she sees sense and we'll sort it out. *Mano-a-mano.*

A pause.

DR FEELGOOD *gets out some cash. Offers it to her.*
TIANA *declines.*

Go on. Top up your phone or something.

TIANA *takes the money.*

A long silence.

So what's up with college, then? This beauty business.

TIANA. There ain't no business.

DR FEELGOOD. What happened to Shanice?

TIANA. She don't want to do it no more. She wants to do construction so she can find a boyfriend.

DR FEELGOOD. She like a challenge then?

A pause.

She's ugly if you want a piece of truth. Whereas you, you shine bright.

A pause.

Like a star. A comet.

TIANA. I ain't in the mood.

DR FEELGOOD. Go on.

TIANA. No.

DR FEELGOOD. Let me take you to Nando's.

A pause.

I ain't really that much older, T. I mean, I may look older but that's the genes and you can't blame genetics and no one bothered about Billie Piper and that ginger git so I'm not a paedo. And I'm good with kids. Carrot and stick. It's all about carrots and sticks.

TIANA. We ain't got nothing in common.

DR FEELGOOD. Yeah we do. Course we do. We got music and fashion. I didn't always want to do this, you know. Serious! You just fall into it. I wanted to – No, you'll laugh. You'll. Okay. Okay. Guess what I wanted to be? No, what did you want to be? What do you want to be? A beautician, right? That's cool and well customer-facing cos I'm customer-facing too and well, you're gonna think, you're gonna think I'm making this up now, but I ain't. A jockey. See? We got things in common, you and me. When you said pony – We connect.

Never got near a horse, though. It looked simple enough. Up and down. And their little silk suits looked well chic.

A pause.

Let me take you to Nando's. And after we could go for a drive. Catch the full moon or something.

TIANA. Okay.

DR FEELGOOD. What?

TIANA. Yeah. Okay.

A pause.

DR FEELGOOD. Me and you, right?

TIANA. Yeah.

DR FEELGOOD. Cos you said yes before and Tanika came.

TIANA. I didn't know you meant it like that.

DR FEELGOOD. Well, I don't like to play things too obvious.

TIANA *puts her coat on.*

What you doing? I meant on the weekend. Jackie might be back by then. Don't want her to think I'm taking advantage.

DR FEELGOOD *opens his tool bag.*

TIANA. It's just Nando's.

DR FEELGOOD. Just Nando's!

A pause.

I was on the bus, yeah? The other day I was on the bus and this man and woman came on. He was maybe fifties looked like a typical inspector, you know, waterproof-jacket type, but she, well, she was pushing sixty, looked rough, hard, make-up couldn't help her, the only thing nice about her was her fur coat. Yeah, she was in a beautiful fur coat and it was a sunny day and talking to the man like, like she was in control, like his fucking mother, or something, with this fag-ash voice and I'm thinking, something ain't quite right. Then there gets on the bus three drunks, two of 'em birds and the bus gets held up cos they're carrying cans and then the woman, this beautifully fur-coated woman with the man's voice goes and flashes her ID and tells them to do what the driver says. I was like fuck, I knew it! And now these coppers are right by me and I've got you know fucking people to see and I style it out and then the drunk bird goes and falls out the fucking doors as the bus drives off and this drunk bird's kicking the bus, telling the bus driver to fuck off. Fuck off, you all can fuck off, she says, her as well, the cunt in the fur coat. You a cunt in a fur coat?

TIANA. What?

DR FEELGOOD. You a cunt in a fur coat?

TIANA. I ain't police.

DR FEELGOOD. I know you ain't police. It's an analogy.

TIANA. No, I ain't a cunt in a fur coat.

DR FEELGOOD. Cos Indian Paul took one out to Nando's five times and got dumped after she'd got a free half a chicken. I want a proper girlfriend, T. A walk in the park, feed the birds and shit.

TIANA. Yeah. Me, too.

DR FEELGOOD. Yeah?

A pause.

TIANA *hesitates.*

What?

TIANA. Nothing.

DR FEELGOOD. Go on. What?

TIANA. I need a favour.

DR FEELGOOD. Here we go and we ain't even been going out five minutes –

He gets out his wallet again.

How much?

TIANA. No, not like – It's a big favour.

DR FEELGOOD. Yeah?

TIANA. But I can't say.

DR FEELGOOD. Funny kind of favour.

TIANA. You got to promise to do it first then I'll say.

A pause.

DR FEELGOOD. A man's got to know what he's promising.

TIANA. I can't.

DR FEELGOOD. A man's oath is a big thing.

TIANA. I know.

A pause.

DR FEELGOOD. It ain't crapping on the next man's car, is it?

TIANA. It ain't that.

DR FEELGOOD. Yeah? Cos I ain't into that.

TIANA. I'll give you something.

DR FEELGOOD. Like what?

TIANA. Right now.

DR FEELGOOD. What, like what, now?

A pause.

TIANA. You gonna do me the favour?

A pause.

DR FEELGOOD. Didn't think you was like that. Freely granting things.

A pause.

If I've got to promise to do a favour that I don't know about. It's got to be a big something for this favour.

TIANA. I know.

TIANA *goes to kiss him.*

DR FEELGOOD. That ain't exactly what I was thinking.

TIANA. You ain't getting a bang.

DR FEELGOOD. I weren't thinking of a bang.

TIANA. Or a blow.

DR FEELGOOD. Do I look like a slag?

TIANA. So what do you want then?

DR FEELGOOD. A wank. Five minutes. Alternate hands.

A pause.

TIANA *nods.*

A pause.

TIANA. We need to borrow your car.

DR FEELGOOD. And something before.

TIANA. What?

DR FEELGOOD. It's my car. I didn't know you were gonna ask for my car.

TIANA. So?

DR FEELGOOD. You can't drive.

TIANA. You're gonna drive.

DR FEELGOOD. Well, that's like two favours now, ain't it?

TIANA. Okay. Okay. Whatever. What's the before?

DR FEELGOOD. A look.

TIANA. At what?

DR FEELGOOD *points to what he means.*

DR FEELGOOD. Quick. Before she comes.

TIANA *takes off her knickers.*

Gimme those.

TIANA *tosses them to him. He puts them in his pocket.* TIANA *flashes him.*

A pause.

I'll think about it.

TIANA. What?

TANIKA *enters carrying two severed dolls' heads of different sizes in either hand.*

TANIKA. What about these?

TIANA. Give 'em back.

DR FEELGOOD. I'm like all mixed up by this side of you.

TANIKA. I couldn't find any balls.

TIANA. I want them back.

DR FEELGOOD. And a bit disappointed.

TANIKA *holds out her arms.*

I'm feeling it. I'm feeling it. (*To* TIANA.) If those are the things you been getting up to.

TIANA. He's going home, T.

DR FEELGOOD. I ain't going nowhere till I've fixed what I said I would. I ain't having Tanika not being able to take a dump.

TANIKA *beams.*

DR FEELGOOD *knocks on the bathroom door.*

Open up. You been in there long enough. To tell you the truth, I don't know how you lot can stand the stink. Could be toxic, you know. All that shit. What's he doing in there, anyway?

He listens.

What you doing, T?

TANIKA. He's shaving.

DR FEELGOOD. Yeah? You shaving, mate? (*To* TIANA.) You should've said he'd grown a bit of beard. Explains all the kung-fu shit.

TIONNE (*off*). Get lost, you pulsating sack of pus!

DR FEELGOOD. Well, that's just great. The first fucking words he says to me.

TIONNE (*off*). Hope you die of an STD.

DR FEELGOOD. I was expecting something a bit more eloquent.

TANIKA. What's an STD?

DR FEELGOOD *walks away, trailing blood, which has seeped out from under the bathroom door, along the floor.* TANIKA *squeals.* DR FEELGOOD *packs up his gear.*

DR FEELGOOD. I'm doing you the favour, mate!

DR FEELGOOD *heads for the door.*

Shaving.

He turns.

While you're in there, shave your balls, mate. Oh, right, I forgot. You don't have none!

He sees the blood.

What the fuck?

TANIKA *giggles.*

What's he got in there?

TIANA *looks at* TANIKA.

TANIKA. It's the dog from number eighteen. We hate that dog.

DR FEELGOOD. A dog?

TANIKA. Or a fox!

DR FEELGOOD. A fox! That's twisted. How d'you catch a fox? Tell him I want a squiz.

TANIKA *bangs on the door.*

TANIKA. T! Open the door! Dr Feelgood wants a squiz.

She listens.

Think you're gonna have to bust it down.

TIANA. Leave it.

TANIKA. Bust it down! Bust it down!

DR FEELGOOD. It's gonna be really toxic with dead animals and shit, Tiana. Someone got to be the adult.

A pause.

Try him again.

TANIKA *knocks on the door.*

TANIKA. Dr Feelgood's gonna bust the door down if you don't come out!

A pause.

He ain't answering.

DR FEELGOOD *runs at the door.* TANIKA *screams. The door doesn't budge.* DR FEELGOOD *feels pain, styles it out.*

T, open the door. Dr Feelgood's gonna bust it down for real this time.

DR FEELGOOD *gets ready again.* TIONNE *opens the bathroom door.*

TIONNE. Come on then! Come on!

TIONNE *grabs* DR FEELGOOD *and they tussle.* TIONNE *manages a punch around* DR FEELGOOD*'s head.* TIONNE *has a moment's surprise at the victory.* DR FEELGOOD *wallops him one.* TANIKA *screams.* TIONNE *collapses to the ground.* TIANA *goes to* TIONNE.

DR FEELGOOD. What the fuck – ? You fucking psycho! He's a fucking psycho.

The stench from the bathroom drifts thick across the flat. DR FEELGOOD *notices something inside it. He is pulled towards it.*

What the fuck you done? What the fuck you done?

TANIKA. It weren't me! I didn't want it. I didn't want it but they wouldn't listen.

DR FEELGOOD *begins to shake and retch, he pulls out* TIANA*'s knickers and breathes into them.*

I found her like that. Found her on her on her knees. Bent over on her knees like a Muslim praying. I wanted to bury her. Bury her like normal in a church with a cross but they didn't want to tell no one so they put her in there with no clothes on.

TIONNE. It's your fault.

DR FEELGOOD. What? Nah, nah, nah you ain't laying this on me.

TIONNE. You did it. You killed her.

DR FEELGOOD. I told her, I told her don't piss up someone else's tree. I told her but the stupid cow went and did it, didn't she?

DR FEELGOOD retches again.

TIANA. Bury her.

DR FEELGOOD. What?

TIANA. In the woods or somewhere.

DR FEELGOOD. In the woods.

TIANA. You must have places to put her.

DR FEELGOOD. Sure I do. I'm the Sopranos. She's got to be taken away. Dealt with properly. Buried like normal in a church with a little cross like she said. She needs a little cross.

TIONNE. Why?

DR FEELGOOD. Why? Why? Because it's how it's done. Because it's fucking unhygienic.

TIONNE. She's clean. I kept her clean.

DR FEELGOOD. You can't just have dead people lying, sitting, in your bath, Tionne. You just – you just can't.

TIONNE. She wants us to stay together.

DR FEELGOOD. Stay to– ?

TIANA. We couldn't think of nothing else to do.

DR FEELGOOD. What? So you put her in the bath?

TIONNE. We're gonna embalm her.

DR FEELGOOD. Oh right. Embalm her. Embalm her. Right. Well, that's really straightforward, isn't it? Seeing as we're in a fucking mortuary. Why didn't you just bung her in the freezer? Ain't that what people do?

TIONNE. She wouldn't fit.

DR FEELGOOD. Oh right.

A pause.

So how you gonna do it? This embalming.

TIONNE. With a hand-pump and a basting needle.

DR FEELGOOD. A hand-pump and a basting needle.

TIANA. Please?

TIONNE. Why you asking him?

TIANA. Cos it ain't working, T!

DR FEELGOOD. I ain't touching this.

TIANA. I'll tell them where she got the brown from.

DR FEELGOOD. Junkies die every day.

TIONNE. She ain't a junkie!

DR FEELGOOD. No one cares. They won't look into how she died or who was about. You ain't important enough.

TIANA. I'll tell them you touched us up. Three kids on their own.

DR FEELGOOD. I never touched you.

TIANA. Yeah but you wanted to.

A pause

He won't cope in there. Not again. They'll mess him up.

DR FEELGOOD. Mess him up? Him?

DR FEELGOOD *moves around the flat, wiping away his fingerprints with* TIANA*'s knickers.*

TIONNE. We agreed.

TIANA. T –

TIONNE. We're gonna kiss and hold her. Talk to her, touch her.

TIANA. It don't look like her no more.

DR FEELGOOD. She smells. Go on, smell the air. That's her. Rotting.

TIONNE. I'll fix her. You think I can't fix her? I'm the man of the house, not you. I'm the man of the house. I take care of her and we're all gonna be together again, her three little birds flying. That's what we agreed. What we said. Bring her out, T, and she'll be dry and pretty. She wants us to all stay together, T. For as long as we can. Like the last time.

DR FEELGOOD. You know, maybe, maybe what she meant by staying together was that she wanted to be cremated and you could have her little, her little, urn sitting up there all nice and tidy and you'll all be together, yeah? Maybe that's what she meant. Not you sitting her down in front of the telly and you all acting like Rod Hull and her like fucking Emu.

TIONNE. Be together till they came.

DR FEELGOOD. You take her to a funeral home and they do all this. They learn to do all this. Spend years. You can't just embalm her with, with Absolut!

TIONNE. Why do I have to hide her away?

DR FEELGOOD. Hide her away? Hide? You mean bury? Cos that's what you do with the dead.

TIONNE. Who says?

DR FEELGOOD. A lot of people say, actually. A lot. Like hundreds. If it was right, if it was right to have dead people hanging about in your bathroom everyone would be doing it but they ain't. (*To* TIANA.) Someone serious needs to speak to him. Who even showed him how to do it?

TANIKA. They got it from the internet.

DR FEELGOOD. The good old fucking internet! You think whatever psychopath who put it on there has a clue what he's doing? (*To* TIANA.) Thought you had a brain in there? I thought you were, I thought –

TIANA. He was crying and crying and she was dead. He wouldn't stop crying.

DR FEELGOOD. Wax masks. Wax masks. That Russian geezer. That's what he's got.

TIONNE. What Russian geezer?

DR FEELGOOD. This geezer in Russia. Wax face and hands. Cos he's all decayed, cos it don't last.

TIONNE. What Russian geezer in Russia?

DR FEELGOOD. He's in the, the Parliament. Their Houses of Parliament so people can look at him. Is that what you want? To hug up to a wax dummy, and when you lift the mask up it's a decaying freak underneath?

TANIKA. A monster?

DR FEELGOOD. Yes! A monster.

TIANA (*to* DR FEELGOOD). Please?

TIONNE. I ain't leaving her like that. In the cold. (*To* TIANA.) We can't leave her in the cold.

A pause.

It's her, T. It still is. If you look properly.

A pause.

Cos I can't find where to put the needle in, T, cos lots of blood came out. Didn't think so much would come out. It's meant to be in the neck. In the neck behind the pulse but there ain't one so I can't find it.

A pause.

We can't leave her like that, T. I need you to help me find it.

A pause.

TIANA. What about after?

TIONNE. I won't shave her legs after. We'll do it how you said.

A pause.

TIANA *and* TIONNE *head for the bathroom.*

DR FEELGOOD. Hey, hey. What you doing? It's your fucking mum, T. It's Jackie. It's fucking Jackie.

DR FEELGOOD *breaks down. They all watch him for a bit.*

TIANA. It's alright. When we get to the real house it's all gonna be alright.

DR FEELGOOD. What real house?

TIANA. And I'm gonna have, I'm gonna have my own beauty shop on the side on top of the one in the West End cos I'll've expanded and I'll've my pony called Clipper and T's gonna have real Uggs and real diamond magnetic Shamballas.

TIONNE. Come on.

TIANA. And we're gonna have massive bathrooms. Bigger than this. Our own bathrooms with jacuzzis and a pool and sauna. Two saunas. And those things that spray water to clean your bum.

DR FEELGOOD. A bidet?

TIANA. Yeah. One of them. A gold one of them. And my name will all be in gold on the door in lights. In really big lights.

A pause.

TIANA *and* TIONNE *exit into the bathroom. They shut the door.*

A long silence.

DR FEELGOOD. I never deal in dirty gear. Want you to understand that.

A pause.

TANIKA. Can you fix my camera?

DR FEELGOOD. Yeah. Course.

He tinkers with it.

Don't know anyone who's died that I've been close to. My granddad's got angina – Ain't never seen a dead person before. You'd think I would have.

TANIKA. Because of your age?

DR FEELGOOD. She made me laugh. Really laugh.

A pause.

TANIKA. Can you fix it?

DR FEELGOOD. No.

A pause.

TANIKA. Take me with you.

A pause.

It don't matter. Ms Jenkins is gonna come. She's gonna come and get me.

DR FEELGOOD. Ms Jenkins?

TANIKA. Yeah.

A pause.

DR FEELGOOD. You're a good kid.

TANIKA. I am.

Scene Nine

Later.

TIANA *and* TIONNE *are on the sofa. They are covered in blood.*

A really long silence.

TIONNE. Maybe –

TIANA. No.

TIONNE. But –

TIANA. No.

TIONNE. We got to –

TIANA. No.

TIONNE *opens his mouth.*

No.

He closes it.

A pause.

TIONNE *gets up.*

T –

She grabs him. They struggle.

We ain't gonna do nothing more to her. We ruined her.

TIONNE. If we drain her –

TIANA. No! We're leaving her, T.

TIONNE. I can't leave her.

TIANA. We're leaving her as she is.

TIONNE. I can't –

TIANA. T –

TIONNE. I can't leave her cos she'll hate me!

A pause.

I prepared her medicine. Me.

TIANA. You did it right.

TIONNE. I don't know.

TIANA. Nothing was different with it, was it?

TIONNE. I can't remember.

A pause.

TIANA. Nothing was different with it. That's why it was your job and not no one else's cos you always do it right. Do it good. How she liked it. It was like Dr Feelgood said. Bad medicine. You did it right. Understand? You did it right.

TIONNE *nods.*

A pause.

TIONNE. What we gonna say when they come, T?

A pause.

TIANA. We say, we say, well, we say we're sorry. We made a mistake. A really big mistake.

TIONNE *nods.*

TIONNE. I'm tired.

TIONNE *lies down on the sofa.* TIANA *gets up, covers him with a blanket.*

A long silence.

A man goes to the doctor. He says he's depressed. He says life seems so harsh and cruel. Says he feels all alone in a threatening world. The doctor replies, the circus has come to town. The great Tagalichi's going to be doing his magic tricks. Go see him. That should pick you up. The man says, but, doctor, I am the great Tagalichi.

A pause.

She told me it when she was in the bath. I thought she never finished it cos she was incapable. But she did.

A pause.

TANIKA *comes out of her bedroom. She's still dressed in her Proteus outfit.*

TIANA. Tionne knows how Mum's Tagalichi joke goes. Tell her, T.

TANIKA *looks at* TIANA *and* TIONNE *and then, slowly, heads for the bathroom.*

T, don't –

TANIKA *looks into the bathroom.*

TANIKA. Ms Jenkins is right! There is a Heaven. There is a Heaven. Mum's gone to Heaven. That's just a nightwalker. A nightwalker with eyes.

TANIKA *takes a photograph.*

TIANA. Tanika –

TANIKA *dodges out of the way and disappears down the corridor.*

TIANA *closes the bathroom door, goes into the kitchen and comes out with tea towels.*

TIONNE. I'm sorry.

TIANA. What for?

A beat.

You didn't make me do nothing. I wanted to do it.

TIANA *puts the tea towels along the bottom of the bathroom door. By now,* TANIKA *has crept back into the room.*

TANIKA. You making it nice for her for when she comes? Cos she don't like monsters. And dogs. She don't like dogs.

TANIKA *exits.*

A long silence.

TIONNE. Do you think he's called them?

A pause.

TIANA. Yeah.

A pause.

Good.

A pause.

TIONNE. Knock, knock?

TIANA. Who's there?

TIONNE. A carrot.

TIANA. A carrot who?

TIONNE. A carotid artery.

A pause.

TIANA. That ain't funny.

TIONNE. I know but I just thought of it.

Scene Ten

Monday, late afternoon.

TIONNE *sleeps on the sofa.* TIANA *cleans up in the kitchen. Their bags are ready. A knock on the door.* TIONNE *wakes up, looks at* TIANA.

TIANA. It's alright. Go tell T they're here.

> TIONNE *exits down the corridor.* TIANA *gathers herself together, opens the door. It's* MS JENKINS.

MS JENKINS. Hi. I'm sorry to – Tiana, right? I'm Ms Jenkins, Tanika's teacher. I came round yesterday, she tell you?

> TIANA *nods.*

Is she there?

> TIANA *nods.*

May I come in?

> *A pause.*

> TIANA *steps aside.* MS JENKINS *enters. She hovers at the doorway. She is affected by the smell, tries to mask it.*

Your mother in?

TIANA. No.

MS JENKINS. She wasn't in the last time I called round, either.

TIANA. Yeah, well, she works.

MS JENKINS. Oh, right. Doing what?

TIANA. Why's it important?

MS JENKINS. It's not. I was just trying to –

> TIONNE *enters.*

Tionne! How are you?

TIONNE. She here for Tanika?

MS JENKINS. Yes, that's right.

TIONNE *and* TIANA *exchange looks.*

A long pause.

TIANA *notices* MS JENKINS*' reaction to the smell.*

TIANA. It's the drains. They're blocked.

MS JENKINS. Oh right.

A pause.

TIANA. Someone's coming to unblock them.

MS JENKINS. Oh good.

TIANA. The caretaker.

MS JENKINS. Good. It's good someone's coming.

A pause.

So Tanika tells me you're at school, Tanisha. Tamaka. Tanika!

TIANA. Tiana.

MS JENKINS. Tiana. Yes. I'm sorry. Tiana. So how's school?

TIANA. Don't go to school.

MS JENKINS. Sorry, college. Hair and beauty, right?

TIANA. Just beauty.

MS JENKINS. Going alright?

Silence.

(*To* TIONNE.) And how are you?

A pause.

You really shouldn't miss out on too much school, Tionne. A bright boy like you.

TIANA. What's she chatting about?

MS JENKINS. Is it bullying?

TIANA. You tell her you're being bullied?

TIONNE. No.

MS JENKINS. He intimated to Mr Mistoffelees –

TIANA. Who's Mr Mistoffelees?

TIONNE. Nothing.

MS JENKINS. Mr Mistoffelees is not exactly –

TIONNE. I ain't being bullied.

TIANA. Who's Mr Mistoffelees?

MS JENKINS. He's a friend.

TIONNE. He's a stupid puppet.

MS JENKINS. Who got you speaking to someone you weren't meant to like.

TIANA. She's got a puppet?

TIONNE. You really coming here for Tanika?

MS JENKINS. That's right. I know it's not normally done but well, we've grown quite close. Since the incident.

TIANA. What incident?

MS JENKINS. One of her friends accused Tanika of stealing her Shamballa bracelet. She didn't tell you?

TIANA. Yeah, she told me and she never stole it.

MS JENKINS. We found it in Tanika's bag.

A pause.

TIONNE. So you're gonna help her, like she said?

MS JENKINS. Well, she is by far my most promising student and she really trusts me.

TIANA. And she tells you what?

MS JENKINS. I'm afraid I can't break her confidence.

A pause.

TIANA. She ain't told you nothing.

MS JENKINS. Well, not yet, no but she tells Mr Mistoffelees everything and once you start talking to him – This is silly,

I really should be talking to your – I'm sorry, do you mind if I – ?

MS JENKINS *pulls back the curtains and opens the window. Light comes in.*

A long silence.

It's funny, at first you wouldn't think anyone was in. Your curtains. The way you always have them drawn. You always keep them like that?

TIANA. We don't always have them drawn. It's just people look in.

MS JENKINS. Oh right. I hadn't thought of that. People looking in.

A pause.

Where's your mother?

A pause.

TIANA. I told you, she's at work.

TIONNE. Sometimes. Sometimes she works.

MS JENKINS. It's just that Tanika said she didn't go to work.

TIANA. So? What's it to do with you?

MS JENKINS. Tanika was so looking forward to it. Coming to school to take pictures. She wouldn't have missed school unless it was something really important.

A pause.

How often does she leave you home alone, Tionne?

A pause.

Tionne, how often?

A pause.

Okay. I'm going to call her.

TIONNE. You can't.

MS JENKINS. I have to. I'm concerned.

TIANA. Right up until the bell rings.

MS JENKINS. This is neglect.

TIONNE. You can't. You can't call her.

MS JENKINS. I'd really like to tell her myself that I'm notifying the Social Services.

MS JENKINS gets out her phone and dials. TIANA's phone rings. TIANA switches it off.

A pause.

It was you, wasn't it?

TIANA. No.

MS JENKINS. I don't believe you.

A pause.

I'm gonna ask you one more time.

A pause.

Tionne?

TIANA. T – Not her.

TIONNE. She left us.

A pause.

MS JENKINS. When?

TIONNE. Thursday.

MS JENKINS. Thursday?

TIONNE starts to cry.

I'm so sorry.

MS JENKINS *hugs* TIONNE.

And she's left you to take care of things, hasn't she, Tiana.

TIANA. You calling the Social then?

MS JENKINS. I have to.

TIANA. No you don't. You don't have to do nothing, miss. Cos I been doing it for time. The cooking, the sick notes, the thank you, Ms Jenkins, for walking my little girl home. Thank you. You're so kind. I wish all her teachers were more like you.

A pause.

MS JENKINS. It's not my decision to make.

TIANA. But it's your decision to come in here with your sympathetic looks and your too-nice smiles and your let's be friends, stepping over puddles of piss to make your promises you can't keep. Thinking you know how to make things better. This is better, miss. This is the best it can get.

MS JENKINS. I understand how you feel, Tiana –

TIANA. Course you do.

MS JENKINS. I wouldn't be doing my job if I just left you on your own, would I? If something happened.

TIANA. Like what?

MS JENKINS. I don't know. A fire. If you had another parental figure – A baby father –

TIANA. He's in South Norwood.

MS JENKINS. Well, what's his – ?

TIANA. He ain't interested.

MS JENKINS. Or a friend.

TIANA. No one's interested.

MS JENKINS. Then I have no choice.

A pause.

It might not be as bad as you think. It'll be just until you find someone. There has to be someone. Or you could get guardianship or maybe –

TIANA. Guardianship?

MS JENKINS. Yes. Something like that. I don't know all the ins and outs of it but I'm sure it could happen. I could look into it. You just have to do it all properly. Through the right channels. And when you're eighteen –

TIANA. Eighteen?

MS JENKINS. It's not that far away.

TIANA. In a home? They can't have two years in a home.

TIONNE. We don't have a choice, T. They won't understand.

TIANA. They will. If we explain. If we explain why, why we did it.

TANIKA *enters from the corridor. She has her suitcase with her.*

TANIKA. I know you'd come!

MS JENKINS. Tanika!

TANIKA. I was peepin'.

TANIKA *hands* MS JENKINS *the camera.*

It break.

MS JENKINS. Is that why you didn't come to school today?

TANIKA *nods.*

It doesn't matter about the silly camera.

MS JENKINS *examines the camera.*

Well, we can still see a few things. You've taken some really good pictures.

TANIKA. Been catching ghosts and nightwalkers.

MS JENKINS. Really?

TANIKA. Are Daphne and Freya in the car?

MS JENKINS. Sorry?

TANIKA. I go to your house.

MS JENKINS. No, they're not in the car. Tanika –

TANIKA (*singing with actions*). *Meunier tu dors, ton moulin va trop vite.*

MS JENKINS. Tanika –

TANIKA. *Meunier tu dors, ton moulin va trop forte.*

MS JENKINS. Tanika, stop.

TANIKA. *Ton moulin, ton moulin va trop vite, ton moulin, ton moulin va trop forte.*

MS JENKINS (*overlaps*). You can't come to my house. I know about your mother. Your brother told me she's gone.

TANIKA. *Ton moulin, ton moulin va trop vite, ton moulin, ton moulin va trop forte.*

MS JENKINS (*overlaps*). Please stop it. Tanika, stop it. Stop it, Tanika. Tanika, shut up!

A pause.

TANIKA. I important.

A pause.

MS JENKINS. I'm sorry I shouted. I shouldnt've have shouted –

TANIKA. She ain't gone. She's dead. And now I living with you.

MS JENKINS. I shouldn't have – You can't live with –

TANIKA. Cos I young like Daphne.

MS JENKINS. I never said she could live with –

TANIKA. I five, too, Mummy.

MS JENKINS. What did I say about lying, Tanika?

TANIKA. You gived me your camera.

A pause.

MS JENKINS. I didn't come here to take you away, Tanika. You didn't come to school today so I came to see why. (*To* TIANA *and* TIONNE.) She's Proteus!

TANIKA. You gived me your camera. I'm the only year five in your photogopy group.

TANIKA *runs into the bathroom.*

MS JENKINS. Tanika!

MS JENKINS *searches for Mr Mistoffelees.*

(*To* TIANA *and* TIONNE.) She's not the only year five to – Disney and Kimone have joined. She had my camera. I entrusted her with it to, to learn how to treat other people's –

She brings the puppet out and heads for the bathroom. She stops. Overwhelmed by the smell.

A long pause.

Tanika?

A pause.

Tanika, come out of there, please.

A beat.

Children, come here.

TIANA *and* TIONNE *stay where they are.*

I said come over here!

TIANA *and* TIONNE *stay where they are.* MS JENKINS *gets out her phone, tries to dial but is hampered by Mr Mistoffelees.*

It's fine. It's fine. Shit.

TANIKA *comes out of the bathroom with her hands behind her back.*

TANIKA. I take them out. Take them out like a jelly gobstopper. See?

TANIKA *holds out her arms to* MS JENKINS, *holding Jackie's eyes aloft.*

Now it real nightstalker and you save me like you promised. You promised, Mummy. You promised.

TANIKA *holds out her arms to* MS JENKINS *to be carried.* TIANA *grabs hold of* TANIKA, *who struggles and cries.*

Get off! Mummy, help me! Mummy!

MS JENKINS *just stands there.*

TIANA. Well, go if you're going, miss.

A pause.

Go on, go!

TIANA *comforts* TANIKA. TIONNE *takes the eyes from* TANIKA, *puts them in his pocket.*

I said go. Go on, get out. Get out, you posh cunt! Get out!

MS JENKINS *exits.*

A really, really long silence.

TIONNE. Well, if you weren't going to a home before, T, you're definitely going to one now.

A beat.

I'm just saying.

A pause.

He shuts the bathroom door. Puts the towels back. TIANA *takes* TANIKA *to the kitchen sink and washes her hands. Then they sit down on the sofa.*

A long silence.

TIANA (*to* TANIKA). Can't believe you did that, T. You're braver than me.

A pause.

(*To* TIONNE.) Can you put them back?

TIONNE *shakes his head.* TIONNE *joins them on the sofa.*

TIONNE. We did it wrong, T. It all went into her face cos we didn't know. We didn't know. That's why her eyes was like that and her skin, her skin's like that cos we didn't have enough ice.

A pause.

T?

A long silence.

TIONNE *laughs.*

TIANA. What?

TIONNE. Nothing.

TIONNE *laughs.*

TIANA. What?

TIONNE. It don't matter.

TIONNE *laughs.*

TIANA. What?

A beat.

TIONNE. You posh cunt!

They laugh.

A pause.

TIANA. I bet she's flying. T, you think she's flying? Flying like Aladdin?

TIONNE. On a magic carpet and God's pouring warm chocolate over her and the sun's licking it off.

TIANA. Flying high and reaching the stars, looking down on us.

TIONNE. And we look just like rats in a tight sewer.

A pause.

Bet she's lit up like one of them stars you see out there. The brightest one.

A pause.

TIANA. I'll find you, T. Find out where they put you. You're gonna have to look after him, you know. Look after each other.

A pause.

And when we get to the real house it's gonna all be different. We're gonna have a bedroom each with our own telly inside. And a playroom in the attic.

TIONNE. And our own laptops.

TIANA. Yeah. And a pool like in *MTV Teen Cribs*. One on the roof.

TIONNE. We gonna have Wii?

TIANA. Course.

TIONNE. And a DVD player better than the one Dr Feelgood took.

TIANA. We don't need no DVD player cos we gonna use the Xbox.

TIONNE. On screens as big as cinemas.

TIANA. And when you go to school, T, there won't be no school uniform. You can wear your Ugg boots. Real ones. Not mash-up ones that go to the side.

TIONNE. And there's gonna be a massive fridge that plays music when you open it cos I'm gonna invent it, T.

TIANA. Justin Bieber.

TANIKA. One Direction.

TIANA. One Direction.

TANIKA. And Cheestrings are inside.

TIANA. And Coke and Strawberry Millions –

TANIKA. And McDonald's chips.

TIANA. Yeah, chips from McDonald's.

End.

WISH LIST

Katherine Soper

'From the gods who sit in grandeur
grace comes somehow violent.'

Aeschylus

KATHERINE SOPER

Katherine Soper's first play, *Wish List*, won the Bruntwood Prize for Playwriting in 2015 and was performed in 2016 and 2017 at the Royal Exchange Theatre, Manchester, and the Royal Court Theatre, London. It has since been performed internationally, including in Germany, Turkey and South Korea.

She wrote *The Small Hours* for National Theatre Connections in 2019, and was an editor and contributor to the Royal Court Theatre's Living Newspaper project in 2020. Her first radio play, *Calls From Far Away*, was broadcast in 2022 on BBC Radio 4. In 2023 she adapted *The Bacchae* for the Lyric Hammersmith. She has been nominated for the Evening Standard Award for Most Promising Playwright, and won The Stage Debut Award for Best Writer.

Introduction
Katherine Soper, 2025

Between 2010 and 2013, I worked in a warehouse in the summers, via a temping agency. And one day, packing some sort of tabloid tie-in merch for the 2013 movie *Epic*, I suddenly thought to myself: I've never seen a play set somewhere like this. I filed it away in my mind – not knowing what a significant moment had just happened.

Around two years later, I'd finished my MA at Central, and I'd done introductory courses with the Royal Court and the Almeida Theatres – and yet I was still struggling to get my work on at scratch nights. Self-producing still seemed insurmountable to me, and my confidence in my work felt very ephemeral. But the purity of something like the Bruntwood Prize is an antidote to that – the anonymity lets the play speak for itself, and it somehow meant I felt braver when I clicked that button to send off my play.

And in line with that purity of intention, the Royal Exchange treated me with such kindness and understanding, every step of the way. Although I'd seen workshops by professional directors during my MA, and I'd been in rehearsal rooms in a student context, I'd never been in a professional rehearsal room and was (maybe unduly) anxious about that. So, the Exchange organised for me to go and sit in on the rehearsals for another 'Bruntwood play': Katherine Chandler's gorgeous *Bird* at the Sherman Theatre in Cardiff. It's always stuck in my mind as such a generous and pastoral act.

Matthew Xia is probably sick of me waxing lyrical about what a brilliant director he is, but I feel incredibly lucky to have had him steering the ship for this play. I'll never forget the moment we first spoke about the play, and he brought a copy of my script out, with my Bruntwood pseudonym ('J Moscow') still on the front, and pencil marks throughout the script. I felt so honoured to have such detailed attention paid to my work – and his empathy and attunement to the script at a really deep level made it clear he was the right director. And he made the right call at every turn – including casting Erin Doherty and Joseph Quinn when I wasn't able to attend auditions for their roles. He promised me over the phone that they were the right choices, and I think both their performances and their subsequent careers have proven him right!

As well as the Royal Exchange guiding me through this baptism of fire, *Wish List* also led to a great relationship with the Royal Court Theatre under Vicky Featherstone: the profoundly rewarding experience of leading their Introduction to Playwriting group; the chance to be an editor in their 2020 Living Newspaper project, which was such an anchor in the most unpredictable days of lockdown; and, most significantly, the truly artistically fulfilling chance to develop a commission with them. It also brought me in touch with artists like Lucy Morrison, Alistair McDowall and Sam Steiner, all of whom have provided me with vital encouragement at critical moments.

I won the Bruntwood Prize five years before Covid. We're now five years out from Covid, and my confidence around my work is at a low ebb again. Given the contraction of the theatre industry, I don't know what the future of my career looks like – a lot of the gambles I've taken haven't worked out, a lot of doors that were once open have now quietly closed, and I have to work very hard not to be discouraged.

But one of the things that maybe people don't realise is just how deeply loyal audiences at the Royal Exchange are. This was reinforced to me recently, when supporters of the Royal Exchange so generously assisted with money to help fund my first short film, which shot in May. That kind of long-term loyalty is profoundly humbling, and emblematic of the spirit that fills the Exchange.

And before *Wish List* was produced, I'd also been in a slightly uncertain place with my writing. I was still trying out a lot of styles and didn't really know what I was good at or what my artistic voice was. A huge part of me wanted to be a really avant-garde writer – but whenever I wrote towards that impulse, it felt like I was trying on clothes that looked amazing on the hanger but somehow, at a fundamental level, didn't really suit me. But sitting in tech rehearsal, something magical happened. I watched a snippet of *Wish List* and I saw my heart in there. I knew, from that point on, that this feeling was what I needed to chase in my future writing. All the other fretting melted away. More importantly than anything else, the Bruntwood gave me my voice as an artist. My gratefulness for that knows no bounds, and that moment in the Studio at the Royal Exchange one September is still my North Star.

Wish List was first performed at the Royal Exchange Theatre, Manchester on 24 September 2016, with the following cast (in alphabetical order):

LUKE MBURU	Shaquille Ali-Yebuah
TAMSIN CARMODY	Erin Doherty
THE LEAD	Aleksandar Mikic
DEAN CARMODY	Joseph Quinn
Director	Matthew Xia
Designer	Ana Inés Jabares-Pita
Lighting Designer	Ciarán Cunningham
Composer & Sound Designer	Giles Thomas

The production transferred to the Royal Court Theatre, London, on 10 January 2017.

Acknowledgements

Enormous thanks must go to everyone at the Royal Exchange, Bruntwood, and the readers, administrators, and judges of the Bruntwood Prize. Thank you for seeing something in my work.

Thanks also to:

Melissa Dunne. Davina Moss. Salome Wagaine. Everyone at Central, especially Sarah Grochala for suggesting I write this idea instead of my other one. The staff of the much-missed Nomad Books café, where the 2014 version was written. Every single member of my extended Penhaligon's family. Citizens Advice and Turn2us for their tireless work and resources. The Howe family. Iliyana Todorova and Lulu Raczka for so much writerly support and reassurance. Nick Hern Books. Jonathan Kinnersley. The brilliant actors who helped workshop the script: Katie West, Jamie Samuel, Ivanno Jeremiah, and Michael Peavoy. The equally brilliant actors who made the play happen: Erin Doherty, Joseph Quinn, Shaquille Ali-Yebuah, and Aleksandar Mikic.

The wonderful Matthew Xia and Suzanne Bell.

Phil, who read this more times than was probably healthy.

Finally, thanks to my parents, and to my brother.

K.S.

Characters

DEAN CARMODY, *seventeen*
TAMSIN CARMODY, *nineteen*
THE LEAD, *thirty-eight*
LUKE MBURU, *sixteen*

Note on Play

The staging of this play is open to interpretation – the stage directions are intended to evoke the literal world of the characters, but do not demand a literal staging.

Scene One

A flat in Oldbrook, Milton Keynes. August. DEAN *is in the bathroom, applying gel to his hair. He does it very precisely and meticulously, applying far more than an average amount and twisting his hair into spikes. It should not be a hairstyle that seems familiar or attractive.*

TAMSIN *enters. Gets her passport, her phone – checking, making sure she's not forgotten anything – looking at her watch, making sure she's got enough time.*

She puts the kettle on and knocks on the bathroom door, deliberately gently.

TAMSIN. Come on. How are we doing?

DEAN. You can go. It's fine.

TAMSIN. Okay.

I just wanna know you'll be all right, though.

DEAN. I will.

TAMSIN. Yeah? You're all dressed then, all ready?

DEAN. Yeah.

TAMSIN. I know you're not.

Pause.

Look, I really have to go in a minute, but I just –

DEAN. You can. It's fine, I said.

TAMSIN. No, like, I don't wanna be worrying about this all / day.

DEAN. I know, I know, I just need –

TAMSIN. Come *on.*

Pause.

Do you want a cup of tea?

Pause.

DEAN. Okay.

She tries to get a cup ready but her hands don't work properly. She swears slightly under her breath.

She makes the tea, and brings it to DEAN in the bathroom.

He takes one sip and then immediately walks into the kitchen.

TAMSIN. It's hot.

He doesn't listen, and puts it in the microwave for five seconds.

I promise you it's hot.

The microwave beeps, and DEAN takes the tea out.

TAMSIN *comes out of the bathroom and watches him – while trying to pretend that she isn't – as he takes another sip, and taps the counter twice with his left hand and twice with his right hand. He's trying to stave off an urge.*

It doesn't work, and he goes and microwaves the cup of tea again.

It's –

She stops herself.

You want me to help you?

DEAN *shrugs.*

Okay.

She gets each piece of his clothing as he checks his hair between each one.

Are we gonna have a good day?

DEAN *shrugs and shifts from foot to foot.*

Do you wanna – [tap]

Together TAMSIN *and* DEAN *tap each item of their clothing four times, twice with the left hand and twice with the right hand.*

Okay?

DEAN. Yeah.

TAMSIN. Are we gonna have a good day?

DEAN. Yes.

TAMSIN. Ten out of ten?

DEAN. I guess.

TAMSIN. Not 'I guess', that's a bit –

She thinks better of this.

Okay. Awesome. Your appointment's at four-thirty, / so if you –

DEAN. I know.

TAMSIN. If you try and get as ready as you can this morning – then I'll call you on my lunch and we can do some exercises and get you out the door. Just if you can make sure you don't put your headphones in –

DEAN. Why?

TAMSIN. Cos I dunno when I'll be able to call, okay?

Is that all right?

Pause.

DEAN. You can't ask me to do that. It's one of the only things / that helps when I need to get ready to

TAMSIN. I know. I know. I know. But I don't wanna risk us missing each other.

Can you do that for me, yeah?

Pause. DEAN *begins to tap again, but* TAMSIN *doesn't join in.*

Dean. I have to go, I've gotta get all the way over to Ridgmont. You need to pick up when I call, okay?

Speak to me. Okay?

DEAN. I hate that you're making me do this.

TAMSIN. I know. But promise me you're gonna answer.

Dean.

DEAN *exits; the* LEAD *enters.*

TAMSIN *hands him her passport.*

She completes a written test, and signs various forms.

She hands her papers and a urine sample to the LEAD, *who also takes a swab from the inside of her cheek.*

The LEAD *gives her a high-vis vest and boots, which she puts on.*

In the moments before the lights come up on the fulfilment centre, TAMSIN *taps the vest and boots in the same way as before – four times each, twice with the left and twice with the right hand.*

LEAD. – and ideally, a target for this size will be four hundred and eighty items per hour. That's eight items a minute, so absolutely achievable, but we'll start you off on a target of four hundred and see how you go. How does that sound?

She's trying to make the best impression possible.

TAMSIN. Yep, really good.

LEAD. We have what we call the 'one best way' of packing – you saw that in the training video – and each item you pack will be examined further down the line, to check that it follows this method. Is that all clear?

TAMSIN. Definitely, yeah.

LEAD. Have you done any packing work before?

TAMSIN. No.

LEAD. Which agency are you with?

TAMSIN. Quartz.

The name is familiar to him.

LEAD. Oh, Quartz. Okay –

He writes this down on a clipboard.

TAMSIN. Also I was wondering / how long

LEAD. Okay. One moment, I just need to fill all this in.

So – there is a bit of terminology to take in but none of this is difficult. If you work hard and you meet your targets, there's always the possibility of transitioning to a permanent associate post.

TAMSIN. Right.

LEAD. In your workstation – you've got the boxes here for 1A7, 1A5, A4, A1, B11 – there'll be other workers keeping those boxes stocked for you – your scanner will tell you the correct size for every item.

TAMSIN. Great. Okay.

LEAD. Right, we're a bit late starting, so if you don't have any questions / I'll just

TAMSIN. I was just gonna ask about how long our break is, cos I need to make a phone call and it / might take

LEAD. Have you got a phone on you?

TAMSIN. ... yes?

LEAD. I'm gonna need to take it, I'm afraid.

You'll get it back at the end of the day, you just can't have it on the floor.

TAMSIN *hands her phone over to him, slightly stunned.*

Anything else?

TAMSIN. ... no.

LEAD. All okay?

She takes too long to answer.

I've really got to go, but chin up, all right? See how you go. I'll be back later.

TAMSIN *is left at her workstation, with* LUKE, *sixteen, opposite her. They have a conveyer belt between them, on to which they need to place the items they package.*

Behind the workstation, a scoreboard of sorts can be seen. On it we can see the time, a counter of the number of items TAMSIN *and* LUKE *have each packed so far in the hour, and their current per-hour average.*

Currently the clock reads 07.16. TAMSIN's *counters are at 0.* LUKE's *counter is at 96.*

TAMSIN *begins familiarising herself with the position of all her equipment, and starts packing.*

After a long enough pause that it's a surprise:

LUKE. Have the boots got you yet?

TAMSIN. Sorry?

LUKE. The boots. They're crap.

TAMSIN. Oh.

LUKE. Or maybe the girls' boots are better, I dunno.

Long pause.

TAMSIN. How lo– sorry, can I ask you something?

LUKE. Yeah.

TAMSIN. How long is our lunch break?

LUKE. Half-hour.

TAMSIN. Okay. Um, and, also – where do they keep our phones and things?

LUKE. Keep packing.

TAMSIN. I just need / to know so I can

LUKE. No, it's fine, just they'll get the hump with you if you don't keep packing.

He probably gave it to security. They've got their office near the entrance.

TAMSIN. The entrance that way?

She points.

LUKE. Yep.

TAMSIN. The one fifteen minutes that way?

LUKE. Well. I did it once in thirteen but that was power-walking.

TAMSIN. And our break's half an hour.

LUKE. Co-rrect.

TAMSIN doesn't quite know how to respond to this. She continues packing.

After a moment:

TAMSIN. And if I needed to make a call?

LUKE. You can whistle for it.

TAMSIN. ... right.

Pause. LUKE *sees that his next item to package is an iPhone. He glances up at* TAMSIN.

LUKE. Hey. Hey.

He has her attention – he lifts up the iPhone.

If only, eh?

TAMSIN. Don't, just.

Don't. Sorry.

LUKE. Okay, okay.

Just trying to lighten the mood.

The two of them package items in silence for thirty seconds or so, with TAMSIN*'s counter on the wall automatically adjusting as she packs.*

She gets to grips with her masking-tape gun, and gets slightly quicker at the packaging as she goes.

The clock now reads 09.55. TAMSIN's counter is at 243, with an average of 240 per hour. LUKE's counter is at 385, with an average of 420 per hour.

TAMSIN *looks around all her cubbyholes for something that isn't there.*

TAMSIN. I don't have any 1A5s left.

I thought he said people would keep these stocked?

LUKE *checks his collection – none there either.*

LUKE. Oh, fucking hell.

TAMSIN *takes out a different size.*

No, don't, they'll notice. It'll rattle around, they'll just unpack it later.

She takes another item and tries to scan it. The scanner doesn't beep.

TAMSIN. It won't let me go to the next one.

What am I meant to do, just – wait?

LUKE. Er.

Looks like it.

TAMSIN. It'll look like I've just slacked off for five minutes.

LUKE. Once they bring them, you can catch up. Go faster.

TAMSIN. If I go any faster I'll make mistakes.

What happens if you don't make your targets?

LUKE. Depends.

TAMSIN. On what?

LUKE *looks up at her and almost laughs.*

LUKE. Don't look so serious!

Um, like, I think it depends on how many warnings you have?

Cos I mean, they don't just chuck you off as soon as you don't make target, but there are. Like. Things they do first.

To try and make you meet targets. I dunno, I haven't had any of that happen yet.

He glances at his next item.

I swear this is like the fifth set of strawberry lube I've packaged in two days, I bet they're going to the same person.

He sees that TAMSIN *is still worrying about her boxes not being available.*

Try not to stress, yeah? They'll bring them.

TAMSIN. When?

LUKE. I don't know, do I? Jesus – look – you take over mine and I'll find where they've got to.

All right?

TAMSIN. Sure. Thanks.

LUKE *only leaves his packing the moment* TAMSIN *takes over, making sure there's absolutely no gap in activity. At a light jog, he leaves the workstation.*

While he's gone, TAMSIN *tries to package his items as quickly as she can, while still looking worriedly at her empty spot opposite.*

Her average begins dropping.

LUKE *returns with an armful of 1A5 boxes.*

LUKE. Bingo.

TAMSIN. Cheers.

He gives her half of the collection and she fits it into her cubbyhole.

TAMSIN *packages the item that had been waiting.*

When's our break?

LUKE. One.

TAMSIN. Sorry I know I just keep asking about lunch – I just, I do actually need to call someone, so.

LUKE. You're not gonna make it back before half-past.

TAMSIN. I'm gonna run, it'll be fine.

LUKE. Like – normally I'd say, all right, maybe chance it, but – you might get half a point for not packing anything while the 1A5s were out, right? So a whole point in one day – I wouldn't do it, man. It's better to like, really hold off on getting points till you get sick, cos that's when they, like, might just fire you if you've got too many points already.

Unless your phone call is, like, five seconds long. Then you might make it.

TAMSIN. They'd genuinely fire me?

LUKE. If it's in the next… how long do points last again?

Three months.

He shrugs.

I mean, it's your choice, but. I stopped trying to run places on my breaks cos it's just using up energy you're gonna need at like five o'clock when you're flagging.

He looks at his current item, a pair of slippers.

Hey, my mum has these.

The clock reads 12.59. TAMSIN's counter is at 245, with an average of 231 per hour. LUKE's counter is at 389, with an average of 404 per hour.

As the clock ticks over to 13.00 and a bell goes, TAMSIN *looks up, startled momentarily.* LUKE *steps away from his workstation.*

Stop stop stop.

TAMSIN *steps away from the item she was packing.*

Are you gonna try and make that call?

Pause.

TAMSIN *shakes her head.*

You okay?

TAMSIN *nods.*

Keep it together, yeah?

They don't want people who get all emotional. They think you'll bait them out or something.

TAMSIN. I'm fine.

LUKE. You / sure?

TAMSIN. Seriously, I'm fine.

TAMSIN begins to walk away, then stops to ask:

How far is the canteen?

LUKE. Ten minutes.

You can make it, just eat fast.

The clock reads 17.29. TAMSIN's counter is at 108, with an average of 228 per hour. LUKE's counter is at 194, with an average of 400 per hour. As the clock turns over to 17.30, a closing bell tolls over the tannoy and they stop packing.

Pause.

TAMSIN. Can we – ?

LUKE. Nah. Not till they say so.

Pause. LUKE *bounces on the balls of his feet impatiently.*

The line out's gonna be *so long* now. Fucking hell.

All the runners and problem-solvers just rush the doors and if you miss the moment right after the bell there's no point.

Fuck it.

He starts rummaging around inside his trousers.

TAMSIN. ... what are you doing?

He emerges with some cigarettes.

Where'd you get those?

LUKE. I have connections in here, don't I?

...I just don't have a lighter. Bugger.

Here.

He offers one to her.

TAMSIN. Serious?

LUKE. Of course, I ain't gonna offer you one and then take it back, am I. Put it away before they see.

TAMSIN. Cheers.

She puts it in her pocket.

LUKE. I got mine in my pants.

TAMSIN. ...

LUKE. So it's not there if my pockets get searched.

TAMSIN. ... fair enough.

After a few moments that feel very long, the LEAD *enters.*

LEAD. This'll just take one moment.

He looks at his clipboard, and gets through his script as quickly as he can.

Luke. Luke Luke Luke. Right – you're not where we want you to be yet but you're up quite a bit, ninety per cent some of the time. Good stuff.

LUKE. Okay?

LEAD. You can come in tomorrow, right?

LUKE. Yep.

LEAD. Okay. On packing again, then. See you at seven.

LUKE. Sweet.

LUKE *leaves.*

LEAD. We've just got a bit of standard paperwork to get through at the end of each day. Performance-related, mainly.

TAMSIN. Okay.

LEAD. So, obviously this is your first day, but this is still a long way from your target.

TAMSIN. I know, I'm sorry. I spent five minutes waiting for 1A5 boxes to be replaced.

LEAD. It's quite a bit below what we'd expect from someone starting out, so, regardless of anything else affecting performance, we want the numbers to match up, okay?

TAMSIN. Okay.

Beat.

Sorry.

LEAD. I've also been told that you went to the toilet twice, and both times you didn't go to the one nearest your workstation.

TAMSIN. Which one is nearer?

LEAD. You went to the one on the west side. There's a closer one on the north-west side.

TAMSIN. I didn't know. They – the floor manager at the time didn't tell me where the nearest one was when I said I was going.

LEAD. I would be able to let you off if it was once, but since it's twice I have to give you a point.

TAMSIN. But you didn't tell me after the first time.

LEAD. I'm afraid it only got written up in the last hour. I hear you –

TAMSIN. It wasn't on purpose.

LEAD. I hear you –

TAMSIN. The only reason it's a point is to stop skiving and I wasn't, I went straight / back to my station

LEAD. I completely understand, but this is protocol. I can't justify not following it. To be honest, normally we'd be giving a point to someone when there's an obvious, extended period where they didn't pack a single item.

TAMSIN. I know. I know. But that's when I / was

LEAD. Normally we'd give a point for that. I can let you off because it's your first day. But I can't do that every time.

We do get a lot of people who aren't right for us. It's fine, because we have a large pool of agency workers to choose from, so if you want we can terminate this assignment now.

TAMSIN. I'm right for you.

LEAD. Okay.

I still have to give you a point.

TAMSIN. That's fine.

Can I come in tomorrow?

LEAD. How are your feet doing?

TAMSIN. Great.

Beat.

LEAD. We'll probably keep you on packing for now so you can come to this workstation again. Okay?

TAMSIN. Yep.

LEAD. You'll also want to put this –

He hands her phone back to her.

– in a locker on your way in tomorrow. You'll need to pay a deposit to be sure you'll have one available every day but it's worth it.

TAMSIN. Thanks.

She puts it in her pocket and takes off her high-vis. Slowly – she's too tired to keep rushing things.

You have far to go to get home?

He keeps looking at his paperwork.

LEAD. That's it, you can go.

Beat.

She starts to leave.

Remember you can't take your jacket home with you. Leave it hanging up.

She turns around, exiting in the opposite direction.

Scene Two

DEAN *and* TAMSIN*'s kitchen.*

DEAN *looks at the plate of food, with cling film over the top, that* TAMSIN *has left for him. He peeps under the cling film for a moment, and then tucks it back.*

He taps each item of his clothing and peels the cling film back.

He sets the plate a safe distance away from him, and taps again.

He picks up a fork, hesitantly, and spears a piece of food.

He puts the fork down.

He taps again.

He picks the fork up again.

He puts it down.

He exits to go to the bathroom, where he spends about twenty seconds on his hair ritual.

He returns, and sits down.

He can't do it.

He tries to put the cling film back on the plate but the feel of the condensation on it makes him anxious. He puts it down and taps again.

He picks up the plate and puts it in the bottom drawer of a kitchen unit.

He returns to the bathroom, and starts doing his hair.

TAMSIN *enters, and takes her shoes off immediately. She sits down and kneads her feet through her socks.*

When she notices some letters, she pounces on them and opens them all up. None of them are the reconsideration result.

After a long pause, she hears the water running intermittently. Realises DEAN *is still up. She manages to force herself over to knock on the door.*

TAMSIN. Hey.

Pause.

'm sorry I didn't call. They took my phone away.

Are you okay?

DEAN. I couldn't go outside.

TAMSIN. I know. I'm really sorry.

Come out here and talk.

DEAN. No.

TAMSIN. I'm not angry with you.

DEAN. Why would you be angry with me? You wouldn't have any right to be angry with me.

TAMSIN. Okay. I just wanna know you're all right.

Pause.

TAMSIN *gets her phone out of her pocket and composes a text to* DEAN.

His phone vibrates – he picks it up and reads it.

He opens the door, coming out into the kitchen.

DEAN. I don't wanna read your stupid text, didn't you see how many times I called you?

She reaches out to his scalp. He avoids her touch.

Don't.

TAMSIN. You're bleeding –

DEAN. *Don't.*

TAMSIN. I didn't mean for you to –

DEAN. You rushed me this morning.

TAMSIN. Because I had to *go*. If you wanna wake up even earlier to give us more time, be my guest.

DEAN. I really wanted to be able to go out.

TAMSIN. I know. I wanted you to as well.

The Jobcentre didn't try and ring or anything?

DEAN *shakes his head.*

We should probably call them and – try and explain what happened. Might come to nothing, but.

DEAN. They're not open now.

TAMSIN. Shit. Yeah.

Beat, and then, slowly:

Would you be able to call / them tomorrow?

DEAN. No.

No.

TAMSIN. Dean, I'm not gonna be able to do it. I'm in work before they open, I get back after they close, I can't ring anyone all day –

DEAN. Neither can I.

TAMSIN. You've phoned people before. I've seen you do it. Don't tell me you *can't.*

DEAN. People I *know.* I won't be able to do anything else for the rest of the day –

TAMSIN. Yeah? What else is new?

Beat.

Sorry. Sorry.

Look, it's just. If we don't tell them straight away what happened then that's zero JSA for at least this week, probably longer cos I think we'd have to apply for the hardship bollocks all over again – and I don't even get paid till I've done two weeks. And I don't know if we still qualify for all the other things like council-tax reduction cos no one I asked would fucking say. Like it depends on my income and I don't even know what that's gonna be, and I just, I have this feeling they might just hit us with a massive fucking bill maybe even going back all the way to your assessment date or something.

DEAN. How likely is that?

TAMSIN. I dunno, do I? That's what I'm saying.

We can try and – leave them a message or something. Maybe see if they can arrange to call you or something, but you'd have to promise to answer…

She looks around.

Where's the folder?

Did you move it?

DEAN *says nothing.*

She starts looking in drawers.

Can't ever find anything in this place, you put something down and it just *vanishes*…

DEAN. Don't –

Too late. She opens the drawer with the plate in.

TAMSIN. Oh Jesus.

You didn't eat *any* of it?

DEAN. I'm going to.

TAMSIN. You're not 'going to', it's in the fucking *drawer.*

DEAN. I was gonna leave it there until I felt ready to / eat it

TAMSIN. It'll be cold.

DEAN. I can microwave it, can't I?

TAMSIN. No, you can't reheat rice, it goes all / funny

DEAN. Then I don't understand why you made me rice!

TAMSIN. Because it's cheap. That's why.

And I thought it'd be – safe. Y'know. It's bland.

I dunno, you can spend bloody hours on your hair –

DEAN. Shut up, shut *up* –

TAMSIN. On your hair, let's be clear about that, on your *hair* – and you weren't even outside all day – couldn't you at least have *tried*?

DEAN. I did.

TAMSIN. Okay. Whatever.

DEAN. I *did*.

TAMSIN shrugs, opening the bin to get rid of the food.

You don't have to do that.

TAMSIN. Are you gonna eat it?

Pause. DEAN doesn't answer.

Then yeah, I do have to do this.

She makes to start throwing it away and then can't do it.

No. No.

She starts to eat some of it herself.

I'm not fucking wasting anything else.

There's nothing wrong with it. You know that.

DEAN starts pulling at a few strands of his hair.

Stop *doing* that, you're gonna –

She tries to pull DEAN's hand away from his hair, and he moves out of the way.

Look, this –

She goes into the bathroom and gets a pot of DEAN's gel.

– this –

DEAN. DON'T.

TAMSIN (*opening it up and scooping gel on to her hand*). It's shit. I fucking hate looking at it.

DEAN. Give it back.

TAMSIN. What does it even do??

This is why I'm too bloody scared to check your bank account, cos I don't even know how much of this you've bought and hidden away.

DEAN. I'm saving it.

TAMSIN. For *what*??

DEAN. Just give it *back*.

Beat – and then TAMSIN *does.*

DEAN *clutches the pot in his hand really hard, has to stop himself from throwing it.*

He goes into the bathroom and locks the door.

TAMSIN. Oh yeah, that's great. Do that.

He begins to apply more gel to his hair.

Beat. She calls through the door:

I'm sorry.

Look – I'm just saying – we can't afford to waste food.

Still through the door:

DEAN. You don't have to spend money getting me food.

TAMSIN. Yes I do, this is the only thing I'm putting my foot down on, / the only thing –

DEAN. You don't –

TAMSIN. – you can do whatever you like with the – the hair and things, but you have to eat.

DEAN. It's not that I don't want to, just –

TAMSIN. What?

No answer.

What is it?

DEAN. Look, I'm not gonna talk about it to you, okay? It's private, and –

TAMSIN. But food's not – it's not a flexible thing, I can't write it off again and go, oh, okay, we'll talk about that in a few months' time, cos look where that got us, / it's your actual *life* here –

DEAN *has been getting more and more frustrated with his hair.*

DEAN. Can you just shut up? I need to concentrate here and you're just – making everything worse – I need you to fuck off for like ten fucking minutes for once – is that like too much for you or something –

TAMSIN. You have *no idea* how much I just wanna leave you to it sometimes. No fucking idea. You should be thanking your lucky fucking *stars* that I haven't because I really, really want to sometimes.

…

Sorry. Sorry. I'm just tired, I've – I've had a shit day, we've both had shit days.

Dean.

She gives up, and is still and exhausted for a few moments.

Then she slowly gets up to wash the gel off her hands, and wash the plate.

After she's finished, she wipes her hands on her jeans, and feels something in her pocket. She reaches inside and takes out the cigarette.

An idea.

She knocks on the bathroom door gently.

No answer.

I've got something for you, I forgot.

DEAN. What?

TAMSIN. Open the door.

Beat.

DEAN *opens the door a crack.*

She shows him the cigarette.

DEAN. Who gave you that?

TAMSIN. Guy at work.

DEAN. Why?

TAMSIN. I dunno – look, do you wanna smoke it or not?

DEAN. It's yours.

TAMSIN. Can share.

She takes a box of matches out of a drawer, then lights the cigarette.

She takes one puff, just managing to stop herself from coughing, and taking care to waft the smoke away, before offering it to DEAN.

It's fine, honestly.

DEAN *comes out of the bathroom, and takes the cigarette from* TAMSIN. *He taps it twice with his left hand and twice with his right hand. Then he takes a drag.*

Good?

DEAN *nods.*

They're meant to calm you down, aren't they? I don't know if it's chemical or just your imagination but I think they're meant to.

I've just had a really bad day.

Beat.

DEAN (*as though it's a stock phrase*). 'You and me both, kiddo.'

TAMSIN. Yeah.

Beat.

Did you move the folder?

DEAN *starts tapping, almost indiscernibly.*

Did you lose it?

It's okay if you did, we can – maybe we can ask them to post us another diary and things?

Before he can speak, DEAN *goes to rearrange his hair very quickly.*

TAMSIN *waits.*

DEAN *returns, and goes to a cupboard and takes out a cardboard folder, which is under some plates.*

He taps it eight times with his left hand and eight times with his right hand, and goes to put it on the table next to TAMSIN.

DEAN *returns to the bathroom and checks his hair again.*

He returns to the table and sits down.

(*In an attempt at levity.*) I really thought you had lost it. You totally had me going.

She opens it and flips through the Jobseeker's Diary inside.

Okay.

This is all really different to the ESA stuff. Um.

So these are the commitments you agreed with them?

DEAN. Yeah.

TAMSIN. Have you done any of them?

Pause.

Did you try?

DEAN. Yeah.

TAMSIN. What happened?

DEAN. I can't look at this stuff for too long without…

Beat.

TAMSIN. I know.

DEAN. They said I had to make a CV and, like, I did try and start, but.

TAMSIN. What?

DEAN. What would you put in one? If you were me?

TAMSIN. Your – skills, and things. Your grades.

> DEAN *isn't impressed with this answer.*
>
> You've got your C in Maths.
>
> You know that if you went back to the unit they'd help you with this.
>
> *Beat.*

DEAN. Did you have to mention that?

TAMSIN. Okay, okay. I'm sorry.

DEAN. For fuck's sake.

> I don't even wanna be doing this in the first place. I'm putting all this effort in and you just like mess with me like that.

TAMSIN. Sorry. Look –

DEAN. I'm in this – bad cycle / anyway –

TAMSIN. Five more minutes. Come on. Please. Let's get this done and then you can do whatever you need.

DEAN. No, I can't, cos I'll have to – eat.

> *Beat.*

TAMSIN. I get how hard this is. I do. I know I'm asking a lot.

> All right, I'm gonna – I'm gonna write down all your commitments here so it's not on the diary, we don't have to get the folder out at all – and you can organise this how you like, doesn't have to be my way – and we'll just, we'll set a time when we try and do a few of them every night.

DEAN. I'll be worried about it all day, though.

TAMSIN. We won't get it done otherwise. You know we won't.

> That sound okay?
>
> DEAN *shrugs.*
>
> Yeah?

DEAN. Yeah. Fine.

TAMSIN. I'll send a letter to the Jobcentre and say we're doing that. Maybe – take photos or something. As evidence.

DEAN. I tried to look at applications. Online ones.

TAMSIN. Yeah?

DEAN. But they always ask about gaps, where you weren't working or in school.

TAMSIN. ...yeah. Right.

I guess you say you were too ill.

DEAN. Are you sure?

Beat.

TAMSIN. I mean, you can't lie, can you? There are – records that you've been on ESA. I mean you can say that the council exempted you from college and things.

If you don't say anything they'll think you've been in prison.

DEAN. They're not gonna hire me either way.

TAMSIN. But it's not – you just have to prove that you're applying, don't you? For now? In the 'outcome' section you can put, I dunno, 'I have tried applying for things but don't know what to say about gaps.'

DEAN. ...

TAMSIN. I know that sounds crap.

Maybe you should put some jokes in there. Liven it up.

Pause.

How're we gonna organise this, then? Do you wanna keep it with the ESA and PIP stuff or is that gonna be confusing?

DEAN. If we put it all in order it'll be fine.

He separates some sheets from the Jobcentre packet.

These are ESA things.

TAMSIN. Are they?

DEAN. It's the report.

TAMSIN. Seriously? What does it say?

She takes the sheets and starts reading.

DEAN. I haven't looked, when it arrived I – didn't want / to –

TAMSIN. Blah blah blah – 'Can get dressed without help or aids'.

...did you say that?

DEAN. No, they asked – they asked if there was any – like, physical disability that stopped me getting dressed. And I said no, but that I needed you to help me.

TAMSIN. 'Is able to go to local shops most days'... 'experiences no distress when interacting with unfamiliar people'. This is bollocks, this is all bollocks, these are just *lies.*

Did they say this was what they were writing? Did they not let you explain?

DEAN. I didn't wanna fiddle with my hair in the assessment so I sat on my hands – and then I couldn't – (*Gestures to mean 'tap'.*) so it was really hard to, like, concentrate on what I was saying.

Beat.

TAMSIN. Was it a man?

DEAN. What?

TAMSIN. Was it a man who did your assessment, or was it a woman?

Beat.

DEAN. It was a man.

TAMSIN. Good-looking?

DEAN. Yeah.

TAMSIN. Good hair?

DEAN *shrugs. Sort of nods.*

Beat.

I should have gone in with you.

DEAN. It's not your fault.

TAMSIN. Yeah, but.

I should've managed all this better. Cos I knew they'd be harsh. I just.

Okay, um, I'm gonna – I'm gonna look at every bit that's not true and write what it's actually like and how the rituals mean you can't do any of this. And send that as a new piece of evidence for the reconsideration. And if they say you have to have another assessment I'll go in with you.

DEAN. I don't like you saying 'rituals'.

TAMSIN. I know. Sorry. They won't understand otherwise, y'know?

DEAN gets up.

DEAN. Um, can I – ?

TAMSIN. Sorry, I know this is a bit – intense.

DEAN. I just need to –

TAMSIN. It's fine, go ahead.

He goes to the bathroom and closes the door. Takes some deep breaths and spends a while cutting bits of his hair.

He opens the door but still stands in the bathroom, talking to TAMSIN *from there.*

DEAN. Is this gonna work?

Beat.

TAMSIN. They cut you off thinking you had nothing wrong with you, that's the thing. Like, *I* would look at this report and go 'Okay, clearly they're fine.' I reckon we send this off, they get you in for another assessment – and I'll – get some hours off work and go with you – and we're golden.

DEAN. Really?

TAMSIN. Yeah. We know what we're getting into this time, we know what they're looking for.

I'll finish this off and then are you okay to eat?

DEAN. Mm.

He doesn't approach TAMSIN, *but holds his hand out.*

High-five.

TAMSIN *grins and gets up, goes over to him and gently returns his high-five.* DEAN *exits.*

She returns to annotate the pages of the report, but before she can really start she's back at her workstation in the warehouse. LUKE *is already there. The clock reads 06.58.*

LUKE (*jokily*). We gotta stop meeting like this!

TAMSIN (*looking up*). Hm?

LUKE. Just – saying hi.

TAMSIN. Hi. Sorry, it's – I'm really tired.

Beat.

I had a late one last night. Not a – fun late one, just.

Yeah.

LUKE. Didja notice that this road – the, um, the one we're on – is called Badgers Rise?

Jokes, right? I lived in MK all my life and I ain't never seen no badger about.

Beat.

What's your name again?

TAMSIN. Tamsin.

LUKE. Luke.

I'd shake your hand but – cardboard cuts.

TAMSIN. Oh – yeah. Me too.

Pause.

The time crawls closer and closer to seven. As it approaches:

Should we –

The LEAD *enters.*

LEAD. Morning.

How are we feeling?

If we can get started –

Tamsin – two hundred and twenty-eight an hour average yesterday – now you're used to everything we need to try and make four hundred.

TAMSIN. Right.

LEAD. Do you think you can do it?

TAMSIN. – yeah. Sure.

LEAD. Four hundred then.

(*To* LUKE.) So you've just about managed your initial target, but most people by this time have managed to bump that up to the mid-four-hundreds at least. So I need you to try and push your rate up to four hundred and fifty, or at least consistently four hundred and twenty or above, okay?

LUKE. Okay.

LEAD. Orders are tailing off a little bit at this point in the month so it should be easy.

TAMSIN. When –

The LEAD *looks at her, slightly startled by the interruption.*

– sorry – um – when do we know, like on average, if we'll be working tomorrow? Do you like – decide based on orders or performance / or

LEAD. I'm gonna get back to you on that, okay? Right now I don't know.

TAMSIN. Okay. Cos I'm definitely available.

LEAD. Sure.

TAMSIN. Just so you know.

Beat.

LEAD. We'll have a little chat in a few hours.

He exits. TAMSIN *and* LUKE *start packing – trying to make up for the minute they've just lost.* TAMSIN *redoes her hair tie and winces.*

LUKE. They've only ever told me at the end of the day. Or sometimes the agency texts the next morning.

TAMSIN. Do you get used to them?

LUKE. What, the leads?

TAMSIN. Well, them too, but I meant – the, uh, cardboard cuts.

LUKE. Oh. Nah, they just get opened up again. I bet I'm gonna have scars, I'm gonna make out I been in a fight…

Pause.

TAMSIN. Can we ask them to open the doors?

LUKE. ?

TAMSIN. Aren't you hot?

LUKE thinks for a second.

LUKE. I've never seen them open the doors on-shift.

Probably worried about theft and that. Fucking everything's about theft.

He sees his next order: it's a vibrator.

Ohhh this is what I like to see first thing in the morning, man.

He shows her.

TAMSIN. I'm like half-asleep, I can't deal with that right now.

He waves it closer to her like it's something gross. She can't help but crack a tiny smile, just cos of how stupid it is.

Get it away!

He's already got it away – he can't afford to package it too slowly.

LUKE. It's called a Humdinger, what does that do?

TAMSIN. I dunno, do I?

LUKE. What, you mean you don't have like, five of them at home?

TAMSIN. Sorry. I'm not that up on sex-toy trends.

LUKE. Oh, well, you work here a few weeks and you'll see loads.

I'm just like preparing you in advance cos they get really weird.

Do people call you Taz?

TAMSIN. No.

LUKE. I bet they do.

She gives him a look.

(*Still bright and unfazed.*) I'm gonna shut up.

TAMSIN. I dreamt about this last night. I dreamt that I was packing boxes in boxes in boxes.

LUKE. I had that after my first day, but it was the – beeping.

Cos I was on picking. They have a different beep on their scanners and after ten hours it gets in your head.

TAMSIN. How's picking?

LUKE. Man. I was like in a trance or something I swear. I don't even remember half of it, you could tell me I passed out and I'd believe you.

TAMSIN. Shit.

LUKE. Yeah.

TAMSIN. Is this better?

LUKE. Nah. Just bad in a different way.

The clock reads 09.31. TAMSIN's counter is at 128, with an average of 249 per hour. LUKE's counter is at 212, with an average of 430.

TAMSIN finishes packing an item, and it's clear she feels slightly faint. She takes a moment to breathe deeply before she takes her next item.

The LEAD *enters. He might swear to himself in his own language as he approaches – he's just had a bollocking.*

LEAD. Right, guys. We're only two and a half hours in and I've been told there's a pretty big shortfall over here. Tamsin – you have to step up, okay?

TAMSIN. Okay.

LEAD (*indicating* LUKE). He's almost doubling you right now.

TAMSIN. Yeah.

LEAD. So it's not impossible, is it?

TAMSIN. No.

LEAD. It's not impossible.

TAMSIN. ... no, it's not impossible.

LEAD. Keep positive about it, okay? You've got a good work ethic and that's great, but whatever you think is the limit you can do, raise it.

TAMSIN. Okay. Yep. Sure.

LEAD. I'll be back soon.

The LEAD *exits.*

LUKE. You okay?

TAMSIN. It's too hot.

LUKE. Keep going, just be a robot for a bit.

TAMSIN. I think I'm gonna – / I can't –

LUKE. Are you gonna faint?

TAMSIN. – what do I do?

LUKE *looks around, checks no supervisors are nearby.*

LUKE. Um, there's a water fountain, right – if you run it's like two minutes that way.

TAMSIN. But I won't –

LUKE. Leg it. I'll cover you.

TAMSIN. Thanks. Thanks.

As in Scene Two, LUKE takes over TAMSIN's work so there is no gap in activity. TAMSIN runs off.

The clock reads 12.58. TAMSIN's counter is at 245, with an average of 251 per hour. LUKE's counter is at 429, with an average of 436.

TAMSIN is back. LUKE struggles with a very large and heavy bag.

He checks the label.

LUKE. It's couscous.

This is forty kilogram of couscous, why would you need that much couscous?

TAMSIN. Wow.

I mean I had twelve MAC lipsticks all going to one person yesterday, so. People bulk buy all sorts.

LUKE. *Couscous* though?!

TAMSIN. Maybe that's the only food they can manage.

LUKE. But forty kilogram at once, the label says it's fifty quid! Though I guess it's cheaper from here.

TAMSIN. But I mean, maybe they can't eat anything else.

LUKE. Oh. Right. Like allergies?

Man, now I'm depressed.

TAMSIN. Try saying 'couscous' again.

The clock ticks over to 13.00 and the bell goes. TAMSIN checks her numbers.

Fuck.

How are you doing four hundred?

LUKE. You'll get faster.

TAMSIN. Like, today?

LUKE. If there's the work they'll ask you back tomorrow. Don't stress your numbers, like.

TAMSIN. Are you going to the canteen?

LUKE. Nah, I want a full half-hour sitting down.

TAMSIN. You're not gonna eat?

LUKE. Had a massive fry-up and a Red Bull before coming – doing an experiment, gonna see if that gets me through.

He sits on his workstation, and takes his boots off, throwing them on the floor, before lying down.

Oh man that's so good. I am really sorry if they smell but that feels so good.

Tell me if you see anyone coming, yeah?

TAMSIN *leans against her workstation, and examines her fingers for cardboard cuts.*

The clock reads 13.15.

LUKE *gets off the workstation, and puts his boots back on.*

Right, your turn.

TAMSIN. Hmm?

LUKE. Sit down. I'll keep watch.

TAMSIN. ... you sure?

LUKE. Yeah, course – go go go, it's already sixteen past! Thirteen minutes!

TAMSIN *sits on her workstation.*

Take your boots off – seriously, it's amaze.

TAMSIN *unlaces her boots and takes them off. It's obviously a relief.*

Pause.

What were you doing before this?

TAMSIN. Oh, we're doing twenty questions.

LUKE. Nah. It's just, you get all sorts here, so I ask.

TAMSIN. Yeah.

She looks around her for something to help change the subject.

Hey, look.

She holds up a Bat Out of Hell II *vinyl that was on the bottom of her next order.*

LUKE. What's that?

TAMSIN. Oh come on.

LUKE. It looks like some goth shit?

TAMSIN. It's Meat Loaf!

LUKE. *What?*

TAMSIN. You know. 'Bat Out of Hell'. 'I'd Do Anything for Love'.

(*Singing.*) 'I would do anything for love – '

Seeing LUKE's *expression:*

No? Okay.

LUKE. 'Meat Loaf'?!

TAMSIN. Yeah.

LUKE. That his actual name?

TAMSIN. ... I dunno. I guess not. But he's – oh my god he's so great. He's like completely, gloriously over the top. Classic power rock.

LUKE. Not my kinda thing.

TAMSIN. Yeah, see, I thought that, but he gets you. Just wait, sit through a few tracks and he gets you.

LUKE. Lemme see?

She hands him the vinyl.

TAMSIN. It's like… pure joy. I promise.

LUKE. I'll check him out later.

TAMSIN. Yeah?

She laughs, and lies down on the workstation.

Report back, tell me what you think.

Pause.

You're so right about badgers, y'know?

LUKE. Right?!

TAMSIN. Never seen one in my life.

Badgers Rise.

LUKE. Yeah, like, rising from *where*??

TAMSIN laughs, and holds up the vinyl again.

TAMSIN. Out of hell. Obviously.

The clock reads 17.30. TAMSIN's counter is at 126, with an average of 247 per hour. LUKE's counter is at 204, with an average of 410 per hour.

The LEAD *is already present. He looks tired.*

I know. I know.

I just need to get used to it all. I can do better.

LEAD. Carmody.

TAMSIN holds her hand up. He gives her a sheet of paper.

Mburu.

LUKE *receives one too.*

These are your scores from today. It's a breakdown, so you can see – right there is your average for each hour, and your average overall, and then the target, and what percentage you've fallen behind.

Take it home and think through how you can improve, all right?

TAMSIN. Sure.

LEAD. So there's not really any excuse for you not to be reaching your targets. Okay?

She nods. He turns to LUKE.

So, a few hours where you hit a hundred-per-cent target, but then that tailed off a lot towards the end of the day, so you need to work on that.

And there's a period – here – where your usual standard, and the standard we want, really slipped – a, a five-minute interval where we didn't record any activity.

LUKE. Right.

LEAD. What was going on there?

LUKE. Back ache. Had to have a stretch.

LEAD. Sure. It's not really acceptable after being here a few months, so I'm gonna need to give you half a point for it.

LUKE. Won't happen again.

That answer's a relief.

LEAD. Brilliant. Brilliant. Okay.

Right.

Can both of you keep tomorrow free?

LUKE. Yeah.

TAMSIN. – Yeah. Yeah.

LEAD. All right. Come in for seven and we'll see how many people we end up needing.

The LEAD *exits.* TAMSIN *and* LUKE *begin unlacing their boots.*

TAMSIN. Sorry, I shouldn't have / let you

LUKE. Bruv. Not like I care. I'm leaving soon.

Is Carmody your last name?

TAMSIN. Oh. Yeah.

LUKE. D'you know Dean Carmody?

Beat.

TAMSIN. Why?

LUKE. Year above me at school. Is he your cousin or?

TAMSIN. – he's my younger brother.

LUKE. Ohhh yeah, you're *old*, I forgot.

TAMSIN. Yeah, yeah, shut up.

LUKE. He's seriously your brother?

TAMSIN. I know he's…

LUKE. What?

She shrugs.

TAMSIN. I dunno.

LUKE. How come I never saw you at school?

TAMSIN. I went to Collier.

LUKE. Oh right.

Hartley wasn't bad, y'know.

TAMSIN. Yeah, but he didn't really…

She thinks better of it.

You know what, I should probably get going, / I need to

LUKE. No, I get what you mean. He was kinda –

TAMSIN (*cutting him off before he can find the words*). I need to get back.

LUKE. But, like, I was in detention with him once and you could tell he was smart.

Like I think it was History work or something, someone was doing their head in over a source question and he just got it, like instantly, and he kind of talked them through it till they understood.

Pause. This is something TAMSIN *can't imagine now.*

TAMSIN. Cool.

Pause.

Want me to take your things out too?

Save you a trip.

LUKE hands her his jacket and boots.

LUKE. Cheers, bruv.

TAMSIN. See you soon.

She leaves. LUKE starts walking the opposite way.

LUKE. Same time? Same place?

TAMSIN. Don't even joke.

Scene Three

A week later. TAMSIN is packing at her workstation, alone. The clock reads 16.27. TAMSIN's counter is at 121, with an average of 243 items per hour.

TAMSIN is going faster than we've seen her so far. She packs for just long enough that the lack of dialogue starts to feel strange.

And then one of her packages contains a yoga DVD. She takes a moment, while getting the box, to look at the back of the DVD.

TAMSIN. Downward Dog.

She packs it.

LUKE swings by, possibly riding on his trolley. (But not for too long. He's breaking lots of health and safety rules.)

LUKE. All right Tammifer?

Tammalamadingdong?

How's it going?

TAMSIN. Where've you been?

LUKE. Ahhh you missed me!

TAMSIN. I've been by myself for days, I've missed humans.

LUKE. Yeah yeah.

TAMSIN. Seriously, I packed a football and had to stop myself stealing it and drawing a face on it.

Where've you been?

LUKE. Picking, right? They were short – needed a big strong boy like me to fill in.

TAMSIN. They said that, did they?

LUKE. Nah, course not.

Pause.

You know how I said packing and picking were equal levels of shit?

Picking is worse. I've decided.

TAMSIN. Right.

LUKE. It's the muscles.

I wish I could have headphones.

TAMSIN. Oh god, me too. That'd be so good.

LUKE. How's it been over here?

TAMSIN. Shit. Fucking shit. Broke three hundred a few times yesterday but I'm not even making two hundred and fifty now.

LUKE. Just remember that the only limitations are the limitations you set for yourself.

TAMSIN *makes a face.*

Arrggh, it burns!

TAMSIN. Yeah, that's right, you don't wanna see my angry face.

There's some writer who said women on their periods could kill bees just by looking at them. My teacher told me.

LUKE. Ah, that stuff's all wank. My mum, like, when she's on her period she just gets sad, not angry. Extra cup of tea and she's fine.

Why, are you...?

TAMSIN. What? No. No.

She looks at the scoreboard. Her average has gone down to 230.

Look, they're so gonna tick you off for standing around.

LUKE *takes a quick look around, making for his scanner again so he can look busy – but his hand cramps and stutters when he tries to pick it up.*

You okay?

LUKE. Yeah, I'm –

His hand gets stuck in a loop of cramping.

I'm fine –

TAMSIN. Hold it up.

He holds up his hand. TAMSIN *presses her palm flat against* LUKE*'s – he winces as his fingers bend back.*

I know. I know.

Push against it.

He does – and she pushes back, letting him stretch his fingers against it.

Did that work?

LUKE. – yeah. Cheers.

Least I'm gonna be hench by the end of the day, right?

TAMSIN. Oh, totally.

LUKE. One of the other guys said he lost a stone in his first month of picking. And he's *old*, like.

TAMSIN. Sorry, I don't wanna be – I really need to keep going, they're kinda losing patience with me.

Beat.

I don't want them to get pissed off with you.

LUKE. I do.

Well, not really. But. Sometimes. Days like this.

TAMSIN. Yeah. I know what you mean.

LUKE. Yeah.

Beat.

He braves a look at his scanner, and winces.

I'm so gonna get a point for this. I shoulda been at north side one minute twenty seconds ago. Twenty-five seconds. Twenty-six.

Pause. In for a penny, in for a pound.

Let's go to the pub.

TAMSIN. What?

LUKE. Not *now*. Obviously. Tomorrow. Or when we both have a day off.

TAMSIN. – I –

LUKE. All my mates have gone Amsterdam. Did some bus deal online and got ten-pound tickets. And I'm here, doing this. I wanna go pub tomorrow.

TAMSIN. Look I can't – I can't think about this right now, I've gotta –

I have to keep going.

LUKE. Okay. Sound.

He begins to wheel his cart away, but has a sudden thought and rummages in his pocket.

Here.

He presents TAMSIN *with a single tealight – he might even chuck it at her so she has to catch it.*

Enjoy. Bag of a thousand tealights split open so I'm guessing they can't sell 'em.

He continues wheeling his cart away.

TAMSIN (*hissing*). Where am I gonna put this?

LUKE looks around, mouths 'in your shirt' and makes hand gestures. TAMSIN puts it inside her shirt, fitting it into her bra and trying not to laugh. LUKE starts to wheel his cart away again.

(*Only half-joking.*) Don't leave me here!

Scene Four

TAMSIN is waiting outside a pub near her house. It's really warm, a kind of golden late-summer evening. TAMSIN could look a bit different here – clothes we haven't seen before, maybe, or wearing her hair down.

LUKE approaches. TAMSIN shields her eyes from the sun.

LUKE. Heyy.

TAMSIN. Hey! Hi. Sorry, I can't –

She shifts herself slightly so the sun isn't in her eyes as much.

Hi.

You okay?

LUKE. Yeah, yeah.

TAMSIN. Um I thought we could – sit here / cos it's –

LUKE. Yeah, yeah –

TAMSIN. So warm and that.

LUKE. Yeah.

He tries to find a position where the sun isn't in his eyes too much, and sits.

Pause.

TAMSIN. Was it okay –

She gestures.

WISH LIST 369

LUKE. Getting here?

TAMSIN. Yeah. Sorry for making you come to my neck of the woods.

LUKE. Oh, nah – why would you wanna come to Conniburrow, like?! – I'm just late cos I got kinda tied up at home.

TAMSIN. Sure, sure.

Pause.

Everything all right?

LUKE. All – ?

TAMSIN. At home.

LUKE. Oh – yeah. Yeah. Just stuff.

Pause.

TAMSIN. It's weird, I kinda didn't recognise you.

LUKE. Yeah?

TAMSIN. You know, without the – without the vest.

LUKE. Ohh.

I think I really work the high-vis, y'know?

TAMSIN. Oh definitely, yeah.

Totally brings out your eyes.

LUKE. Yeah, my bright orange eyes.

Pause.

TAMSIN. Um. I was gonna say – d'you wanna…

Beat.

LUKE. What?

TAMSIN. D'you wanna buy me a drink?

LUKE. Oh. Uh –

TAMSIN. You don't have to.

LUKE. No, like, it's fine, but I'm six/teen

TAMSIN. Sixteen.

Fuck, yeah, I forgot.

Pause.

Would they actually ID you though?

LUKE. I dunno, I ain't been here before – look, I'll give you the change and you go get us both something.

He starts counting out notes and change.

TAMSIN. What d'you want?

LUKE. Get me a, get me a Kronenbourg.

TAMSIN. Cool.

Don't worry, I won't spend all of it.

She goes inside.

LUKE *checks his palms for sweat and rubs them on his trousers. Then cracks his knuckles for good measure.*

He looks at the field across from the pub. Gets out his phone and takes a photo of it, and one of the sky.

TAMSIN *returns with two beers and some change. Gives* LUKE *one of the beers.*

LUKE. Thanks.

Quiet.

TAMSIN *concentrates on rearranging the change into little coin stacks, in ascending value.*

When LUKE *notices her:*

TAMSIN. You carry this much change around, you must be raking it in.

LUKE. Oh, totally, yeah.

More like –

What's less good than raking?

I've only got like a really tiny rake.

He mimes a miniature rake. TAMSIN *grins into her glass before taking a sip.*

TAMSIN. Oh god that is really nice.

Thanks.

LUKE. S'fine.

A kind of awkward, kind of peaceful pause.

TAMSIN. Maybe I should get drunk for tomorrow.

LUKE. Oh, mate, don't do it. I did a day hungover and it was shite. Would not recommend. Day felt like five times longer than normal.

TAMSIN. Really?

LUKE. Mm.

It was, the night before was when all my mates were leaving, and they were like, we've got fifteen hours on a bus, obviously we need to be proper smashed, right, so we all stayed up and kicked around near The Point till their bus came at like… 2 a.m. And then it was just me, smashed, 2 a.m., at The Point which is like a fucking graveyard now anyway, I was like… even without work tomorrow this would be depressing.

Pause.

TAMSIN. Has it been bad without your mates?

LUKE. Just fucking dry, you know?

It's okay, but. *That* during the day, just me and my *mum* in the evenings, like…

TAMSIN. I'd've left by now if I were you.

The warehouse I mean.

LUKE. But… Tamsin. I'm packing at ninety per cent! You don't just walk away from skills like that!!

TAMSIN. Seriously though.

Beat.

LUKE *shrugs.*

LUKE. I mean, I wouldn't be able to get anything else before I go to college, y'know?

I tried to get a paper round first, cos that's like, classic – and exercise – but. This was the only thing going.

I guess picking is exercise, though. Kinda.

TAMSIN. Kinda. Yeah.

Pause.

What're you doing at college?

LUKE. BTEC Diploma.

(*Warning her jokily.*) Don't say it!

TAMSIN. I – wasn't gonna say anything.

What's it in?

LUKE. Uniformed Public Services.

TAMSIN. What's that, like, army?

LUKE. Well, yeah, that's part of it but I'm gonna try for emergency services cos I really wanna work in an ambulance crew.

TAMSIN. Wow.

Wow. Yeah, that.

Beat.

That's so good. Good for you. I'll drink to that.

Pause.

Hang on, that's how you know all the first-aid stuff, isn't it!

LUKE. Yeah.

TAMSIN. I thought maybe you were just making it up.

LUKE. Nah! I did a Red Cross course and everything. I've got a certificate.

TAMSIN. Right.

So what did you have to get for the BTEC? Like, good Biology grades, or?

LUKE. Five Cs including English and Maths.

TAMSIN. Okay. That's not too bad.

LUKE. Ehh. I only got Maths by one mark.

TAMSIN. Maths is okay when you get down to it.

LUKE. No it's not. Don't lie to me.

TAMSIN. It is, it's sort of like a game. I was all right at Maths. And Physics. Space and star cycles and things.

LUKE. Ahh, we must have done different exam boards, I dunno any of that.

TAMSIN. White dwarfs and stuff?

LUKE shakes his head.

Oh, it was cool – like you know how a star before it's a star is just this big cloud of gas, right? Like made of hydrogen and stuff?

LUKE. No, but, sure.

TAMSIN. Okay, basically… so gravity means the hydrogen all kinda clumps together and it gets really really dense and really really hot, and then after a while the hydrogen's under *so* much pressure clumping together that it starts to make helium, and that makes energy, and it basically keeps going like that in a cycle for billions of years. And it's like a massive plasma fireball type thing.

LUKE. Okay.

TAMSIN. But then, hydrogen starts running out – and so then it can't make helium, so *then* it can't make energy any more, and so the, the middle of the star – the core, shrinks into like this tiny little white dwarf and all the outer layers expand and kind of… burn out and turn to dust. And the star basically dies.

LUKE. It dies?

TAMSIN. Yeah.

Beat.

LUKE. Wow.

You are such a neek.

TAMSIN. Fuck off.

LUKE. It's cool!

TAMSIN grins.

TAMSIN. No it's not.

LUKE. It is! I couldn't do any of that bollocks. Why aren't you going to college?

TAMSIN shrugs. She fiddles with one of the coins. She flips it and covers the result with her hand before looking.

TAMSIN. Um.

My GCSEs were – kinda crap.

I think Collier really regretted letting me in, in the end.

LUKE. Why?

TAMSIN. There was just loads going on at the time. With, with my mum, mostly. I was doing all these hospital visits, so.

LUKE. Right.

TAMSIN. And.

No going back now.

You remember what Dean was like at school? Like, a bit – a bit weird?

LUKE. Yeah.

TAMSIN. He kinda got worse.

Pause.

Like, pretty bad.

I kind of have to look after him.

LUKE. Oh.

Right.

TAMSIN. I mean it's fine. It's fine really, I'm not being like 'feel sorry for me'.

LUKE. Okay.

TAMSIN. It's just that all that stuff's kind of, y'know. Top priority.

Pause.

Yeah.

Pause.

We – like, we used to live a bit further out, near Willen Park – this was years ago – and my mum got this letter through the door – some neighbour had posted them to everyone, warning about a boy who'd been hanging round the houses who looked 'menacing', that if we kept seeing him we should tell police. And we read the description and it – mentioned the hair.

LUKE. Oh man.

I get those looks too sometimes. If I'm out with my friends.

TAMSIN. Really?

LUKE *shrugs.*

LUKE. You can get why.

TAMSIN. But you're not –

Beat.

I dunno.

LUKE. It's crap. I know.

TAMSIN. I get why she thought that about him, though.

Cos he looks like a fucking weirdo, he comes off like the kind of person who mumbles to themselves on the street, you know?

LUKE. He can't help it though, can he?

TAMSIN. No. He can't. But I just.

Beat.

I dunno.

She searches for something else to change the subject.

Your mum's car is the one with the Jesus thing on the dashboard, right?

LUKE. Yeah.

TAMSIN. She always picks you up.

LUKE. Yeah. She does.

TAMSIN. That's really nice.

LUKE. I mean. Yeah.

She gets proper, proper lonely.

TAMSIN. Right.

LUKE. So.

Like she didn't say anything but I knew she'd've been sad if I went to Amsterdam. And now she keeps saying she don't want me to move away after college.

Pause.

Sorry, that was…

TAMSIN. Don't worry.

Pause.

LUKE. I should probably bounce.

TAMSIN *checks her watch.*

TAMSIN. Yeah. Me too.

She doesn't move.

I can't go in tomorrow.

LUKE. What, you / can't?

TAMSIN. No, I, I physically can, just.

I *can't.*

They're gonna counsel me.

LUKE. You make it sound like they're gonna shoot you or something. 'They're gonna *counsel* me!'

TAMSIN. You can laugh, you're making ninety per cent of your target.

LUKE. Oh yeah, ninety per cent of my target, I am *living the dream.*

Just don't argue with them.

TAMSIN. I know, I know. But it's like you said earlier, it's…

LUKE. Take it on the chin, think about other shit like –
I dunno – star life cycles, whatever – wait for them to stop talking, and just – go with whatever they say.

TAMSIN. That's what you'd do?

LUKE. Yeah.

I mean, in a few years that whole place's gonna be run by robots anyway. Just tell 'em what they wanna hear and move on, y'know?

Pause.

TAMSIN. How do I get what *I* want though?

LUKE. Um. Like to persuade someone, you use rhetorical questions.

And facts. And emotive language.

TAMSIN *grins.*

TAMSIN. You wanna write a letter to the DWP for me?

LUKE. If you'll spell-check it, sure.

Beat.

TAMSIN. Don't head off yet.

LUKE. It'll get cold really soon though.

Pause.

How far away is yours?

Scene Five

TAMSIN *and* LUKE *enter the flat.* DEAN *is in the bathroom, headphones in.*

TAMSIN *approaches and knocks the door gently.*

TAMSIN. Dean?

He can't hear, so she sends him a text message. He reads it and takes his headphones out.

DEAN. What?

TAMSIN. Everything okay?

DEAN. Fine.

TAMSIN. Yeah?

I've got a friend coming over, do you wanna say hi?

DEAN. Are they there?

TAMSIN. No –

She bats LUKE *away.*

– they're coming over in a few minutes.

LUKE *dutifully goes to wait outside.*

DEAN. Who is it?

TAMSIN. It's a boy from work who used to go to school with you. Luke Mburu. Not someone new.

Do you wanna come out and say hello when he arrives?

DEAN. I'm okay.

TAMSIN. Or – not right away, but you could come out when you feel ready? Before he leaves?

DEAN. How long is he staying?

TAMSIN. Dunno. Few hours I guess.

He remembers you.

Said you used to be good at history sources or something, I dunno.

DEAN *taps the tub of hair gel, psyching himself up to:*

DEAN. Okay.

He taps the tub some more.

TAMSIN. Yeah?

DEAN. Yeah.

TAMSIN. Awesome.

She begins to walk away from the door and then remembers to say:

Thanks.

TAMSIN *goes to open the door and lets* LUKE *back in. She speaks to him with her voice lowered, so* DEAN *doesn't hear.*

He's gonna come out in a moment.

Just don't – don't judge him, okay? If he does something that seems weird or his face makes weird expressions or – he can't help it. And like, don't mention people from Hartley or anything, cos it'll embarrass him –

LUKE. I know. Bruv, gimme some credit here.

TAMSIN. Sorry. I'm –

LUKE. Chill.

TAMSIN. Okay. Okay.

DEAN. Tamsin?

TAMSIN *goes into the bathroom.*

Can you...?

He indicates a small mirror on the counter.

TAMSIN. Sure.

She holds it up so DEAN *can see the back of his head, as he continues to work on his hair.*

Outside the bathroom, LUKE *looks at the Jobcentre forms on the table.*

He sees a few items of TAMSIN*'s clothing on the floor, and gingerly picks them up, looking at each one with a slight curiosity, feeling the texture. He folds them neatly over a chair.*

TAMSIN *and* DEAN *come out of the bathroom.* DEAN *is awkward throughout, but is making a lot of effort.*

DEAN. Hey.

LUKE. Hey.

Beat.

How's it going?

DEAN. Okay. It's going okay.

He reaches up to fiddle with his hair for a moment before stopping himself.

LUKE. We've just been at The Cricketers.

Beat.

DEAN. Right.

LUKE. Y'know it?

DEAN. No.

Beat.

LUKE. Me neither – I live in Conniburrow, so. Don't usually come by Oldbrook.

Beat.

DEAN. You, um. You work with Tamsin?

LUKE. Yeah. Yeah. We're master packers, aren't we?

TAMSIN. Speak for yourself.

LUKE *notices his shoes.*

LUKE. Tamsin, do you want me to take these off inside?

TAMSIN. It's fine.

LUKE. You sure? / Cos I can –

TAMSIN. Seriously, it's fine.

LUKE. Some people are – y'know. Weird about it. I'll go to someone's house and forget and then I can feel their eyes on my shoes like *arrgh*...

DEAN. It's not a big deal for us.

LUKE. Right. Okay. Sound.

Pause.

(*To* DEAN.) Hey. Do you remember how in Hartley there was all them words on the walls when you first walked in? You remember that?

DEAN. Yeah.

LUKE. What were they? Like, Commitment, Passion...

DEAN. Endeavour.

LUKE. Endeavour, yeah yeah yeah. At the warehouse – 'fulfilment centre', sorry – they've got the same thing. Not, like, the same words, but right near the door they've got like this massive slogan thing: Work. Enjoy. Improve.

Beat.

Dunno why I brought that up, it's – not really the same thing –

DEAN. It's marketing.

LUKE. Yeah. Yeah, it is. You're right.

DEAN. It's trying to make you feel like you're important.

LUKE. Yeah.

Beat.

Man, what the hell is that about, am I right though?

DEAN. Yeah. Weird.

LUKE. Yeah.

Pause.

DEAN. – I'm gonna go to bed, is that –

He looks at TAMSIN.

TAMSIN. Yeah, that's fine, you go.

Just before DEAN *has left the room,* TAMSIN *approaches him.* LUKE *may studiously look away.*

She still doesn't want to say anything in front of LUKE, *but clasps* DEAN*'s shoulder in a way that says 'well done'. He acknowledges it, but if he says anything it's too quiet to hear.*

He exits.

TAMSIN *turns back to* LUKE.

LUKE. I dunno why I said that stuff about my shoes –

TAMSIN. Nah, don't worry! Not gonna give you half a point for it or anything.

She laughs.

That was – like I don't think he's ready to, y'know, go for a pint with us or whatever, but –

I don't remember the last time he spoke to someone like that.

Just – yeah. Cheers.

LUKE. No problem.

He fist-bumps her.

Pause.

TAMSIN *notices the clothes on the chair, and snatches them up.*

TAMSIN. Sorry, place is a complete –

Smells them.

– need to go in the wash –

She puts them away hurriedly.

Sorry.

LUKE. I was gonna ask.

TAMSIN. Yeah?

LUKE. When I see a star, how do I know if it's dying?

This is really gonna distract me now.

TAMSIN. Well. You can't really see white dwarfs, they're too small.

LUKE. If you had a telescope though?

TAMSIN. It'd have to be, like, industrial level. I dunno much about it.

I'm sorry it's such a mess in here, I didn't think I'd –

LUKE. I've got a Kit Kat.

TAMSIN is confused. LUKE holds up the Kit Kat, then explains:

I just – found it in my pocket. D'you want some?

TAMSIN. – *obviously* yes. There's only one answer to that.

LUKE. Might be a bit melty though.

He breaks it in half, starts eating one stick and puts the other on the table.

I thought it was one with four sticks for a minute and got *really* excited, but this'll do for now.

TAMSIN *sits down and has a nibble of the second half.*

TAMSIN. They're really small, actually. I swear they're bigger than this.

Unless it's just *me* getting bigger.

LUKE. Nah, that's Chunkys.

TAMSIN. … actually, yeah.

Pause.

LUKE. Also… also also…

He fishes his phone out of his pocket, switches the screen on, and hands it over to TAMSIN.

Look.

TAMSIN. ... I can't get in, you've got a passcode.

LUKE. Oh – sorry –

TAMSIN. You and your fancy phone!

He takes it back and fiddles around with it.

LUKE. I was looking up – when I was outside – arrgh, why won't it come up...

He gives up and discards the phone.

Look – MKC does part-time courses. So you wouldn't have to be in all day every day. And it's like just round the corner. So you wouldn't have to leave Dean for hardly any time at all.

TAMSIN. Do they give you commission to recruit people or something?

LUKE. Course, I only do warehouse work as like my passion project, yeah?

TAMSIN. Cos, y'know, if this is a pyramid scheme you have to say.

Beat.

LUKE. You'd be fine. You wouldn't have to worry about not knowing anyone, cos I'd be there. I'd hook you up.

Pause.

TAMSIN. I'd have to ask for all this special treatment. Again.

LUKE. That's okay.

TAMSIN. I ask for so much already.

Pause.

And what would I even do afterwards?

LUKE. Dunno. Don't matter.

TAMSIN. It does matter.

LUKE. No, / cos

TAMSIN. If Dean's the same as he is now I won't be able to go and do any work, so what's the point?

LUKE. I just think you'd be *good* at it. I think you'd have fun. I think there's no point *not* doing it just cos you're scared / it won't work.

TAMSIN. Oh my god –

LUKE. You know I'm right, Taz.

Beat.

You could do one year, part time. Resit your GCSEs, they have like a special course for that. And then you can stop and look after Dean, right, or you might like get an A and then you can go and do part-time A levels or a BTEC or – whatever, I dunno, what would you wanna do?

Beat.

TAMSIN. Physics. Obviously.

And maybe like.

Law or something?

LUKE. Okay. I think I've still got my booklet thing at home, I'll bring it in for you, yeah?

Beat.

TAMSIN. Yeah.

LUKE. Okay.

Pause.

TAMSIN. Jesus, I haven't drunk in ages, I think the beer went right to my head.

LUKE. Eat something. Eat the Kit Kat.

She lies face-down on the floor, and then pushes herself up on her arms.

TAMSIN. Downward Dog.

Wait, no, Upward Dog.

LUKE. What you on about?

TAMSIN. Oh my god, my back feels so much better. Man.

She tries to transition into Downward Dog, and her socks make her slip.

Ow. Ow. Ah.

LUKE. You okay?

TAMSIN. Oh yeah, yeah.

She goes into Child's Pose.

(*As if she can't quite believe it.*) I'm gonna go to college.

After a few moments in Child's Pose – with LUKE *watching her – she lifts her head up and quickly checks her watch, before reassuming her position.*

LUKE. What time is it?

TAMSIN. Are you tired?

LUKE. No.

TAMSIN. Okay.

I'm gonna… wind this back…

Beat.

LUKE. What time is it now?

TAMSIN. Seven-thirty.

LUKE. Sick.

Beat.

Yo. Tamsinator.

Tasmania.

TAMSIN. … yeah?

LUKE. You gonna get off the floor or you gonna just stay there?

TAMSIN. … I'm gonna get off the floor.

She turns over to lie on her back.

In a moment.

Yoga's meant to be good for anxiety, right?

Yoga and smoking.

LUKE. Why you anxious?

TAMSIN. I'm not.

Pause. LUKE *joins* TAMSIN *on the floor.*

Are you going to sleep?

LUKE. I'm just closing my eyes.

Pause.

TAMSIN. Alabama... Alaska... Arizona... Arkansas...

LUKE. What you doing?

TAMSIN. Sending you to sleep.

It's a rhythm. It's calming.

LUKE. You're *so weird*, man.

TAMSIN (*protesting jokily*). I'm not!

LUKE. And I'm not tired.

TAMSIN. Yeah, I know, I know, you're just closing your eyes.

Pause.

I keep like. Thinking the post is gonna come.

LUKE. ... it's night-time.

TAMSIN. Yeah I know.

Beat.

LUKE *sits up.*

LUKE. Hey.

TAMSIN. Mm?

LUKE. You know that album with the – y'know, with the motorbike on the front?

TAMSIN. *Bat Out of Hell II.*

LUKE. Yeah, yeah. What was that song you sang?

TAMSIN. I didn't sing anything.

LUKE. No you did, you sang a line from one of them.

TAMSIN. 'I Would Do Anything For Love (But I Won't Do That)'?

LUKE. Yeah! Yeah yeah yeah. I'm gonna look it up on YouTube.

He fiddles with his phone for a moment.

TAMSIN. It's like twelve minutes long.

LUKE. ... ah, I'm out of data anyway.

Do me a clip of it.

TAMSIN. What?

LUKE. I'll get a beat going, you do vocals.

TAMSIN. No.

LUKE. But you said it was really good! Are you gonna leave me hanging?

TAMSIN. That's a really weird thing to ask, Luke.

LUKE. No it's not, I always do this with my friends, we're like famous for it at school. It's – it's like, a capella or whatever. It's good for you, yeah, it releases endorphins.

TAMSIN. If Dean doesn't have his headphones on it'll disturb him.

LUKE (*calls*). Dean?

No answer.

He's fine.

TAMSIN. I mean – it's still twelve minutes long but I could – I could give you a really condensed version.

LUKE. Sick.

TAMSIN. Um – okay.

Beat.

So I think it starts off with all these motorbike noises –

You have to imagine there's like hairspray and dry ice everywhere. It's 1993 but still basically feels like the eighties.

And then there's the piano riff that goes like –

She imitates the piano riff.

Do you know it now?

LUKE. Gimme some bars. First verse.

TAMSIN. Okay, it starts with – um –

She hums/sings her starting note.

Just, um, making sure –

It's like –

Doing her best Meat Loaf impression, she starts to sing.

The lyrics TAMSIN *chooses can be improvised – she might not remember all of them and substitute other words. It should definitely feel silly. When appropriate,* LUKE *could even join in somehow, singing or doing a drumbeat. She should include the penultimate line about 'screwing around', because after taking a moment to come down from the end of the song she says:*

Cos that's what it is, apparently. A long massive denial of cheating.

LUKE. If he takes that long to say he won't cheat on her, doesn't that mean that / he's gonna –

TAMSIN. He's probably gonna cheat on her? Yeah, maybe. That tends to be how it works.

TAMSIN *really slowly leans in and kisses* LUKE *on the cheek – but doesn't pull away.*

He turns his head and kisses her properly.

They're both nervous.

After a moment, TAMSIN *breaks away, almost laughs.*

LUKE. What? What's funny?

TAMSIN. No, nothing.

It's okay.

It's okay.

She kisses him again.

Scene Six

The fulfilment centre. The clock reads 17.29. TAMSIN's counter is at 370, with an average of 284.

The bell goes for the end of the day. TAMSIN stops, and notices her count.

TAMSIN. Wow.

The clock reads 17.36. The LEAD walks in briskly.

LEAD. Okay.

Pause. He catches his breath, sees her looking at the clock.

This won't take too long.

TAMSIN. I had the weirdest packages today.

LEAD....

TAMSIN. Like I had about five separate packages that were just bottles of gin. How weird is that? I guess cos it's Friday people are like 'Arrgh, I need a proper pick-me-up tonight.'

Beat.

LEAD. You know why we're having this meeting, right?

TAMSIN. Yep.

She realises she needs to say it.

Cos I've got two points.

LEAD. Yeah. And if you get another point we would, company policy means we would be obliged to release you from your current contract. So this is really your chance to think about your productivity, and improve it before it gets to that point.

Normally by now, after a couple of weeks, we would expect people to be making one hundred per cent of their original target, if not more.

So we need to look at why that's not happening and identify some immediate practical goals.

Can you identify any specific errors or choices that have contributed to your failure to meet standard productivity targets?

TAMSIN. Sometimes I get new cardboard cuts and that slows me down.

LEAD. Okay. Good. Can you think of any immediate practical goals that can increase your productivity in this regard?

TAMSIN. I get cuts when I rush, so.

LEAD. Well, one thing I've noticed is that when people are using the same hands to do the same things, hour on hour, they find carpal tunnel tends to set in and that increases the chance of injury. So you might want to consider changing what each hand is doing every so often.

Shall we put that down as a suggested objective?

TAMSIN. Okay.

LEAD. If you can think of something else we can put something else down.

TAMSIN. I just think changing hands would slow me down more. Cos I have to get into a rhythm to even make these numbers.

LEAD. Okay.

TAMSIN. But we can put that down.

LEAD. Sure.

He writes for a moment.

Do you consider that you possess any psychological barriers to your productivity?

TAMSIN. Sorry?

LEAD. I've got a space here if you can name any psychological barriers.

Pause.

TAMSIN. I try really hard.

LEAD. Just one line. Doesn't have to be negative.

TAMSIN. I got 370 just now.

LEAD. Do you want to do better?

TAMSIN. At the end of the day and everything.

LEAD. Tamsin. Do you want to do better?

TAMSIN....

Yeah.

LEAD. So let's say that what you struggle with is maintaining a positive attitude to your targets.

He writes.

Right – only a few more – do you believe that your only limitations are the limitations you set for yourself?

TAMSIN....

Do you want me to –

LEAD. In those words is fine.

TAMSIN. My only limitations are the limitations I set for myself.

LEAD. Okay. Right. Thanks.

The LEAD *writes a few sentences on his clipboard.*

Sign here –

She does, and he sets his clipboard aside.

Okay. Let's talk.

Beat.

You're with Welling, right? Your agency?

TAMSIN. Quartz.

LEAD. Right. Have they got anything else they could line up for you?

TAMSIN. Are you firing me?

LEAD. I'm just asking. Do they?

TAMSIN. No.

LEAD. You've checked?

TAMSIN. Obviously I have.

LEAD. And you're grateful, in this environment, for this job existing? And you being able to have it?

TAMSIN. ....yeah.

LEAD. Okay. So the priority is keeping it.

TAMSIN. For now. Yeah.

LEAD. Sure.

But whatever's going on for you out there, whatever people are saying to you, you have to leave it at the door.

TAMSIN. But it's – I wouldn't care if it was just hard work. That's fine, I can work hard, whatever. It's not like I think I'm too good for this cos I don't.

LEAD. Good.

TAMSIN. It's all the other stuff.

When you assume I'm gonna steal things, that makes me *want* to, cos y'know, why not, not like you're gonna trust me either way, right?

LEAD. Do you think I'm important? You really think they wouldn't fire me in a second if they had a reason?

I have to be twice as professional. I *have* to be able to say yes I timed their toilet breaks, yes I tried all of the above tactics when they were falling short on target, yes I did everything I could.

And this has never been a stopgap for me.

TAMSIN. I know.

LEAD. I've got a daughter who grows out of her clothes and school shoes every year. You know how much that costs?

TAMSIN. Yeah. That's…

LEAD. Look. There are people at the top of this. And as far as they can see, they're doing the right thing. They don't see it from this – angle, they don't see it from here, because they just get numbers in the red and they work out how to put them in the black. And it will be the same anywhere else you go.

So you have to remind yourself that no one is targeting you. None of this is personal.

TAMSIN. They wouldn't do all of this if they didn't think we'd skive off at any moment.

LEAD. Honestly? I don't think they think about you at all.

I mean – do you think about where your clothes come from? How much that child earned?

He goes back to paperwork. TAMSIN *doesn't move until he notices she's still there.*

That's it. You can go.

TAMSIN. Can I come in tomorrow?

The LEAD *makes some calculations in his head.*

LEAD. We've already covered tomorrow, I'm afraid.

Quartz should text you to confirm but I'll probably need you back 7 a.m. Sunday. Okay?

Beat.

TAMSIN. Yeah, sure.

LEAD. You can spend some time at home.

TAMSIN. Yeah.

LEAD. Is your brother disputing the decision?

TAMSIN. Sorry?

LEAD. His Fit for Work decision.

Is it getting looked at?

TAMSIN. – yeah. Yeah, we've sent off for a reconsideration, so.

LEAD. Good luck. I'll keep my fingers crossed for him.

Beat.

TAMSIN. Thanks.

Scene Seven

TAMSIN *lights the tealight on the table, and sits down, resting her chin on her hands and fixing her gaze on the candle.*

She might put her hands together, as if in prayer – or whisper urgently to herself.

Slowly the room's light returns, but is still quite low when a decisive 'thunk' comes, loud enough that the item feels like it could have been dropped from the sky.

TAMSIN *springs awake immediately, somehow knowing what has arrived.*

She collects a large brown envelope, sets it on the kitchen table and stares at it.

She takes a deep breath and opens the envelope. Out of it come numerous documents – photocopies of sick notes, a WCA report, various letters of correspondence.

TAMSIN *sifts through all of these on the kitchen table until she finds the most recent one. She reads it.*

It's the wrong news.

TAMSIN *searches for her phone – it's somewhere underneath all the papers.*

She composes a text, sits down, and buries her head in her arms.

DEAN *emerges from his room, in his nightclothes and a hat, holding his phone.*

DEAN. Did we not get it?

Pause.

Are we gonna appeal?

Pause. As if she didn't hear him:

Are we gonna appeal?

TAMSIN *slowly sits up.*

TAMSIN. It says we can't.

DEAN. What?

TAMSIN. At the bottom. 'You must seek a mandatory reconsideration before you can appeal a decision.'

DEAN. I thought we did. I thought this was a mandatory reconsideration.

TAMSIN. I think it's…

There was some reason they couldn't. Hang on.

'…your adviser's letter dated 6th August requesting a mandatory reconsideration… Before this can be undertaken, we have to *review* our decision and provide you with an explanation of our reasons…

'We attempted to contact you by telephone on the 19th August and did not receive an answer…

'This means we have been unable to proceed with a mandatory reconsideration…'

Um…

Ah – 'We have taken your adviser's disputes into account in our review, but it must be noted that the Health-Care Professional is considered to be impartial and medically informed…

We accept that you have difficulties that… blah blah blah… but consider that said health conditions do not limit your functional abilities sufficiently for work for Employment and Support Allowance purposes'

Pause.

Look. Didn't even put a dot at the end of that, that's how much time and effort they're putting in. Look.

DEAN. Maybe they're dyslexic.

TAMSIN. I'm not gonna make excuses for them.

I don't know what we do now. I.

Pause.

DEAN *is tapping on the table.*

When he feels TAMSIN *looking, he takes his hands away from the table and sits on them.*

We're gonna make it without them. Okay? Fuck them. Fuck them and their fucking review and reconsideration and all that bollocks, I don't fucking care, we can do this ourselves, we can – I can work, and – this – this isn't fucking *fair.*

I can't keep doing this.

I can't. I'm so fucking *tired.*

And you just –

You act like you don't even *miss her*

Pause.

DEAN. I don't wanna talk about that.

TAMSIN. No. Obviously not. Obviously you don't fucking want to.

DEAN. It's too –

TAMSIN. What?

DEAN *tries to say something and can't find the words.*

What?! What is it?

DEAN *goes into the bathroom, and closes the door.*

He takes up one of his pots of hair gel.

He steels himself, and then throws it into the bathroom bin.

He does the same thing with his comb – his scissors – all his pots of gel – then takes the rubbish bag and goes to put it in the larger kitchen bin. Every single time he throws something away it's agony for him.

You don't have / to

DEAN. Shut up shut up I just need –

After putting the bag into the bin, he forces himself to sit down again, and sits on his hands.

He remembers something, and goes into his bedroom.

He brings out two more pots of gel, that haven't even been opened. He bins them, and then sits on his hands again.

Are you at work tomorrow?

TAMSIN. I think so.

DEAN. Oh. Okay.

After, could you help me with –

I'm going to try and stop with the, with the…

I might cut it tomorrow. So I can't do anything.

TAMSIN. Are you sure?

DEAN. Yeah.

TAMSIN. Okay, if you're – you know, if you're positive about this.

DEAN. I want to try and cut it out.

He tries to smile at his own joke.

Um.

Just make things easier. Cos I know it's all stupid. I know that.

Beat.

Is that the right thing to do?

TAMSIN. I only want you to do what you're comfortable with.

DEAN. I'm comfortable with this.

TAMSIN. On a scale of one to –

DEAN. Ten. I'm ten comfortable with it.

It'll be easier when the days get shorter.

Cos I can try and go outside more when it's dark, when it's not...

Yeah.

Beat.

Can you –

TAMSIN. What?

DEAN. Cos I know they're still there, can you – (*Gestures to mean 'take them out'.*)

TAMSIN. Okay.

She takes the bin liner out and opens the front door.

Um. It's Saturday, so.

DEAN *looks at her, not understanding.*

It's gonna get collected tomorrow.

DEAN. That's fine.

TAMSIN. You sure? Cos then they're – [gone]

DEAN. I don't want to be able to go and get them.

TAMSIN. Okay.

Last chance...?

DEAN *nods.*

TAMSIN *leaves with the bin liner.*

Scene Eight

TAMSIN *gets* DEAN *out of bed. He puts his hat on, and refuses to let her help him.*

TAMSIN. Let me.

He shakes his head, and puts on his clothes himself, tapping them all the while. It's obviously difficult and distressing for him.

Come on –

DEAN. Shut up / I'm trying to –

TAMSIN. Don't tell me to shut up.

DEAN. – just, *please*, I'm trying, okay?

Pause as he finishes.

TAMSIN. Are we gonna have a good day?

DEAN. Yep.

TAMSIN. Are you sure?

DEAN. Just gimme a bit of space.

She does.

I'm gonna have a good day.

TAMSIN. Do you feel calm?

DEAN. Yeah.

I don't want you to be late, you should go.

He is tapping in rhythms of four the whole time.

TAMSIN. Please eat something today, okay?

DEAN. I will.

TAMSIN. Even if it's not what I made you, it's fine if you just want toast or something.

DEAN. I don't / eat

TAMSIN. I know you don't eat bread, it was just, it's an example.

Can you promise me?

DEAN. What?

TAMSIN. That you'll eat something.

DEAN. I already said.

Are you gonna go?

I don't want you to be late.

TAMSIN. ... All right.

I'll get back soon as I can.

(*Getting as close to him as he will let her.*) You're okay. You can do this, yeah?

TAMSIN *exits.* DEAN *is left continuing to tap in these patterns of four even after she's left.*

With nothing to focus on, he begins to go into the bathroom, and then stops himself. Tries tapping the kitchen table.

He goes into the bathroom, taps the sink, and runs some water over his hands. He almost wets his hair with it a few times, but manages to stop himself, his hand stuttering.

He dries his hands, returns to the kitchen, and taps the table. Getting stuck on a loop of tapping, he then sits on his hands.

He gets a can of soup from a cupboard, empties it into a pan, and then lights the hob.

He manages to stop himself going back to the bathroom by tapping on the kitchen countertop, but eventually it becomes less effective.

Eventually he goes back to the bathroom and wets his hands again.

He forces himself to dry his hands before he can let himself put the water in his hair, and goes back into the kitchen.

He's so distracted that without thinking he touches the pan with his left palm and burns himself.

He tries not to touch it with the other hand, but the need to complete the pattern is obvious – his hand stutters in mid-air. He tries to physically restrain himself but it's agony.

The lights go down the moment he burns his right palm.

Scene Nine

The fulfilment centre. The clock reads 15.21. TAMSIN's count is at 91, with an average of 258 per hour.

The LEAD *approaches* TAMSIN.

LEAD. We need to have a chat.

Stop packing, I've only got a moment and I need you to pay attention.

She stops.

Don't tell anyone about this, okay?

TAMSIN. ...okay?

LEAD. Can you promise me that?

TAMSIN. I promise.

LEAD. It's really really important you don't say anything, this is jobs-on-the-line sort of stuff.

TAMSIN. I won't.

LEAD. Okay. Now – none of this is set in stone and I'm not making any guarantees. But – we've got a few permanent positions coming up. Same as what you do now, but –

Actually, keep packing. I don't want any gaps.

She starts again.

I can't give one of them to you while you're making seventy-per-cent target.

TAMSIN. Okay.

LEAD. You understand that, right? It'd look sketchy, and it's not worth my job if someone decided to investigate. But you've been here nearly three weeks – in nine weeks, if you're still here, managing one hundred per cent target, and not got any more points, I'll have some evidence to put in the form and your previous points'll have dropped off, so it'll all check out okay. And then we can put your salary up to the permanent rate, and your hours would be contracted.

TAMSIN....

LEAD. Like I said, I can't promise anything. And you *have* to keep your head down. But if you do.

TAMSIN. Do you get to choose?

LEAD. I can make recommendations.

TAMSIN. Okay.

Beat.

LEAD. Don't rush to thank me or anything.

TAMSIN. No no, that's –

LEAD. I mean, do you want it?

TAMSIN....

Yeah. I do.

Thank you. Genuinely.

LEAD. Sure.

Numbers up, okay?

The LEAD *exits.*

The clock reads 17.10. LUKE *comes by with a trolley of totes.*

LUKE. Yo yo yo.

TAMSIN. Hi.

TAMSIN *just keeps packing as he speaks.*

LUKE. Tried to swing by earlier but they're riding me really hard today. Worst leaving present in the world.

Wagwan?

TAMSIN. This your last day?

LUKE. Yeah.

TAMSIN. When does college start?

LUKE. Tomorrow.

TAMSIN. Wow. Wow, that's – quick.

LUKE. Yeah. Well, they're 'letting me go' anyway cos I been here twelve weeks – I was gonna say like 'Oh so you're cancelling now the free trial's ending?' but I didn't think they'd get the joke.

I found the booklet, though, my mum's gonna bring it when she picks me up.

TAMSIN. ...thanks.

Beat.

LUKE. You okay?

TAMSIN. Do you know what you're starting out with, have you got your, um, your timetable yet?

LUKE. It's like... leadership and teamwork and things.

TAMSIN. Cool. Awesome.

You're gonna be really busy, aren't you?

LUKE. I mean. I guess, but I'll still have / time for –

TAMSIN. Not, not in a bad way, but you will.

(*Mumbling.*) You should get on, they'll be... pissed off...

LUKE. I'm leaving tomorrow, don't make a difference now.

TAMSIN. I'm not, though.

LUKE. Not what?

TAMSIN. Leaving.

Beat.

LUKE. You're staying on?

TAMSIN. Hopefully. Yeah.

LUKE. Seriously?

> TAMSIN *can't bring herself to answer for a split second too long.*

Why? Did / the

TAMSIN. Luke. Don't. Don't do this.

LUKE. I'm just asking.

TAMSIN. Thing is. This – *this* doesn't matter.

> You're gonna be fine, you really are. Don't worry about all the other crap, yeah? Tell me you're not gonna worry.

LUKE. ....okay.

TAMSIN. You're gonna be really, really, *really* good.

> So, it's – it's okay. I promise.
>
> I'm gonna – my average is already shit today, so...

She starts packaging again.

LUKE looks at her for a while, and eventually pushes his trolley away. Once she can't hear him any more, TAMSIN *stops for a moment and steadies her breathing.*

Trying to force herself back into her routine, she packs a few items, and then finds that her next order is a massive tub of hair gel – industrial size. The gel is the same design or brand as every single one of Dean's pots.

She looks around for a moment, as if wondering whether someone is playing a trick on her.

She begins to package the tub of gel, her hands slightly unsteady.

She's about to put it on the conveyer belt, and falters, clutching the package to her chest – but then looks at the scoreboard. Her average has dropped.

She taps it twice with her left hand and twice with her right hand, and puts it on the conveyer belt.

The clock reads 17.30. The LEAD *approaches.*

Can I go?

LEAD. I'm sorry?

TAMSIN. I know what you said, and I swear I'm gonna keep my head down. I'm gonna do better than today, I absolutely completely promise I am, I just I need to go *right now.*

LEAD. ...this isn't gonna happen again, all right?

TAMSIN *tries to shrug off her orange vest and boots as quickly as possible.*

Give it to me.

Breathe. Okay?

Go.

She does.

Scene Ten

DEAN *is sitting in the bathroom, wearing his hat, and continually tapping with his fingertips.*

TAMSIN *enters, dropping her bag, and calling out immediately:*

TAMSIN. Dean?

Are you okay?

She knocks on the bathroom door – but urgently this time.

Dean??

Pause.

DEAN *slides the bolt of the door, but doesn't open it.*

TAMSIN *goes into the bathroom.*

She notices his hands.

Oh god…

They're both burned, in exactly the same place. TAMSIN *touches one of the burns for a moment –* DEAN *winces and recoils.*

Sorry – sorry.

Put them under some water.

She takes hold of his hands again, and tries to put them under the tap. He jerks back.

DEAN. No –

TAMSIN. Dean, come on. Put them under the water.

He struggles and won't let her.

Come on.

Look, okay, tap for me.

She lets go of his hands and offers her own palms as a surface for him. He taps them three times with his left hand and three times with his right.

She tries to take her hands back but he grips on to them.

Again? Okay.

He taps her palms three times with his left hand, three times with his right.

She gently takes his hands again and puts them under the cold tap.

See? Doesn't sting.

Pause.

What happened?

DEAN *shrugs.*

What happened?

DEAN. I…

Pause. She waits.

I panicked.

TAMSIN. Why?

Pause.

Cos you didn't have your gel, and all your – ?

DEAN *nods.*

How did it happen?

Pause.

What were you doing?

DEAN. Cooking.

TAMSIN. But I made you food.

DEAN. Take my mind off not being able to…

He trails off.

TAMSIN. Do your hair?

DEAN. …yeah.

Pause.

TAMSIN. Both of them?

DEAN. I tried not to, but – after I did one, I.

I did try not to.

I just.

TAMSIN. Do you want me to take you to A&E?

He shakes his head.

I think we should go.

He shakes his head more vigorously.

DEAN. 'm fine.

TAMSIN. I don't know how to treat this, I…

DEAN. I'm not going outside.

Pause.

TAMSIN. Do we have any cling film left?

DEAN doesn't answer, but TAMSIN goes into the kitchen and searches through the drawers until she finds a roll. She returns to the bathroom and shows DEAN.

Is this okay?

She tears off a piece.

I'm just gonna wrap it over the...

Gently, she takes DEAN's hand from under the tap, turns the tap off, and covers one burn in a layer of cling film.

DEAN. Is that what you're meant to do?

TAMSIN. Yeah. I think so. Someone told me.

Is that...?

DEAN tests out his hand, bending it slightly. It's painful.

Don't bend it there, just –

She takes his hand back and unbends it, before starting to wrap the other one.

I was thinking – a few days ago – it was really sunny on my way in and I like started thinking about this time when – I don't know how old we were, but it was the summer holidays – and you were sitting on the doorstep – and I was listening to that Discman we had.

So I must have been. What. Ten?

And I took my headphones off and asked what you were doing and you were memorising all the states of America. And I ended up doing it as well. And we just spent – it must have been weeks – testing each other again and again on being able to recite them. And write them down alphabetically. And we did it right before bed every single night. And Mum got completely sick of us. I don't even remember why we did it, but. It was kind of amazing.

Why the states? Why not the counties? I don't know any of the counties.

Keeping his hands straight, DEAN *taps the edge of the sink with his fingertips – four times with the left and four times with the right.*

Slowly, DEAN *walks out of the bathroom, out of the kitchen, into his room.*

TAMSIN *watches from her position on the bathroom floor.*

After a moment, DEAN *opens his door, and addresses* TAMSIN *from there.*

DEAN. Are you all right?

Long pause.

TAMSIN. Did you order some more gel?

DEAN. Yeah. I thought I should probably…

Pause.

TAMSIN. No, it's, it's fine.

DEAN. I got the cheapest one I could find.

TAMSIN. I know.

DEAN. Cos I know we can't –

TAMSIN. I know.

Good stuff.

When DEAN *speaks, the words sound foreign and unfamiliar to him.*

DEAN. Do you want a cup of tea?

Pause.

TAMSIN. Yeah. Thanks.

They both come into the kitchen.

Being careful and awkward, hampered by his hands, DEAN *goes to put the kettle on to boil.*

He gets a mug ready, and puts a teabag inside.

After pouring the water, he goes to hand it over to TAMSIN – *before taking it back and putting it in the microwave.*

While waiting for the microwave to count down, TAMSIN *notices the tealight on the kitchen table.*

She considers it for a moment, searches for some matches, and lights it.

End.

untitled f*ck m*ss s**gon play
(srsly, this is not the title)
(oh well)

kimber lee

'It is particularly sad and ironic that this controversy should surround a piece of theatre such as *Miss Saigon*, a tragic love story in which a young woman sacrifices her life to ensure that her Amerasian son may find a better life in America.'

Cameron Mackintosh

'Some people who are irritated by these criticisms of *Miss Saigon*'s enduring popularity will say, It's only a show, nothing more.

But the enjoyment of the show's fantasy is precisely why the show matters. Fantasy cannot be dismissed as mere entertainment, especially when we keep repeating the fantasy...

Racism and sexism are not incompatible with art... Our enjoyment of a work of art does not mean that the work cannot be racist or sexist, or that our enjoyment does not come from a deep-seated well of derogatory images of Asians and Asian women.

The unsettling paradox here is that we can indeed love and desire people whom we see in completely racist and sexist ways. That is the real, unintended universal truth of *Miss Saigon.*'

Viet Thanh Nguyen

KIMBER LEE

Kimber Lee's plays include *the water palace* (Susan Smith Blackburn Special Commendation), *to the yellow house* (La Jolla Playhouse), *untitled f*ck m*ss s**gon play* (inaugural Bruntwood Prize International Award, world premiere Royal Exchange Theatre/Young Vic, UK), *saturday* (Colorado New Play Summit), *tokyo fish story* (South Coast Rep, TheatreWorks/SV, Old Globe), *brownsville song (b-side for tray)* (Humana Festival, LCT3, Long Wharf Theatre, Philadelphia Theatre Company, Seattle Rep, Moxie Theatre, Shotgun Players), and *different words for the same thing* directed by Neel Keller (Center Theatre Group).

She has developed work with Lark Play Development Center, Ground Floor/Berkeley Rep, Page 73, O'Neill National Playwrights Conference, Hedgebrook, Ojai Playwrights Conference, Bay Area Playwrights Festival, ACT Theatre/Seattle, Premiere Stages, and Magic Theatre. She is a Lark Playwrights Workshop Fellow, Dramatists Guild Fellow, member of Ma-Yi Writers Lab, the inaugural winner 2019 Bruntwood Prize International Award, 2020/2021/2023 Susan Smith Blackburn Prize Finalist, Edgerton New Play Award, Herb Alpert Award in the Arts, Ruby Prize, PoNY Fellowship, Hartford Stage New Voices Fellowship, Hodder Fellowship, Helen Merrill Award, and Hermitage Artist Retreat Fellow. MFA: UT Austin.

Introduction
Kimber Lee, 2025

Receiving the inaugural Bruntwood Prize International Award in 2019 gave me the warmest welcome to the UK that I could have ever imagined. Connecting with so many UK theatre workers and having my play introduced to them through the Bruntwood process was an incredible gift that led directly to so many new opportunities as well as one of the most beautiful collaborations I've ever experienced, working with director Roy Alexander Weise on the world premiere production of my play at the Royal Exchange Theatre and the Young Vic in 2023.

In this industry, it can be challenging for playwrights to be seen at all, let alone have their work read and carefully considered. If you are a Global Majority writer, it can be even more difficult to be visible beyond a checked-box tokenism. What the Bruntwood Prize did for me in the UK was to give me a little boost up, so that my work had a chance to speak for itself and be heard and engaged with in a meaningful way. The great care for the plays that come through the Bruntwood process, the actions they take to engage with the winners to explore ways to bring their work to production, whether at the Royal Exchange or elsewhere – this commitment is also what sets them apart. And this means so much to a playwright, because we write to be performed, to be inhabited by actors, directors and designers, and received by an audience.

I'm always going to be grateful to the Bruntwood Prize community, and especially to every reader and every person on staff who worked so long and hard on the rigorous, meticulously organised selection process. Thank you with all my heart for your dedication and passion, for believing in new plays and the people who work so hard to write them.

*untitled f*ck m*ss s**gon play* was first produced by the Royal Exchange Theatre, Factory International for Manchester International Festival, Young Vic and Headlong, and performed at the Royal Exchange Theatre, Manchester, on 24 June 2023, with the following cast:

AFI/GORO	Jeff D'Sangalang
ROSIE/CIO CIO	Lourdes Faberes
EVELYN/RICHARDS	Jennifer Kirby
KIM	Mei Mac
NARRATOR/BRENDA	Rochelle Rose
CLARK	Tom Weston-Jones

Director	Roy Alexander Weise
Designer	Khadija Raza
Costume Designer	Loren Elstein
Lighting Designer	Joshua Pharo
Composer	Ruth Chan
Sound Designer	Giles Thomas

The production transferred to the Young Vic Theatre, London, on 18 September 2023.

untitled f*ck m*ss s**gon play was first written and developed with the support of the Lark Play Development Center in NYC in 2017 and in 2018 the Ground Floor at Berkeley Repertory Theatre.

The play was also developed during a residency at the Eugene O'Neill Theater Center's National Playwrights Conference in 2019. (Wendy Goldberg, Artistic Director; Preston Whiteway, Executive Director.)

The play also received a workshop at the 2019 Ojai Playwrights Conference.

Characters

KIM, *female. Asian American. Early twenties (or can pass for early twenties)*
ROSIE/CIO-CIO, *female. Asian American. Forties–fifties (or can pass for forties–fifties)*
AFI/GORO, *male. Asian American. Twenties–thirties*
CLARK, *male. White. Twenties–early thirties*
EVELYN/RICHARDS, *female. White. Twenties–early thirties*
NARRATOR/BRENDA, *female. Actor of color. Thirties*

And THE BAND. *Is there a live band? Maybe.*

Note on Text

Stage directions in parentheses are not read aloud.

Actually anything in parentheses is not read aloud, though the NARRATOR will read all stage directions that are not in parentheses.

The NARRATOR speaks through a microphone.

Translations in square brackets can be projected as subtitles, or spoken by the NARRATOR, or both.

1906

Date of the NYC premiere of Puccini's opera, third draft, Madama Butterfly *at the Metropolitan Opera.*

NARRATOR (*on a mic*). Lights up on a muddy road through a muddy village, which, though muddy, is also misty and mysterious.

There's music – a swelling overture of some kinda vaguely shakuhachi/shamisen type of thing with a Western vibe laid over the top for dramatic tension.

Peasants shuffle to and fro, some might have baskets on their heads; they gesticulate, like peasants do.

KIM enters, she is young, virginal, frightened, plucky, hopeful, noble, dirt poor but very clean otherwise, and has really great skin.

A massive horn blast from a steamship arriving in the nearby harbor shakes the air.

The peasants gape at the sky in awe and exclaim unintelligibly: (*Like maybe they just mutter the same word over and over, like 'ohayo gozaimasu' for instance.*)

Another blast from the ship (*closer, louder*) the peasants exclaim and scurry.

KIM tries to scurry, takes one step, and falls down.

KIM. Oh!

NARRATOR. ROSIE enters, an older peasant woman wearing the standard Asian peasant pajama set but with a Western vest over the top and a pair of bright-red cowboy boots.

(*She drags* KIM *to her feet.*)

ROSIE. Kim!! The Americans are here! It's our chance to escape this cesspool of a country!

KIM. What?

ROSIE. Don't you want to go to America?

KIM. Uh –

ROSIE. It's our only hope!

KIM. Oh my god! Really? But I don't have any money for a ticket!

NARRATOR. ROSIE slaps KIM's ass.

ROSIE. That's your ticket right there, my little cherry blossom!

KIM (*shy, embarrassed*). Oh, Mother!

ROSIE. Just follow my lead and we'll wave sayonara to this shitstain of a village and be on our way to a new life in America where there are equal rights for women! Stand up straight, shoulders back, tits up – here comes your future!

NARRATOR. (*They stand at the side of the road.*) ROSIE arranges KIM's clothes and hair for the sexiest effect.

KIM stands quietly, like a doll being dressed.

(*Lights shift*), a romantic haze floods the stage as:

CLARK enters.

He is tall, he is boyish and rugged and handsome and clearly does weights, cardio and High Intensity Interval Training at least four times a week – he looks like he could lift KIM up and break her in half over his knee, but he also exudes a very attractive manly gentleness and social-consciousness which we can discern in the way he regards with revulsion the oily conniving peasant men scurrying around him, trying to sell him their daughters.
The scurrying peasants part like the sea as CLARK strides through the village.

(*Text in square brackets should be projected as subtitles, or spoken by NARRATOR, or both.*)

CLARK. Maki. [Greetings.]
Kimono sushi ohayo ichi ni san. [We come in peace from the West.]

Maguro! Saba! [We bring news of the modern world to you!]
Kyoto dojo katana – [We hope to open trade and avert any
conflict with –]

NARRATOR. His eyes meet KIM's across the scurrying crowd.
She lowers her eyes modestly, ROSIE grins and pulls her
over to CLARK.

ROSIE. Welcome to our humble village, most Number One
American Son.

CLARK. Onigiri. Sake. Hashi…? [Thanks. I'm happy to be
here. And this is…?]

ROSIE. This is Kim.
Would you like to come over for dinner?

CLARK. Honto go! [Would I ever!]
Okonomiyaki. [Say eight?]

ROSIE. Maybe earlier – at six?

CLARK. Kurosawa. [Wonderful.]

NARRATOR. He gently lifts KIM's chin, her eyes flutter shyly.

CLARK. Fujisan momotaro. [I can't wait.]

NARRATOR. He bows over her hand, kissing it respectfully yet
also kinda sexy-sexy like.
KIM's eyes go wide, she's never felt man-lips on her skin
and it awakens something inside her… something *sexy* like.

(CLARK *smiles and strides away, the villagers murmuring
around him.*)

KIM (*holding the hand* CLARK *kissed*). What is happening?

NARRATOR. ROSIE cackles (*delighted*) whips out a shamisen
and plays an upbeat song as the scene shifts – maybe
something like 'Proud Mary', the Tina Turner version but
with a shamisen.

ROSIE. You are my golden ticket, girlie –

KIM. What? But…

ROSIE. – the way out of this stinking mudhole!

UNTITLED F*CK M*SS S**GON PLAY   423

I mean do you really want to stay in this hut for the rest of your life?

KIM. Uh –

ROSIE. What other possible future is there for you?

KIM. I had so many dreams.

ROSIE. Psshh – what dreams? You can't eat dreams.

KIM. Well, but there was that one about having some kind of rice delivery business, I was going to call it 'Rice Now' but… but then the rice famine happened and the investors pulled out, so…

ROSIE. So… no dreams.

KIM. Goro the fishmonger's son has offered to marry me.

ROSIE. Goro the fishmonger's son is not a dream.

KIM. He likes my rice delivery idea. He was gonna do a fish side to go with it: 'Rice Now, Fish Later'.

ROSIE. Listen to your mama, you foolish girl. You gotta learn how to defer gratification. If you do your duty, you will have a rice delivery *empire* in America. And fishmongery? Really? Nothing gets that stink off you at the end of the day, trust me.

NARRATOR. GORO scurries past with a giant basket of fish on his head, leaving a strong smell of fish in his wake.

GORO. Hey Kim!

KIM. Hey Goro!

GORO. The mackerel are running today! I'll save one for ya!

ROSIE. Kim. My girl. Be better than Goro the fishmonger's son. Be better than all of this.

KIM. I mean…

ROSIE. Why have the gods made you so beautiful? For nothing?

KIM. I mean –

ROSIE. It's so you can go to America! Shake that tight ass and we will rise up from the mud and fishy smell of this place!

NARRATOR. (KIM *looks at her hand where* CLARK *kissed it.*) A waft of romantic CLARK-haze across the stage, KIM looks off into the distance, bravely.

KIM. Very well. I will do what I must do, Mother.

ROSIE. Great, now go take a bath. And be sure you get *everything* clean.

KIM (*shy, embarrassed*). Mother!

ROSIE. You never know where the night will take you, it's best to be prepared. I left some cherry blossom soap by the tub and we don't have a razor but I gave my fish knife a good going over with Kenji's sharpening stone, so, you know… be thorough.

NARRATOR. KIM bows, exits.
ROSIE cackles and plays the shamisen again, perhaps 'Celebration' by Kool and The Gang.

(*She sings and whoever is helping with the set change sings along.*)

DANCE BREAK.

Happy villagers, happy in their simple village way.

ROSIE *and others*. Ceee-leh-brate good times come on! duh nuh nuh nuh, nuh nuh, nuh nuh…

(ROSIE *and the others continue to sing the first refrain and verse of 'Celebration'.*)

Meanwhile, a tiny hut-like dwelling has emerged…

So the interior of the hut is Asian in the sense that there is probably a lot of bamboo that has been distressed with a dark-brown stain to make a properly dark, mysterious locale; might be some noren curtains in the doorway, printed with bamboo patterns; cushions on the floor (*no chairs*) a low table, lots of oil lamps and candles.

Maybe the whole place looks like Pier 1 and Cost Plus had a three-way with Ikea and this hut is their bastard mixed-race child.

(ROSIE *fluffs up a futon bed nearby, exits.*)

(*Lights shift to*) evening, after dinner.

CLARK, KIM, and ROSIE sit around the low table, sipping after-dinner tea.
KIM is decked out in full kimono with her hair done up high and tight, full of flowers and sparkly ornaments.
CLARK can't keep his eyes off her, she keeps her eyes modestly lowered.

CLARK. Furikake. [Your hair looks really nice.]

NARRATOR. KIM covers her mouth and smiles, with a little shy shake of her head.
ROSIE brings a plate of mochi to the table (*grins*) offers a gold paper crown to CLARK.

CLARK. Desho? [What's this?]

ROSIE (*sneaky grin*). Dessert hat.

CLARK. Sashimi! [How fun!]

NARRATOR. ROSIE puts a golden cloth on KIM's head, hands them each a mochi, directs them to feed a bite to each other, which they do.

ROSIE. And I now pronounce you...
(*Whispers.*)... husband and wife!

CLARK. Tataki? [What was that?]

ROSIE. Mochi is yummy!

CLARK. Ah, dojo, dojo! [Yes, it is!]

(ROSIE *stretches and yawns elaborately.*)

ROSIE. Welp! I'm all tuckered out, I think I'll turn in. Enjoy your mochi, kids.

CLARK. Daiko, Rosie. [Thank you, Rosie.]
Yamamoto. [Goodnight.]

NARRATOR. ROSIE leaves, but we see her eyes peeking through the bamboo wall.
CLARK inches closer to KIM, who brings out a fan and hides her face shyly.

CLARK. Pachinko. [Don't be afraid.]

KIM. Oh... hee-hee.

CLARK. Kim.

KIM. Yes?

CLARK (*savoring her name on his tongue like a fine port wine*). Kiiiiiiiimmmmmm...
KimKimKim...

KIM. ...yes?

CLARK (*points at himself*). Clark Jackson Lincoln Garfield.

KIM. Coo-lah-rak... Jehck-uh-som-rinkuh... Guh-rah-ruh-feeduh.

(*He laughs, charmed.*)

CLARK. Sakura tatami obi. [You have captured me with your maiden's heart.]

KIM. Okay.

CLARK. Shohei ohtani. [Look at me.]

NARRATOR. She meets his gaze shyly, he gently touches her cheek.

CLARK. O-bun furoshiki. [You are like the moon and stars.]

KIM (*fluttery, flattered*). Ohhh...

NARRATOR. Her eyes flutter bashfully, he grasps her chin. They gaze at each other, the sexual tension building.

CLARK. Gomi leah nanako, tabi yo, hayao miyazaki. [You fill the sky, my sky, your silvery light.]

KIM. And you are the sun, warming me with your kind, round American eyes, and your – wow, you are really the largest man I've ever seen up close, your chest, your arms, your –

UNTITLED F*CK M*SS S**GON PLAY 427

NARRATOR. He presses his man parts onto her lady parts.

KIM. – whoa.

NARRATOR. He kisses her passionately, her shyness seems to have worn off because *dayum* – she's a natural at the exotic sexy-sexy stuff.

CLARK. You taste like moonlight and jasmine and mystery!

KIM. You taste like freedom!

NARRATOR. They make out, rolling around on the cushions – (*At one point she thumps at his arm, he stops, she pants heavily.*)

KIM. Sorry. Couldn't breathe there for a second.

CLARK. Yes this feeling is so powerful –

KIM. – no your arm was on my windpipe. Anyway. Carry on.

NARRATOR. More making out, he stands with her in his arms like she is a twig, carries her to the futon where they continue to get it on.

(*Lights dim, and*) ROSIE pulls down a curtain around the bed.
She whips out her shamisen and plays a slow-jam version of 'The Rhythm of the Night' by DeBarge.
(*Lights fade to black.*)
An inexplicably and overwhelmingly loud, long blast from the steamship's horn – is there something orgasmic about it? Maybe.

Peasants scurry around the stage, changing the scene to:

Four Years Later.

The hut has not aged well, the noren curtain hangs in shreds, the walls are just flat-out busted, one pale lamp burns on the low table near a large photo of ROSIE, who has died.

KIM stands gazing out the window toward the harbor.
She is still pretty but her Asian pajamas are very raggedy, her hair is unkempt, and her face is smudged with grime like she works at a Jiffy Lube auto-repair shop.

Also she has a runny nose.
Another blast from a ship.

KIM. Oh! He has come back! I see his ship glide into the harbor like a swan or maybe a crane! At last, he has come back for us as he promised!

NARRATOR. She hugs ROSIE's photo.

KIM. At last, Mother! I will fulfill your dreams!
I must take a bath!

NARRATOR. She wipes her nose and runs offstage.

CLARK enters, stands outside the hut with EVELYN, his white American wife.

CLARK. You are the best, most noble woman I know, Evelyn.

EVELYN. Oh, Clark.

CLARK. How many other wives would stand by their husbands after learning of his terrible, dark past?

EVELYN. How could I abandon you to the nightmarish burden you have carried these past four years?

CLARK. You have saved me from my dark memories, Evelyn. They are so dark. So oily and greasy and dark –

EVELYN. I know. Let's say no more about it, darling. We must do what we must do.
We will take the child and never return to this place.

CLARK. Yes, but I –

NARRATOR. (*He breaks off as*) KIM runs in, hair wet from her bath.

KIM. My love, I knew you would not forget me!

(*She stops short when she sees* EVELYN.)

Wait, who is this?
Who is she?
Who are you?

EVELYN (*to* CLARK). Well.
She's every bit as pretty as you said.

CLARK. Kim, shogun origami. [Kim, it's been a long time. You look well.]
Edamame, Evelyn. [This is my wife, Evelyn.]

KIM. Your *wife*?

NARRATOR. CLARK nods, EVELYN holds up her ring hand. KIM falls to her knees.

KIM. But... *I'm* your wife.

NARRATOR. She runs to the hut and brings out the gold paper crown, now a little worse for wear.

(CLARK *looks puzzled.*)

KIM. Don't you remember? Rosie brought us the wedding mochi?

CLARK. Where is Rosie anyway, I –
Oh wait. Oh no. Oh wow.
Are you telling me that was... wasabi shoyu? [A wedding?]

KIM. Yes, a wedding.
And Rosie died.

CLARK. Tamago. [I'm so sorry.]

EVELYN. Clark, what's going on? You know I don't speak her language.
Did she say she's... your wife?

CLARK. No no no no! Of course not! *You* are my only wife, Evelyn –

(KIM *gives an anguished little cry and falls to her knees again.*)

– what happened with Kim was – you know, there were all these trade deadlines and treaties – everything was passing before my eyes –

KIM. Passing!

CLARK. When I got back home, it was like I woke from a bad dream and there you were –

KIM. Bad dream!

CLARK. You saved me from myself!

EVELYN (*touched by his declaration*). Oh, Clark!

KIM (*despairing*). Oh, Clark!

NARRATOR. CLARK and EVELYN embrace, make out a little.
The kissing goes on maybe a tad longer than is really comfortable for everyone.
KIM (*watches them*) moans a little in despair, then she resigns herself, walks tragically into the hut, and returns with a child – which may be played by a very large doll dressed as a peasant child. (*But even if you use a real child, he or she should never move or show emotion, the others should pick him or her up and use him or her like a prop.*)

CLARK and EVELYN stare at the child.

(KIM *prostrates herself before them.*)

KIM. Please, I beg of you! Take my son with you to America!

(*Pause.*)

Please! He must have the life I am unable to give him! Take him away from the dirt and the grime and the greasy fish oils of this place! I am begging you please please –

EVELYN. Okay.

KIM. – what?

EVELYN. We'll take him.

NARRATOR. Evelyn holds out her arms, the child runs to her, she scoops him up.

EVELYN. See you back at the ship, darling.
Don't dawdle.

(*She exits.*)

NARRATOR. KIM weeps on the ground, CLARK pats her head awkwardly.

CLARK. Tamago. [I'm sorry.]
Tam, tam, tamago. [I'm so, so sorry.]

KIM. You will give him everything I wanted for him? He will have the world?

CLARK. Haribo! [Yes!]

KIM. Then go! Leave me!

NARRATOR. He reaches for her, she turns her face away from him.
He pats her hair and leaves.
KIM drags herself to her feet, wipes her runny nose on her sleeve like the peasant she is, goes into the hut.
The candle by ROSIE's photo has burned low, flickering.
KIM pulls ROSIE's fish knife from under the futon.
She presses the point against her chest, then stomach, then her temple, between her chest and stomach – trying to find the best place, she's never done this before.
She sighs, hums a little vaguely Asian lullaby (*then says*):

KIM (*soft, tragic, noble*). You were my sun, now our son is your sun.
The moon is down.

NARRATOR. And then suddenly, she slices herself across the throat in one quick move,
SHNICK,
and slumps over, very gracefully, her hair spreading on the floor very poetically, her hand extended open with the knife fallen on the floor in a perfect line pointing to ROSIE's picture.
The candle sputters and goes out.

Blackout.

1949

(*Date of the Broadway premiere of* South Pacific.)

NARRATOR. A muddy little village on a muddy little island somewhere in the South Pacific.
A sweaty marketplace, island people scurrying to and fro, some with baskets on their head.

KIM enters carrying some mangoes on her head – young, virginal, frightened, hopeful, et cetera.
Sounds of a war plane passing overhead.
The island people look skyward, muttering in some vaguely Polynesian way (*like 'lani kai' and 'pahoa'*).

A muffled but very deep boom from the direction the plane went in – the villagers (*'oooh' and 'aahhhh' and*) point to the sky in wonder.

Another, louder boom – the villagers cringe, cry out, and scurry around
KIM falls down, her mangoes go flying, she crawls around picking them out of the mud.
A man named AFI runs on, pulls KIM to her feet.

AFI. The Americans are here!

KIM. Ouch, my mangoes –

AFI. It's our chance to escape this cesspool of an island!

KIM. Uh –

AFI. We can start over in America!

KIM. But Afi, I don't have any money for a ticket! You spent the dowry my father gave you for our wedding on drinking and gambling and trying to corner the pineapple market!

NARRATOR. AFI slaps KIM's ass.

AFI. That's your ticket right there, my little hibiscus flower! I knew that ass would be gold one day. Don't you want a new life in America where there are equal rights for all men regardless of skin color?
Stand up straight, shoulders back, tits up – don't mess this up for me or I'll make you pay.

NARRATOR. They stand at the side of the road, AFI pushes KIM forward.
(*Lights shift*), a romantic haze floods the stage as:
CLARK enters with RICHARDS, another soldier.
CLARK is tall/boyish/rugged/handsome, does weights/ cardio/Interval Training, et cetera, et cetera.

Scurrying peasants part like a field of grasses, and sound like one too since they are all wearing grass skirts (*as* CLARK *strides through the village*).

CLARK. Katsu. [Greetings.]
Lau lau lychee tako. [We parked our planes in your sugarcane fields.]
Puu-puu saimin. [Don't tell anyone.]
Hanalei kona – [We stopped by for lunch and a strategic foothold in the Pacific theater –]

NARRATOR. RICHARDS puts the moves on a peasant girl.

RICHARDS. Well, well – lookee what we have here…

(CLARK *grabs his arm.*)

CLARK. Richards!

RICHARDS. Aw, come on, Clark – just a little harmless R&R!

CLARK. For god's sake, man! You don't treat these people like that!
(*To the girl.*) Kahlua. [Sorry about that.]

NARRATOR. CLARK looks up and sees KIM, their eyes lock.
Heat crackles between them.
AFI grins and pulls her toward CLARK.
She resists weakly.
AFI slaps her butt, she cries out.
CLARK strides over to them.

CLARK. Lani kai! [Leave her alone!]

AFI. Welcome to our humble village, most Best Quality American GI.

CLARK. Waikiki. Lei. Poke…? [Thanks. I'm happy to be here. And this is…?]

AFI. This is Kim, my… sister.

KIM. That's not tr–

(AFI *elbows her in the ribs.*)

– ow –

AFI. Would you like to come over for dinner?

CLARK. Ono! [Would I ever!]
Lolo leelo? [Say eight?]

AFI. Perfect!
Here's the address.

NARRATOR. AFI gives him a ti leaf with directions written on it.

(CLARK *looks at* KIM *again, nods and smiles, her eyes flutter shyly.*)

CLARK. Maui manoa. [I can't wait.]

NARRATOR. He bows, does sexy-sexy hand kissing, exits. KIM's eyes go wide from sexy man-lips, et cetera.

KIM. What is happening…?

She looks at her hand where CLARK kissed it, rubs it against her face (*and then there's a split second of déjà vu: 'wait a minute…'*)

(*She shrugs it off.*)

NARRATOR. AFI (*laughs*) whips out a ukelele and plays an upbeat song as the scene shifts – maybe something like ukelele 'I Feel For You' by Chaka Khan.

AFI. You're our golden ticket to the future, baby!

KIM. But isn't it weird that I'm engaged to you but you want me to go with him…?
That doesn't make you feel weird?

AFI. No. Why would it?

(*Beat.*)

KIM. Yeah I still think it's kinda –

NARRATOR. AFI smacks her across the face, she goes flying.

KIM. Oof!

AFI. Don't you want to eat something besides papaya?

KIM. But what about my dreams –

AFI. Oh my god –

NARRATOR. He smacks her again.

KIM. Owf...!

AFI. Stop being crazy! You don't got any dreams!

KIM. Well there was my idea for a mushed-up fruit and ice stand, where we'd mush up fruit and ice and call it 'mushie' sell it to the field laborers, but then we could never figure out where all that ice would come from since refrigeration is such an issue...

AFI. I'm supposed to smack you again but this humidity is really getting to me...

(She looks at him, they both look around suddenly – a moment of awareness...? – then back to –)

KIM. Goro the fishmonger's son has offered to marry me if you don't want to.

AFI. Goro the fishmonger's son. Seriously. You really just said that to me.

KIM. He likes my mushie idea. He was gonna do a fish side to go with it: 'Mushie and Sushi'.

AFI. Listen to me, dummy. If we go to America, you can have anything you want! You don't have to grow old bearing the children of a man who thinks fish oil is hair care!

KIM. Fish oil has many health benefits —

AFI. Come on, Kim! Be better than Goro the fishmonger's son, can't you? Be better than all of this, all of these greasy, sweating, mongoose villagers just putting one foot in front of the other for the rest of their greasy mongoose lives.

KIM. I used to have a pet mongoose named Buboy. He was so loyal.

AFI. All right fine, fuck it – if you won't dream for yourself, can't you just help me get my dream? Huh? What about *my* dreams?? You don't wanna marry me, fine – but at least don't bogart my American dream with your selfish, puritanical ways! If you wanna stay in a place where you gotta hide your gifts under a fishwife's muumuu that's fine but you don't gotta drag me down too! Let me live, Kim!! LET ME LIVE!!

(*Beat:* KIM *shrugs.*)

KIM. Okay.

AFI. Great, now go make me a fish sandwich and then take a bath.
And be sure you wash *everything*, I hear these American GIs like a clean, well-lit workspace.

KIM (*giggly, embarrassed*). Afi!

AFI. You never know where the night will take you, it's best to be prepared.
I left some hibiscus and gardenia soap by the tub and we don't have a razor but I gave my abalone knife a good going over with Kenji's sharpening stone, so, you know… be thorough.

(KIM *bows, exits.*)

NARRATOR. AFI cackles and starts playing the uke again, perhaps a slow-jam version of 'Give It To Me Baby' by Rick James.
Meanwhile, our tiny Pier 1-love-child, hut-like dwelling has emerged…

(*Lights shift to*) later in the evening, after dinner.
CLARK and KIM at the low table, sipping after dinner rum drinks with tiny umbrellas.
KIM is decked out in full muumuu/hula dancer costume with her hair cascading over her shoulders, full of flowers.
CLARK can't keep his eyes off her but she keeps her eyes modestly lowered.
AFI brings a plate of sliced mango to the table, glances back and forth between them.
He offers a crown of hibiscus flowers to CLARK.

CLARK. Hana? [What's this?]

AFI. Dessert hat.
Island custom.

CLARK. Pali! [Wonderful!]

NARRATOR. AFI puts a chain of flowers around KIM's neck, hands them each a slice of mango, directs them to offer a bite to each other, which they do.

AFI. And I now pronounce you... mananwife!

CLARK. Kamehameha? [What was that?]

AFI. Mango is yummy!

CLARK. Ala moana! [Yes, it is!]

(AFI *stretches and yawns elaborately.*)

AFI. Welp! Past my bedtime!

KIM. Afi...

CLARK. Malasadas, Afi. [Thank you, Afi.]
Ono. [Goodnight.]

NARRATOR. AFI leaves, but we see his eyes peeking through the bamboo wall.
CLARK inches closer to KIM, who brings out a palm frond and hides her face shyly.

(*At certain moments, a very, very slight edge of impatience creeps into* KIM*'s voice though she quickly goes back to smiling, sweet and shy.*)

CLARK. Kama maka mooka. [Don't be afraid.]

KIM. I'm not.
And those aren't actually words you just said.

CLARK. Kim.

KIM. Yes...?

CLARK (*savoring her name on his tongue like a fine port wine*). Kiiiiiiimimimim...

KIM. Mmhm, that's my name.

CLARK (*points at himself*). Clark Jackson Lincoln Garfield.

KIM. Clak... Jahck-som-rinkoo Gahffd.

(*He laughs, charmed.*)

CLARK. Hana hana ono kelikimaka. [You have captured me with your maiden's heart.]

KIM. Okay.

CLARK. Hapa. [Look at me.]

NARRATOR. (*She meets his gaze shyly, he gently touches her cheek.*) His touch sets her on fire.

CLARK. Hulihuli loon. [You are like the moon.]

KIM (*fluttery, flattered*). Wooooowww, I feel so… no man has ever made me feel the way you make me feel… you're so tall and… wide and… big…

NARRATOR. Her eyes flutter bashfully – (*he grasps her chin*) et cetera.
They gaze at each other (*the sexual tension building*), et cetera.

CLARK. Mahi mahi, hana, loon. [You fill the sky, my sky, your silvery light.]

KIM. And you are the sun, warming me with your big American (eyes) –

NARRATOR. He leans in and kisses her, they make out, sexy futon time, et cetera, et cetera.
(*Fade to black as*) a warplane engine roars to life, in a slightly orgasmic kinda way? Maybe.

Four Years Later.

In the busted-ass hut one pale candle burns on the low table near a large photo of AFI.
KIM stands gazing out the window.
Raggedy muumuu, unkempt hair, grimy Jiffy-Lube face, runny nose.
The warplane thunders past overhead.

(KIM *looks up and waves, jumping up and down with excitement.*)

KIM. Oh! He has come back! I see his plane glide into the harbor like a – well, no actually not into the harbor is it,

UNTITLED F*CK M*SS S**GON PLAY

why'd I say 'harbor'? – plane glides into the… the – the cane fields like a – what lands in the cane fields, maybe a, a pelican…? Never mind, not the point –
At last, he has come back for us as he promised!

NARRATOR. She goes to AFI's photo, throws it down.

KIM. At last, Afi! I will leave you behind in this place and your shadow shall not fall on me anymore!

NARRATOR. AFI's ghost enters, KIM screams and falls to the floor.

AFI'S GHOST. Think again, you silly bitch!

KIM. Noooooooooooooooooo!!

AFI'S GHOST. You better not fuck this up again because where ever you go, I go too, remember that! And I wanna go to America, dead or alive, I don't care! You'll never be free of me, I curse you for all time! You shouldn't have given me that rancid fish sandwich!

KIM. I didn't know it was rancid! Goro said it would keep at least three days!

AFI'S GHOST. I don't care! My death was still by your hand, your fishy, fishy hand! Now stop fucking around and go take a bath!

NARRATOR. She wipes her nose and runs offstage.

CLARK (*enters*) stands outside the hut with EVELYN (*his white American wife*).

CLARK. You're the best, Evelyn.

EVELYN. Yes. Yes, Clark. I know.

CLARK. How many other wives would stand by their husbands after learning of his dark island deeds?

EVELYN. Not any. But let's say no more about it, darling. We will do what we must.

We will take the child and never return to this place.

CLARK. Yes, but I need you to know that I know that you are my only –

NARRATOR. (*He breaks off as*) KIM runs in, hair wet from her bath.

KIM. My love, I knew you would not forget me!
(*She stops short when she sees* EVELYN.)
Who the fuck are you?

EVELYN (*to* CLARK). Well.
She's every bit as pretty as you said. A bit *earthy*, though.

CLARK. Kim, manolo blahnik. [Kim, it's been a long time. You look well.]
Hula puka aikau, Evelyn. [This is my wife, Evelyn.]

KIM. Your *wife*? No, no. *I'm* your wife. Remember?

(CLARK *makes a 'sorry no' face,* EVELYN *holds up her ring hand.*)

NARRATOR. KIM starts to fall to her knees, then runs into the hut instead.
She brings out the withered hibiscus crown, now a little worse for wear.

KIM. Ring any bells? No?
Surely you remember the matrimonial mango? Who could forget matrimonial mango??

CLARK. No really, I have no idea what you're – oh wait. Oh no. Oh wow.
Are you telling me that was… hoku hula? [A wedding?]

KIM. Yes, a wedding.

CLARK. Oops.

EVELYN. Clark, you know I don't speak her language.
What is she saying?

CLARK. That she's my… my… wife…?

EVELYN. What?!!

CLARK. No!!

EVELYN. Then what did you just say??

CLARK. 'She's my wife…?'

EVELYN. You said 'wife'?

CLARK. No she said, 'wife' – ?

EVELYN. *How could you do this to –*

Thing is, I can't really tell what you're saying, the upward inflection is confusing me. So you're saying… she's your wife? Your – (*downward inflection*) *wife*.

CLARK. No no no no! Of course not! *You* are my only wife, Evelyn –

(KIM *gives an anguished little cry and falls to her knees again.*)

– what happened with Kim was just – you don't know how I suffered here, the darkness of the – war was in the air, the sky was – just full of – full of war and the whole island was on fire, I was on fire –

KIM. Me too – fire!

CLARK. But when I got back home, you saved me from the fire!

EVELYN (*touched by his declaration*). Oh, Clark!

KIM (*despairing*). Oh, Clark!

CLARK. Oh Evelyn!

NARRATOR. CLARK and EVELYN embrace, make out, et cetera.

(KIM *watches them from the ground, moaning, glancing over to see if they're done, moaning a little more.*)

Finally, KIM's resigned, walks tragically into the hut, and returns with the prop child.

(CLARK *and* EVELYN *stare at the child.*
KIM *prostrates herself before them, her cries are still mostly heartfelt but sometimes tapers off a tiny little bit into a tone of 'yeah, whatever, I see how this is gonna go.'*)

KIM. Please, I beg of you! Take my son with you to America… please!

(*Pause.*)

He must have the life I am unable to give him! Take him away from the dirt and the, the – you know, the grime and the greasy fish oils of this place! I'm begging you! Please, oh please. Oh please. Oh ple–

EVELYN. Okay.

KIM. – what?

EVELYN. We'll take him.

NARRATOR. She holds out her arms, the child runs to her and she scoops him up.

EVELYN. See you back at the plane, darling.
Don't dawdle.

(*She exits.*
KIM *weeps on the ground,* CLARK *pats her head awkwardly.*)

CLARK. Lomi-lomi. [I'm sorry.]
Lomi, lomi, lomi-lomi. [I'm so, so sorry.]

KIM. You promise to give him everything!

CLARK. Kelikimaka! [Yes!]

KIM. Then go! Leave me!

(*He reaches for her, she turns away, he pats her and exits.*
KIM'*s weeping subsides, quicker than in the previous scene.*)

NARRATOR. KIM drags herself to her feet, wipes her runny nose on her sleeve like the peasant she is, and goes into the hut.
The candle by AFI's photo has burned low, flickering.
KIM pulls AFI's abalone knife from under the futon.
She presses the point against her chest, she tests the edge of the blade with her finger.
(*She sighs.*)
She hums a little bit of a Polynesian lullaby (*then says*):

KIM. Be the sun of my son for you are no longer mine.
The moon sinks behind the mountain.

NARRATOR. She raises the knife.
(*A beat in which we see her thinking 'Is this really the thing I do here…?' – then she shakes it off.*)
Sudden slice across her throat,
SHNICK,
slump,
hair spreading poetically,
hand open like a fallen water lily petal.
The candle sputters and goes out.

Blackout.

1953

The final year of the Korean War, the setting for M*A*S*H, *and also in the 1950s–1960s there were a bunch of books/movies/musicals like* The World of Suzie Wong, The King and I, *etc.*

NARRATOR. So here we are again at the busted-ass specifically vaguely Asian hut.

There's some brown hills that could be southern California or could be South Korea – both look the same, as we learned from the TV show *M*A*S*H*.
Some kinda plinky-plunky vaguely 1950s Asian music.
KIM runs on in some Asian-like streetwalker get-up, which still manages to give the impression that she works in an auto-repair shop.

(*She's carrying her son/doll, and she gazes eagerly out the hut window, then stops.
She looks around the hut quickly, and down at her clothes: 'Wait just a fucking minute… wasn't I just here…?'
She shakes it off and continues with the scene, but keeps having little flashes of awareness.*)

CLARK and EVELYN enter (CLARK *wears a US Army uniform*).

CLARK. Bi bim bap! [I've come back!]

KIM. You did! Four years later but okay!

CLARK. Bulgogi. (You look great, Kim.)
Chodang gol, Evelyn. [This is my wife, Evelyn.]

EVELYN. Hi.

KIM. Wow. That's... disappointing.

CLARK. We've come for my son.

KIM. Oh?

CLARK. You knew that.

KIM (*I don't like the way this seems to be going*). Maybe... or maybe not.

NARRATOR. KIM edges toward the back door, EVELYN boxes her out like a true center in the NBA.

EVELYN. You begged us to take him.

KIM. Did I?

CLARK. You did. Just now.
Pakjiehae – [Remember?]

KIM. That's a name, not a verb.

CLARK. Don't you want our son to have the best life possible?

KIM. Changed my mind. He can have a below-average life here with me.

EVELYN. So pretty, but pretty selfish.

CLARK. Kim, be reasonable – at least I came back –

KIM. But he's my son!

CLARK. Mine too! Give me the boy!

KIM. I don't wanna!

NARRATOR. KIM turns and runs
CLARK runs after her, wrestles her to the ground, takes the child and throws it to EVELYN who is back for the pass like an NFL wide receiver.

(EVELYN *catches the kid and keeps running, calling back over her shoulder.*)

EVELYN. See ya back at the jeep, Clark!

NARRATOR. KIM weeps on the ground, CLARK pats her head awkwardly.

CLARK. Well.
Kimchi. [I'm sorry.]
Kimchi chigae. [I'm so, so sorry.]
Uh… [Uh…]

KIM. You got what you came for, now go! Get out!

NARRATOR. He reaches for her, she slaps his hand, he exits. He comes back in, puts his service revolver on the ground beside her.

CLARK. Just in case of burglars or… raccoons.

NARRATOR. He exits.
KIM stops crying abruptly.
She doesn't even wipe her nose, just lets it run like the peasant she is.
There's no dim, romantic candles flickering – it's broad daylight, harsh and unrelenting.
She looks at the gun.

KIM. I will never see my son again.

NARRATOR. She squints up at the sun.
She sits up, puts the gun to her temple, pulls the trigger –
POW –
She slumps.

Blackout.

1975 – Part One

(Bet you can guess why 1975. And what musical is set in Vietnam in 1975. Bet you can.)

NARRATOR. The aforementioned hut, including the much-described vaguely Asian foolery, this time somewhere approximating Southeast Asianness.

KIM runs on carrying her son, wearing a different set of grimy Asian pajamas.

(She looks at her clothes, around at the hut, realizes where/when she is.)

KIM. Aw, crap.

NARRATOR. *(This time, she is actively – but not desperately, not yet, she has hope she can get away – looking for an escape route.)* She finds a gun just sitting in the middle of the floor.

KIM *(not gonna get me that way)*. Yeah, right – not today, motherfuckers!

NARRATOR. She throws the gun out the side window *(and starts to run out the door)*.

(CLARK and EVELYN appear out of nowhere blocking her path, smiling, reaching for the child.)

CLARK. Hi Kim!

Phố Bác Hồ! [Surprise! I'm back!]

KIM. No Kim here! My name is Charlene!

EVELYN. She's so pretty, just like you said –

KIM. Wrong hut! Kim is the next hut past the rubber tree!

CLARK. Bánh mì? [Is this my son?]

EVELYN. He's so cute! What a little doll! Come to Mama!

NARRATOR. She spreads her arms, the child/doll flies into them.

KIM. Give him back!

EVELYN (*to* CLARK). Meet you at the helipad, darling!

KIM. Nooooo!

(*She tries to run after them,* CLARK *grabs her.*)

CLARK. Nong, nong… [Easy now…]

KIM. It's so fucked up that you think you're saying words.

CLARK. Hey listen – it's not like I have a choice here. This hurts me just as much as it hurts you.

KIM. Oh really?

CLARK. The tide of human events has carried us away on its unjust back! You can't understand the complexity of my position – my analyst says that I'm just as much of a victim as you are –

KIM. Uh-huh.

CLARK. – because I feel so awful about this! What can I do?! You think I like hegemony?

KIM. Well I don't know what to think, Clark! You come here, we fall in love, we get it on, you go away for *four years*, and then one day you just waltz back in the door?? With a *wife* – ??

CLARK. But I came back, didn't I?! I'm trying my best –

KIM. No! No! You get no points for *trying*! Fuck your trying!

CLARK. God you're hot when you're pissed off!

KIM. I'm aware!

NARRATOR. He grabs her face and lays one on her.
She fights, but the sexual chemistry is overwhelming and she succumbs to his magic man-lips.

KIM. Oh, Clark!

CLARK. Oh, Kim!

NARRATOR. The sex happens abruptly, then a couple beats of afterglow.

A horn honks.

CLARK. Whoops – there's my ride!
Hey um so… you stay here, I'll be right back.

NARRATOR. (*He exits.*)
KIM (*sighs*), sits on the ground, flinches, feels around in her waistband and discovers the gun she threw out the window.

KIM. Of course. Well… fool me once…

NARRATOR. She (*sighs, exasperated*) points the gun at her stomach.

KIM. Fool me twice, shame on me.
Shame on me.

NARRATOR. *POW!*
Slump.
Blackout.

1975 – Part Two

NARRATOR. Yeah, here again – hut, plinky music, and so forth.
But KIM is onto this shit now.
She stands in her tattered ao dai-like dress, with her Jiffy-Lube cheeks, looking wildly around the stage.
EVELYN sprints across suddenly, carrying the child/doll.

KIM. Give me back my son, you bitch!

NARRATOR. KIM starts to chase her, CLARK (*appears*) blocks her path.
KIM (*stumbles back, but doesn't fall, then*) notices for the first time there's a gun in her hand.

KIM. Oh shit –

CLARK. Oh, Kim.

KIM. Oh man.

NARRATOR. (*They look at each other.*) KIM looks around for an exit, there are none.

CLARK (*half-hearted*). Um – no, stop, don't.

KIM. You know what? You're right. You talked me out of it. I think I'll –

CLARK. Oh for god's sake –

NARRATOR. CLARK puts his hand over hers, turns the gun into her abdomen.
(*She looks up at him, he's implacable.*)

KIM (*just get it over with then*). Goddammit.

NARRATOR. She squeezes the trigger –
POW
Blackout.

(*The following scenes should roll through in rapid succession, and each time her clothes get more and more soaked with blood till by the end she's dripping with it –*)

1975

NARRATOR. Lights up.
AFI hands KIM a knife, she cuts her own throat.
Blackout.

1985

NARRATOR. Lights up
EVELYN hands KIM a gun, she shoots herself.
Blackout.

1995

NARRATOR. Lights up
CLARK leads KIM onto a bridge, KIM jumps.
Blackout.

2005

NARRATOR. Lights up
Oxycontin falls from the sky.

KIM. THIS IS SUCH BULLSHIT.

NARRATOR. KIM takes the pills and ODs.
Blackout – a heavy boom, like a giant door slamming shut.

Mushed-up crashed together kaleidoscopic bits of songs and voices pulse in the dark in an arrhythmic heartbeat pattern, kinda mesmerizing and queasy, like being squeezed through some kind of temporal, sonic birth canal.
A great whooshing and:

2023

NARRATOR. It's twenty-fucking-twenty-three, do we think this makes a difference?
Guess we'll see.

(*In the dark, we hear easy-listening instrumental versions of songs like 'Bette Davis Eyes' or 'The Girl from Ipanema' for example.*)

Lights up on GORO, Assistant Manager in the seafood section at Whole Foods in Harlem.

He's slicing fish into fillets like a boss – seriously, he's really good at it and it's kinda sexy – and talking to a very old woman named CIO-CIO, who sullenly stacks two-for-one crab legs on a tray.

GORO. And my dad was a fish guy, and his dad was a fish guy, and *his* dad was a fish guy – yep, pretty much all the way back. Fish guys. What can I say, it's just in the family. And the thing about it is that even though the trappings of the business have changed – like I'm not tryna do any commercial fishing myself nowadays, no thank you, that shit is dangerous, I know, I saw *Deadliest Catch* and those dudes are straight-up nutso – but um yeah, as I say, although the accoutrements have changed, what with shipping and planes and whatnot, fish flying all over the world – you know what hasn't changed? The fish, man. Fish are fish. And in my family, we know fish. I can tell you whether a fish is fresh, what type of water it swam in – salt or fresh – whether it has been frozen, how far it's traveled, what bait they used to catch it, how old it was when it was caught, what it was eating, and whether it had a bad attitude – all that, without even looking. One small sniff and I know it all. I'm not bragging. Well, I guess I am, but what's wrong with that? In my family there was always this thing about 'no bragging'. If I'd even smile about my work, my dad would just – *bap* – up the back of my head, cuz he thought I was bragging. But what I think is – if you can back it up, it's not bragging. Look at LeBron James. And we are the best fish guys ever in the history of fish guys, and it's not bragging, it's the truth. We are the LeBron James of fish guys. The best. Period.

NARRATOR. CIO-CIO makes a movement that *might* be a shrug, continues to stack crab legs. He holds up a prawn.

GORO. Oh man she used to love these. She liked making this killer cioppino.

CIO-CIO (*grunts*).

GORO. Well, I guess that's what I'm trying to figure out. How a guy with my instincts could get so wrapped up in someone who clearly was never interested at all. I'm not gonna lie, it sorta haunts me. Like, worse than the actual fact of the break-up is the thought that somehow, I got fooled. Someone slipped me some grouper disguised as king salmon. I keep replaying what happened, trying to find clues. Should I have known? *Could* I have known? Should I have seen past her discerning taste in shellfish? Should I have known there could never be a future with her even when she talked so enthusiastically about opening a poke bar together?

CIO-CIO (*grunts*).

GORO. We were gonna call it 'Poke-Okey-Dokey'.

CIO-CIO (*grunts*).

GORO. Thanks, I did too. Anyway – all gone now, all those dreams. So strange and confusing, like... like building a house that you never get to live in. Fish don't have this problem, you know. I mean yeah they don't live in houses but also, they don't play games with love. When it's time to mate, boom. Eggs and sperm, everybody delivers the goods, no vacillating, no questions, no subterfuge. Simple. Traditional. Like me. Ahhh, well – you know. Clams in, clams out, my grandpa used to say. Any sense of control over your life is an illusion, things go the way they go, whatever will be, will be. What you gonna do? The heart wants what it wants. And in the end, it doesn't matter a whole lot, not in the greater scheme of things, like as in, if one were to consider the situation in the context of the multiverse, then who gives a shit, amiright? Through that lens, we're all just krill crawling around the ocean floor for a day. So who cares if a girl I liked, who I thought liked me, turned around and crushed me under her heel like two-for-one escargot? No one. Nobody cares and that's okay because it doesn't matter and I'm over it.

CIO-CIO (*grunts*).

GORO. For real. I'm over it.

CIO-CIO (*grunts*).

GORO. Exactly. 'Plenty of fish in the sea.'

NARRATOR. CIO-CIO pauses almost imperceptibly, makes a very slight but kindly meant pawing movement with a crab leg.

UNTITLED F*CK M*SS S**GON PLAY   453

GORO nods.

GORO. Thanks. I really appreciate that.

NARRATOR. They go back to work.
CIO-CIO finishes the box of crab legs
She looks at GORO.

GORO. Done already? Wow – great job, Cio-Cio san.

CIO-CIO (*tilts her head slightly*).

GORO. No, I think that's all good. We don't seem to be that busy, so, um...
why don't you take your lunch now?

CIO-CIO (*sighs*).

GORO. It's fine, really. I'm just gonna Windex the display cases up front, then when you get back, I'll get my break.

CIO-CIO (*looks at him*).

GORO. I hear ya, Cio-Cio san. Thanks – you too.

NARRATOR. She exits into the back room.
Instrumental version of 'Let's Get It On' by Marvin Gaye starts playing, and I mean, for Muzak, the beat is slightly dope.
GORO's head starts bobbing to the beat.
Then his hips sway a bit, his shoulders bump.
Suddenly he busts out singing –

GORO. We're all sensitive people...

(GORO *sings the first verse of 'Let's Get It On'*.)

NARRATOR. At this point, bomb-ass dance moves have been fully busted, and it turns out GORO can sing the fuck outta that shit.

(GORO *keeps singing up until the refrain.*)

And so on and so forth...
Does he get down with the whole damn song with his sexy, bad-ass self? And does he grab a mic from the stack of sourdough-bread chowder bowls?
Maybe.

Does CIO-CIO enter and sing back-up vocals and do they proceed to bust a move, Motor City style?
Could be.

(*The song ends.*)

CIO-CIO san picks up her reusable grocery bag and sweater, pats GORO, and exits.
Muzak morphs into Kenny G (which doesn't sound all that different, really) and plays us out of the Whole Foods and into:
A nice apartment on a nice block on the Upper East Side, New York City.
Maybe it has the floor plan of that ol' hut, but we don't really notice that amidst all the blandly tasteful beige-sand-taupe-beach-pebble-wheat-colored Ethan Allen/Crate & Barrel/Pottery Barn puke in the room.

(*There are three doors visible: stage-right, the front door that goes to the outer hallway and elevator; stage-left, a swinging door that leads to the kitchen; and a double-door door upstage next to the cream-colored mantel over a shiny brass fireplace insert.*
There are stairs that lead to a second floor.
There are long ivory and taupe silken drapes along one wall upstage-right, behind a lovely rustic reclaimed wood bespoke dining table and chairs.
The soporific stylings of Kenny G float through.
The dining table is set for six.)

KIM stands in the center of the room, wearing a stylish Lululemon activewear ensemble and breathing hard like she just finished running a five-K, eyes wild and hunted, darting around the room in confusion.
She wonders where the music is coming from – she wonders also what IS that music, like *IS* it music, what's happening why does it feel like someone is pouring tepid molasses into her ears??

KIM. This isn't real.

NARRATOR. A very real sizzling and smell as ROSIE enters from the kitchen, carrying a tray of Asian sizzling beef and

a dish of potstickers with dipping sauce and garnished with
a mango cut to look like a lotus blossom.
Oh man. It smells *delicious*.

(*The* NARRATOR *smiles and steps into the scene,* KIM *sees her.*)

Mmmm that smells so good! Aren't you hungry, Kim?

KIM. Wait a minute… you… you're…

NARRATOR. Can I help you with anything in the kitchen, Mrs –

ROSIE. Oh, please – call me Rosie!

NARRATOR. Sure, Rosie!

ROSIE. And you are so kind to offer, but you are a *guest*, you are Afi's *guest* –

KIM. *Afi's* guest?? Afi is here…?

NARRATOR. Business associate, partner really – but I'm so happy to be here. I don't get out much.

ROSIE. Yes and we are so pleased to have you here for Afi's special night – anyway, I've got everything under control, if I can just – Kim? Kim! What are you doing, for goodness' sake?!

KIM. Huh?

ROSIE. Go change your clothes, we have company!! (*Smiles at* NARRATOR.) Please help yourself to wine, Brenda – we'll be ready to sit down any moment!

NARRATOR (*who we now call* BRENDA). Brenda. Huh. All right then, that's a name. I guess.

(*She grins at* KIM *and eats a potsticker.*)

BRENDA. Ohmahgah! So yummy!!

ROSIE. Thank you!

BRENDA. Where did you get these?

ROSIE. They are a special home-made recipe from my great-grandmother, who made them for her village festival every summer in the mountains of southern —

(*A burst of giggly laughter, and* EVELYN *and* AFI *enter from upstairs.*)

Oh, here they are!

EVELYN. Oh, Afi!

AFI. No, it's true, though. I would never lie to you.

EVELYN. You better *not*. Cuz I would *find out*. And then you'd be *in trouble*.

AFI. Oooo, could I please?

EVELYN. What, you silly boy?

AFI. Be *in trouble*?

(*They share a sexy-sexy look.*)
(KIM *stares at them.*)

KIM. All right then. That's new.

ROSIE. Kim!! What are you babbling about!! Go put on some decent clothes! (*Smiles at* BRENDA.) Please do have some wine!

BRENDA. Don't mind if I do. For you?

ROSIE. Oh, hee hee – no, I'm still cooking in there, don't want to set the house on fire!

BRENDA. No, we don't want that! Do we, Kim? Ha ha!
Afi, Evelyn – wine?

AFI. None for me, thanks.

ROSIE. He gets the redness. You know. In the face. And the – (*gestures to neck and chest and stomach*) all over, really.

BRENDA. Ah.

EVELYN. I think the redness is adorable.

AFI. You would, you angelic supportive weirdo. Okay then, I'll have a glass.

(*A brief canoodling.*)

ROSIE (*exiting into the kitchen*). Aww!

KIM. Eww.

AFI. Oh shut up, brat! Not like you and Clark were any different when you got engaged.

KIM. ... Clark? I – what? Is he – *what*?? WHERE IS HE??

AFI. Oh ha ha ha, very funny –

EVELYN. I'd love some wine, thank you, Brenda.

AFI. – and what the hell are you *wearing*? It's an engagement dinner, for god's sake! Not your, your – mooey chai class or whatever.

KIM. Can I have some wine?

BRENDA. Do you think you should?

KIM. Oh, yes, I do, I do think I should.

BRENDA. But – you're not worried about the redness – ?

KIM. I think it's safe to say the redness is the least of my worries in this moment.

BRENDA. You know, my sister is a nurse, and there is a medical and biological basis for the redness, you should really be careful about your intake of –

KIM. Sure okay.

(BRENDA *pours.*)

Yeah I'll tell you when to stop, lady.

(BRENDA *pours more.*)
(KIM *gulps down the whole glass, gestures for a refill.*)
(AFI, EVELYN, *and* BRENDA *chatter in the background,* ROSIE *clatters pots and pans in the kitchen and sizzling and steam puff into the front room through the swinging door.*)

(THE PALE ROSÉ BUBBLE.)

(KIM *sips her wine, and a pale, rosy flush steals across the stage, enclosing her in a pale rosy bubble of light.*

AFI, EVELYN *and* BRENDA *sip wine and chat continuously under the following but their voices are muted, as if heard through a fabric wall.*)

Hmmmm
MmMmMmmmmHm
Sometimes I think
My body is completely separate from me
Like a
Like a
Space suit
a Me Suit
I come home from space and take off my Me Suit
and hang it on a hook on the wall
Me Suit
Where did it come from
Why do I wear it
What if I put on another one
would she be me
or he
Hmmm
Sometimes I think
I would like to go out into space without my Me Suit
Without any suit at all
Just let me be raw pink purple red jelly boneless skinless coagulation
pulsing through space it would feel
Free
wouldn't it?
Weightless and light
But
This is ridiculous of course
No one goes out without their Me Suit
No one does that
Or
Or
Or if they *do*
If they *do* do that
go out without their Me Suit
I think
I think maybe they go and *they never come back*

(*She feels her cheeks.*)
uh ohhhhhhhh
oh noooooooooo
It's here
The Redness

(AFI, EVELYN, *and* BRENDA *invade* KIM*'s rosy bubble, which makes a distorted 'boingy' sound as they enter.*)

AFI. I could not disagree more – it's not a serious wine.

EVELYN. Oh, Afi – you're such a purist! That's so deathly *cute*.

BRENDA. I think it's a nice quaffing wine, for summer, when it's hot –

AFI. And that's fine, Brenda, but I would never consider cellaring a *rosé*.

I mean, come on. Why would anyone do that?

BRENDA. Why, Afi! You're a wine snob! I never knew this about you!

EVELYN. He does have classic highbrow tastes, you should see him schooling the sommelier at Jean Georges –

AFI. If it's a crime to have a discerning palate and a taste for the best in wine – *and* women – then I am guilty as charged!

(*Tasteful laughing, quaffing – except* KIM, *who:*)

KIM (*a honk, really*). *HAH.*

BRENDA. I donno if you're guilty, but you're definitely under indictment!

EVELYN. Oh, Afi! You're so goofy! You're so mortally adorable I just wanna urrrrrr I WANNA SCRUNCH YA.

AFI. Oh? How would that work, exactly, this *scrunching* –

EVELYN. Shall I show you?

BRENDA. You guys are too much!

KIM. You said it, Brenda – (*Sotto voce to* BRENDA.) *if indeed that is your name.*

(*They all sip their wine,* KIM *chugs hers till it's gone. She stumbles over to the side table to get more – the movement causes her bubble to stretch and separate, leaving* AFI, EVELYN, *and* BRENDA *in their own bubble.*
ROSIE *comes out of the kitchen with some food, puts it on the table.*
KIM *drunkenly moves around to the couch, her rosy bubble bumps against* ROSIE, *but* ROSIE *is impervious to rosy bubbles, and does* not *get enveloped.*)
(ROSIE *watches* KIM *stumble to the couch, 'tsk-tsk', then she notices, through the filter of* KIM'*s bubble the* NARRATOR'*s empty chair and mic.*
She looks at the others in their bubbles, only BRENDA *notices her noticing them*
BRENDA *watches as* ROSIE *steps out of the living room, to the mic.*)

ROSIE. I would like to say at this point, that *personally*, I think this is all – it's an overreaction. But kids these days, they will always find fault with something. It's in their nature. Fault-finding. There is some deeply-seated need to find fault. With everything. It has to do with the kind of people they are, whether they are positive or negative people. I have taught myself to be positive, to always look for the 'plus side'.

(*The bubbles around the others murmur a little 'boing boingg'…*)

When I was young, there was movie called *The World of Suzie Wong.* I loved this movie. And they didn't know any better back then, so of course it's not perfect. But what is? I can still love it.
What does that mean?
To love an imperfect thing?
I don't know.

(*Bubbles murmur.*)

I know how it felt. Like I had jumped to my feet, but inside, in my soul. My soul jumped to its feet. To see faces that looked like mine, in a place where I had never seen them, somewhere I never thought they could be – an American movie screen. With an American movie star, William

Holden, so handsome and kind. So romantic and loyal – and for the record, it was *not* a tragic ending. He doesn't abandon her. He defends Suzie Wong to the other bad, prejudiced white people. He loves her, despite their many differences, he loves her *because* of the differences. He doesn't want just a normal wife, this man.

To me, this was wonderful.

Because – and it was just the way it was, we accepted it – we knew that this is America. That this is not our country. We understood that we were being allowed to live and work and make a life in a country that did not belong to us, you see? And yes I was born here, but being born somewhere does not mean that you are not also a guest – every day someone asks me where I'm from. And we try very hard to be good guests – and to be quite honest, when I was growing up, seeing Asian characters in films was not at the top of the list of things we worried about. My goodness. Between raising a family and putting food on the table, who had time for worrying about whether there were Asian characters in a movie? If I wanted to see Asian faces, all I had to do was turn sideways and *wahh* – there would be ten of them staring back at me. My parents, my brothers, my sisters, my aunts and uncles and cousins. No shortage of Asian faces in my household, believe me.

(*Bubbles murmur.*)

But you know. When that film came out. And there was this Asian woman, a Chinese woman as the star? It took my breath away and I was startled – I hadn't known how much hunger there was inside of me for that and suddenly it rose up inside of me like a storm, like a flood and I was submerged in my hunger for her face, my eyes devoured her face on that screen. All of the Asian people in that film – how hungry I was for those faces, for those lives.

And she was mixed, yes, but this only enhanced her beauty, those wide eyes with only a slight tilt upward at the corners, and she had a lovely full figure, and she was so full of life. What Asian woman wouldn't feel well-represented by such a lovely girl? And she was still so innocent, so pure, despite being forced to turn to prostitution to support her illegitimate child. And the story wasn't only about her being a – a *compromised* woman – no, no, no. Those parts of the film only lasted a few minutes here and there, and they were always very, um, blurry so you didn't see anything naughty. No, if that's all you focus on, you miss the point, that this was really a love story, about the love of a mother for her child. It showed, um, it showed the strength and nobility of soul in Asian women. Her pluck and resourcefulness and bravery. Why is it a stereotype to show that we will do anything, give everything, even our lives, for our children? Wouldn't any mother do this? Why is it bad to show that Asian women are like any other woman in this respect? I don't think it is. It is not bad to me. And she was so good that William Holden decides to marry her in the end. Even though her illegitimate baby dies in the monsoon and she is distraught with grief, she is always strong and gentle, and William Holden rescues her from her life in Hong Kong and they live happily ever after. So there you go, you see – they do not always die in the end. Sometimes they are rescued by William Holden.

(*Bubbles murmur.*)

And all these women, these actresses, they are all so beautiful, they speak so beautifully, they are strong and good and sometimes very talented in martial arts. Even if the portrayal is not completely… factual, in a sense? It's just a story, for goodness' sake, just a movie – and for a movie, of course they will pick out the exotic aspects of our culture, it's meant to be entertaining, so people can escape their daily lives and have an adventure. And to be acknowledged at all is not… well, it is not *nothing*. And is, in fact, something to be grateful for – a crumb from the table is still food, even if it leaves you a tiny bit hungry. It is not necessarily a bad thing to be a tiny bit hungry, it gives you something to work for. I find nothing to be ashamed of in any of that. Because some of us remember a time when we were not seen at all. We were just an invisible multitude that moved across the land and *poof*! Things magically appeared! Gunpowder! The transcontinental railroad! Hand-pulled noodles! I save my outrage for real things, things of consequence in the world. Abused children, public education, the climate crisis. How Asian people are portrayed in American culture – is it really of such concern? Does it really affect anything of consequence?

Does it?

(*Bubbles murmur.*)

Case in point: my daughter. She's...
Sometimes I wonder if she has too much freedom. And not enough struggle. So she doesn't know how to be properly grateful for either one.
She's doing some kind of internet movie with friends from the Art Institute, something about being trapped inside a mirror – or was it a window? – I can't remember, something about a mirror that reflects a person that is not you, but then the mirror person comes alive and takes over the... something? And the real you is trapped somewhere?
The art they make, these liberal political activist types – it's all so *earnest*, so wracked with their own guilt, so angry, so intent on *putting someone in their place*. I don't know. It sounds like complete nonsense but you know – the kids these days must have their creative expression. It's unpaid, of course. Sixteen weeks of full-time work for no pay, on a depressing, angry student film. What about something nice once in a while? Why not something *happy*, like, like – *Music Man*? *Music Man* is so nice. Everyone likes *Music Man*.

(*Bubbles murmur.*)

Our son, on the other hand. Afi. He's doing very well, very well, indeed. He and his business partner Brenda have just gone public with their company, 'Fish in a Barrel' – can you imagine? Millions of dollars because people will pay $19.95 plus tax to eat fish and rice in a bowl for lunch. My goodness. They're opening stores all over the country. It's quite a sensation. But you know – with him, the hard work pays off. He went to Harvard Business School.

(*Bubbles start rising, getting bigger.*
Do we worry about popping? Maybe.)

I don't know why Kim struggles the way she does. She's her own worst enemy, you know, and I'm her mother and I love her and I don't like being the one to have to say this but if there's a choice between straight line and crooked, guess which path she always, *always* goes down. Drawn to trouble. Like a magnet. And all self-inflicted wounds as far as I can tell – her employment difficulties, dim prospects, digestive issues. Complain, complain. All day every day, just around and around in a circle. Milk gives her a stomach ache, nobody at work likes her, someone at the Whole Foods asked her where is the Chinese food aisle. I think it may have something to do with low self-esteem but I don't understand where she would have gotten that – certainly not from me. She just can't ever accept things as they are, that some things just *are the way they are*, she wants always for things to *be as they should.* Which – I have tried, over and over, to explain to her that we don't get to decide, we don't create these circumstances, they simply *are* as they *are*, and there is no use in being so rigid, so brittle. Brittle things break. You must learn to lean with the wind, not push against it in that way. You cannot win against the win. No win. No win wind. No winning with the wind, the wind wins when it wins. Bend, don't break. Stumble, don't fall. Be all you can be. If you fall behind, run faster. Fall down nine times, get up twenty, thirty, a hundred, a thousand – it doesn't matter how many times. What matters is you get up. *You get up.* YOU GET UP.

(*BZZZZT! the apartment front-door buzzer, really loud, POPS all remaining bubbles.*
ROSIE *snaps out of her reverie and goes back into the kitchen –* BRENDA *watches her.*)

(CLARK *enters, brings his own sort of golden glow into the room and he is devastatingly handsome. I mean, what the fuck? The updating of men's clothing has done only amazing things for him, he looks amazing.*)

(*His eyes meet* KIM*'s, he smiles and I mean – holy crap! He needs to stop, or everyone is going to burst into flames from his hotness.*
He crosses to KIM*, his golden glow spills over her and he lays one on her – the kiss deepens a little further than was expected, due to the aforementioned hotness, to which* KIM *is highly susceptible.*)

CLARK. The bodega didn't have any cocktail napkins, so I went to the Fairway and they had only dinner napkins, but my parents didn't raise a quitter and I said 'Oh it's ON, now!' and then what did I do?

EVELYN. I don't know! What did you do!

AFI. What!

CLARK. I Uber-ed to the fucking Paper Source on 75th and 3rd and had some finest quality organic cotton paper napkins embossed with a golden 'A' and 'E' and – BOOM! Happy engagement, kids!

AFI. That's so incredibly generous of you, man!

EVELYN. Eeeeee! Clark! You're so amazing, these look amazing, ohhhh – (*she chokes back tears, to* BRENDA) Don't these look *amazing*??

BRENDA. Awwwww! The little golden A and E! For Afi –

BRENDA/EVELYN. – and Evelyn!! Awwwww!!

(ROSIE *bursts back in with yet another platter of food.*)

ROSIE. Perfect timing!

(*Everyone cheers, golden light glints off the package of napkins as* CLARK *joins the party; he opens the package and expertly fans the napkins, placing them artfully on a side table with the beverages.*)
(KIM *watches as everyone floats over to the dinner table, bits of conversation float around as they eat and talk and laugh in golden slow motion.*
KIM's *rosy glow wears off somewhere in the middle of dinner,*

right about here →)

CLARK. And then I said, 'Hey man, you better tie your shoe!'

(*They all laugh hysterically.*)

ROSIE. Oh, Clark! You're so funny!

AFI. Hilarious, man!

EVELYN. I love the way you tell stories!

(*Laughing, laughing.*
CLARK *glances over at* KIM, *who is standing in the same spot.*)

CLARK. Sweetheart, come sit down.

(KIM *doesn't move.*)

AFI. 'Hey man – '

CLARK/AFI. 'You better tie your shoe!'
AH HAH AHAHAHAHAHHAHAHAHHHH!!

(CLARK *looks at* KIM.)

Kim. Honey? Earth to Kim, come in, Kim –

ROSIE. Kim!! Your husband is talking to you!

KIM. Yeah… I don't think so…

AFI. Oh my god.

EVELYN. Is she all right?

BRENDA. She's maybe been through a lot… lately…?

EVELYN. Oh. Has she tried therapy? Because I know a terrific therapist, down in the East Village –

CLARK. Anyway – I'd like to make a toast.

(*They all look at him.*)

When I first met Afi, he was being stuffed into a recycling bin behind the dining hall by the varsity lacrosse team, and I thought how strange it was that a grown man could fit into a recycling bin.

(*Laughter around the table.*)

And I was also glad that I played rugby because those lacrosse guys ended up getting suspended later that year for setting fire to the arts and humanities library.

(*Laughter.*)

But I digress. And all kidding aside, I made a new friend that day, and though I didn't know it, also the person who would introduce me to the love of my life.

(*Murmuring, 'awww', etc.*)

Afi and Evelyn. If you have even half the happiness I've found with Kim, you will be the luckiest couple on earth.

ROSIE. Hear, hear!

BRENDA. That was so nice! So nicely put!

ROSIE. You have such a gift with words, Clark!

(*They all drink the toast.*)

KIM. *Hah!*

BRENDA. Pardon me?

KIM. Thass was a hoot! Thass what thass was!

(*Buzzkill.* ROSIE *glares at her.*)

A… hoooo… t…

(*Pause.*)

Yeahhp… thiss the nice part, I guess. Where everyone is… happy… wedding mochi…

AFI. Can you please get a grip?

KIM. Oh, Afi. Afi, Afiiiiii. I sorry that sandwich was rancid. I dint mean that to you.

AFI. Oh my god – what are you talking about?

KIM. I know, I know – this your happy time, iss the happy time. Shhh. I know what comes next, but I won't say. So you can enjoy your happy time. Especially all the – (*makes vulgar fucking gesture*) yeahhhhhh, baby. Go 'head. Get it, Afi.

ROSIE. Kim…

KIM. Yep, thass my name, so they say, but let's look into that a lil bit, shall we? Why is so many Asians call 'Kim' in this place? Huh? Why so Asian name here? Iss not even a girl's name, iss a LAST NAME, a SURNAME, why's name girl baby 'Kim'?? Shhh, so dumb. Iss *Korean*, iss KOREAN LAST NAME, what you gonna do, name girl KIM KIM?? Hahhhhh iss fuckin *joke*.
Thass for start.

AFI. Mom – make her stop –

KIM. And oh yeah I juss remember –

ROSIE. KIM!! STOP IT!!

KIM. I AM NOT LOTUS FLOWER!! OR EXOTIC INNOCENCE MODEL MINORITY DOCILE!! OR LUCY LIU!! Or A&P class girl Grace Chung. Or barista Louisa Changchien.

CLARK. Just let her go, maybe she'll get it out of her system.

KIM. I also donno where is the best Chinese food nearby. And I'm not fluent in Japanese. I don't wanna die so my son can have a better life. I just I just I just –

EVELYN (*like the Dog Whisperer*). Oh, Kim. Shhh. Shhh now.

KIM. I'm just me –

EVELYN. I know you're in pain.

KIM. – why does it always happen… why do I always… why does it always end the same way…?

EVELYN. Hey, I get it, I know.

KIM. Oh? Do you?

AFI. Evelyn, you don't have to engage with her when she's like this. It's very sweet of you to try but –

EVELYN. I know, because as a *woman*, as a fellow sufferer of injustice, I have been where you are, Kim.

BRENDA (*maybe not, lady*). Mmm – has she…?

ROSIE (*under her breath*). Well maybe she has, she's done everything else.

(BRENDA *and* ROSIE *cackle and slyly give each other dap.*)

EVELYN. The hardest thing in the world is to resist striking back when you feel like things are so unfair, like the world isn't being very fair, you feel like, 'Hey, I'm doing all the right things, why aren't you being fair?' I know.

KIM. Hey lady *you donno know me.*

EVELYN. I know you have hurt. We all do. We've all been through so much, haven't we? As a woman, as a feminist,

I know these battles – I have fought them my whole life! Not being chosen as Senior Class President though I was much more qualified than the *boy* they elected! Being second in my class at Harvard! Driving a hand-me-down BMW that didn't even have a sunroof! Keys to an executive washroom which is *two doors* away from my office instead of part of the suite like the other VPs! Being passed over again and again for CEO! Beauty is wound, my friend – my goodness, the judgement we endure just because we know how to apply a little lipstick! So look – I know the corrosive nature of the struggle for acceptance and validation and autonomy, what that can do to your faith in humanity, and I know how difficult it is to keep the faith when the world wants to put its limits on you, to define you in their small box marked 'Woman' or 'Wife' or 'Chorus Dancer' –

KIM. uh-huh

EVELYN. But I believe in you, Kim. I believe that you can be strong enough to put yourself aside, and hold space to celebrate with Afi and me. To know that whatever you have experienced in the past, in this room, you are loved and accepted for who you are, and your truth is honored. I know what you've been through. I've been there, believe me – I have been there.

(*Pause.*
KIM *looks at* EVELYN *with intensity, it's not clear if she's thinking about hugging her or strangling her.*)

CLARK. Sweetheart, please – can we just all go sit together and celebrate this wonderful union?

(*Silence.* CLARK *and* EVELYN *exchange a meaningful glance,* EVELYN *crosses back to* AFI, *squeezes* CLARK*'s arm as she passes.*)

KIM. *I saw that.*

BRENDA. Oh boy.

CLARK. Kim, please calm down.

KIM. You think I don't know what's going on here?

CLARK. Come sit, I promise you, there's nothing –

EVELYN. Clark. Tell her the truth.

CLARK. What??

EVELYN. I told Afi. And he's fine with it.

AFI. Yes. I'm fine with it. I'm cool like that.

EVELYN. It was before Afi and were together, of course.

AFI. But I'm cool with it. It happens, you know.

CLARK. Wow.

KIM. Uh-huh. And…?

CLARK. Kim, this is… well it was a long time ago…

EVELYN. Not that long. Not really.

KIM. … that you and Evelyn were fucking…

ROSIE. Don't say 'fucking' it's so vulgar! Say 'had an affair' –

CLARK. Yes so, we had an affair –

KIM. After we were married.

CLARK. Maybe…?

KIM. Yeah.

CLARK. But it ended! That's the most important part of the story, it ended! And we, Evelyn and I, agreed it was a terrible mistake!

KIM. Did you? That's too bad.

CLARK. I know it's a lot to take in, and I didn't want you to ever have to know, but… in the interest of transparency – I'm so sorry, Kim –

KIM. Okay.

CLARK. What?

EVELYN. What?

KIM. I know you and Evelyn used to fuck, and I don't care. Can we move on?

CLARK. Oh. Uh. Okay.

AFI. Huh. Interesting. I would have expected a bigger reaction.

KIM. Well, Afi. I guess I'm cool like that.

AFI. Yeahh... okay...

EVELYN. Well it's really a relief to have it all out in the open –

ROSIE. Of course, and it doesn't mean anything! Now we can have all the incomes in one big family, and we'll all gather in the Hamptons for the holidays every year with the –

KIM. NOPE!!!!!!!

(KIM *throws her glass at the wall.*
Stunned silence, everyone stares at her.)

I know what you're doing, you assholes. Trying to make me think that I'm – drive me to – you know – SCHNICK!!

ROSIE. Language, Kim!

AFI. Mom, don't start on her. It won't help.

ROSIE. Well.

KIM. Stop talking about me like I'm not here!!

AFI. Hey! How about you calm down!!

(CLARK *crosses to* KIM, *who backs away warily.*)

KIM. I think I'm gonna go now.

CLARK. Kim, come on – your mother made this wonderful food for everyone. Don't you want to sit and eat?

KIM. Nope!!

CLARK. Kim –

KIM. I'm not falling into your traps!! Not again!! HOW STUPID DO YOU THINK I AM??!!

CLARK (*moves closer to her, hands out to her*). Shh, shh – no one thinks you're stupid –

KIM. Hey! You better *fall back*, buddy –

CLARK. Come on now. It's me. Clark. I would never –

KIM. HAH!!

ROSIE. Kim, stop being ridiculous and come eat your dinner.

KIM. How could *you* do this, this – all of this!? You're my *mother*!

ROSIE. Oh, here we go again –

KIM. How could you let me be *sold to a* –

ROSIE. – it's all my fault, everything is my fault, all your failures, all your pain and worry and problems, all me, not you, it's always my fault –

KIM. YOU WERE SUPPOSED TO PROTECT ME!!

ROSIE. Enough of this silliness. Kim, calm down immediately and stop embarrassing the family in front of company!!

CLARK. Kim, darling –

(CLARK *makes a move to grab her, she dodges him and runs to the front door, stage-right (1), scrabbles at the handle, gets it open and runs out.*
Everyone looks at each other: EVELYN *looks concerned in the way of sisterhood,* BRENDA *looks concerned, narratively speaking,* ROSIE *eats sizzling beef,* AFI *shrugs.*)

(KIM *runs back on, coming in from upstairs.*
She looks around in dismay.)

KIM. Crap!

CLARK. Kim! Wait!

(KIM *sprints out the front door (1) again, again runs on from upstairs.*
She looks around, out of breath.)

KIM. Are you fucking *kidding me*???

(*She runs out the kitchen swinging doors, stage-left (2), comes back on through the front door.*)

GAAAAHHHHHH!!!!

(*She runs up the stairs but enters through the kitchen doors.*)

(*Out of breath.*) God. Dammit.

(*She runs to the double-doors upstage (3), wrenches them open and out tumbles an avalanche of dark bamboo screens, low table, palm fronds – detritus from the earlier scenes in the love hut, including an array of the weapons used in the suicides.*)

The fuck is this shit??! Some kinda twisted *recycling program*?!!

CLARK. Now, Kim – let's stay calm –

KIM. You know, it's funny how often in my life people have said that to me. And what I think is, actually, I *am* calm. I'm already a pretty calm person, a quiet person. I keep my TV at a low volume, I don't use my cellphone in public, I try to approach people in the least threatening way possible even if it's to ask them to take their foot off my windpipe – and maybe being *quiet* is not the same as being *calm*, but. I think that's what you actually mean, right? You want me to be quiet. To SHUT UP. To not raise questions or a fuss or my own son. To die beautifully, tragically, nobly, sacrificially, and silently.
I might as well not be here at all, you could use my Me Suit.

ROSIE. Your what?

KIM. Not important. Anyway. Oh lookee what we have here.

(KIM *picks up a gun from the junk on the floor.*
The others gasp.)

I know how it ends and *I don't wanna do this anymore.*
Now which one of you assholes is gonna to tell me how to get out of this shitshow?

(BRENDA*'s eyes involuntarily glance at the drapes along the upstage-left wall.*)

AH-HAH!!!

CLARK. Please, Kim. Just – sit with me and talk. We can –

(*He blocks her way, lunges, a struggle for the gun which* CLARK *wins, he throws it away.*

KIM s*prints away, he chases her around the room,* AFI *and* ROSIE *and* EVELYN *join in, trying to corral* KIM *like she's a runaway horse.*
BRENDA *sips wine and watches.*)

KIM. Y'ALL BETTER GET OUTTA MY WAY IF YOU DON'T WANNA END UP ON THE FLOOR – !!

EVELYN. Stop, Kim – you don't know what you're doing –

AFI. Clark's a good guy, Kim!! He's stood by you all this time!! Why are you putting him through this?!!

ROSIE. You spoiled brat!! I knew we should've drowned you in the well!!

I mean the hospital!! Left you in the hospital!!

KIM. AAAAAAAAAAAAA!!!!

(KIM *lowers her shoulder NFL-tackle-style and lays them out, one by one, until only* CLARK *is left between her and the drapes.*
She fakes left and goes right, but he's got some defense and he boxes out.
And yeah, I've again mixed NFL and NBA terminology in the same paragraph of stage directions. So what. That's the least of your worries, at this point.)

(*A standoff.*)

Move.

CLARK. No.

KIM. *Move. Your ASS. OUT OF MY WAY.*

CLARK. NO. I'm not giving up on us.

(KIM *laughs mirthlessly.*)

KIM. Is that what you think this is about? You giving up or not giving up?

CLARK. Well… uh…

KIM. Get out of my way, Clark.

CLARK. No, Kim! I can't let you go, I love you too much! I will always love you in spite our differences, in spite of the difficulty of trying to understand you and – *why*?? Why are you like this?

KIM. GOOGLE IT, MOTHERFUCKER!!

(KIM *makes a move to get past, he blocks her.*)

CLARK. Shh I need you to stop yelling and calm down –

KIM. TOLD Y'ALL TO STOP TELLING ME TO CALM DOWN OR – !!

AFI. Or what? What are you gonna do??

KIM. *You have no idea what I can do to you, Afi.*

AFI. Oh come on –

KIM. *Would you like a fish sandwich??*

(AFI *blanches.*)

BACK THE FUCK UP.

CLARK. I feel like you're determined to make me the bad guy here, and I honestly don't know what I did to deserve that. If you could just – explain to me why you feel this way –

KIM. IT'S NOT ABOUT MY FEELINGS, ASSHOLE!! STOP MAKING IT SEEM LIKE I AM THE PROBLEM HERE AND YOU'RE SO REASONABLE!!

BRENDA. Kim –

KIM. YOU.

BRENDA. Me?

KIM. Yes, you, don't play like you don't know.

(BRENDA *gazes at her placidly, starts putting food in her pockets.*)

BRENDA. Welp. Been nice having a break, but I suppose it's about time we get back. Don't worry. All of this is gonna play through, the way it always does, and you won't remember.

KIM. I remember you. *I know you know what I know.* You do! You know!

BRENDA. Do I?

KIM. You saw it! In the hut! The *huts*!! All those times, every single time! I was alone and you saw! And you wouldn't help me…? Why wouldn't you do something, you knew, you saw it – why why??? Aaaaaaaaaa…

(*She has flashbacks of* CLARK *leaving her, taking her child, the suicides – this pain starts to have a tinge of reality, poignancy.*)

It happened, it happened, it happened to me, it's in me – it's not wiped away, it stays somewhere, you know – it stays inside me, every time. Every time. With the knife, with the gun, down the well, off the bridge, the poison, the fire, the water, the hands around my neck, the sword through my belly, the rape, the beating, the hanging, the pillow over my face – I remember them all. I remember them all. The way I was torn, and crushed, and dragged, and burned, and cut. I feel it in my body, all those deaths. Over and over and over. But that wasn't the worst.
Not the worst.
The worst…
My son… alive in my body, then warm in my arms, his little hands, his tiny fingers clasped around my thumb like a starfish all night, all the nights I didn't sleep, waiting for his father to come back, dreaming of the world outside that hut. And when they came, when they took him from me, when they tore him from my body, his hands his feet his cheeks, everywhere his little body touched mine he took my skin on his skin when they pulled him away and I was left peeled and raw, missing skin a red patchwork on my body angry bleeding burns in the shape of him.
That.
Over and over.
Do you have any idea what that feels like?
Can you even imagine?

(*Pause.*)

Now how do I get out of here??

BRENDA. Ah. See, this is where I think you are a little confused and you don't understand that –

KIM. WAY OUT!!

BRENDA. – YOU'RE ALREADY OUT! THIS IS OUT!!

KIM. It can't be… no… this can't be all there is, I…

(*Beat.*
KIM *sprints over and pulls the drapes aside, revealing a sliding glass door – harsh searing white light floods the stage, bleaching everything and obscuring what lies beyond the door.*)
(KIM *and* BRENDA *exchange a long look,* KIM *slides the door open.*
Wind blows in.
KIM *tries to see what's beyond the door, but she can't see anything.*)

What about this?

(BRENDA *shrugs.*)

BRENDA. I honestly don't know.

(*Do we believe her?*
I don't know.)

We could stop here. We could stay here. It's not so bad, is it?

(KIM *stands on the threshold, the wind blows harder.*
She's scared.
She looks at BRENDA, *then takes one step across the threshold.*
Lights flare white-hot and burn everyone's eye sockets and KIM *disappears from view.*)

(*Blackout.*)

(*We could stop here.*)
(*We could stay here.*)
(*Or…*)
(*In the black, a sound comes up, waves of a sound that slowly resolves into a voice, a very distorted and sloweddown voice…*

Lights and sound bump up –)

GORO. Hey! Hey, Kim! Come on, girl, wake up!

(KIM *opens her eyes and she's in the seafood section at Whole Foods in Harlem.*)
(*She's lying on the floor,* GORO *leaning over her, concerned.*)

Oh my god!

(KIM *sits up slowly.*)

Are you okay? How do you feel? Okay? Not okay? Do you want me to call someone for you? Call 911?

KIM. Goro…?

GORO. Yeah, hi, hi – I just – are you okay?

KIM. Yeah…?

GORO. Oh my god, girl – shit was *crazy* – you came in and like you were yelling and running and – like someone was chasing you, right? Like straight-up yelling and carrying on and throwing seafood condiments and sourdough chowder bowls at people, and I was like 'Oh shit, it's Kim' and you were like '*Lemme outta here, you assholes!! You don't know who I am!!*' and I was like 'But I *do* know who you are!! Come down off the sushi display case please!!' and then right when the store manager was about to call the cops you just – PADONK! You just like passed the fuck out right on top of the crab legs display and fell to the floor and then we had to get a – never mind, not important – and then you were just laying there for like, the last twenty minutes and then, and then – and then you woke up.

KIM. Where…?

GORO. The seafood section at the Whole Foods in Harlem. New York.

KIM. Harlem.

GORO. New York.

(KIM *looks around.*)
(GORO *watches her closely.*)

KIM. I... don't think I've been in this one before.

The layout is... different.

GORO. Yeah, you go to the one in Columbus Circle, right?
Yeah. I get it – they got an escalator.
Hey, are you...? Are you sure you're okay? What year is it?
Who is the President of the – no that's too disappointing to think about –
Okay – where do you live?

(KIM *looks around.*)

Or maybe, how many fingers am I holding up?

KIM. Goro.

GORO. Nope, it's two. Oh god, I hope there's no permanent damage –

KIM. Goro.

GORO. – okay how about – What's my name? Do you know me?

KIM. ...Goro.

GORO. That's right! That's good, so your memory is pretty, um, I guess, intact or whatnot if you can remember me –

KIM. I've known you longer than I've known almost anybody.

GORO. Yeah. You have.

(*Pause.*)

Well... do you wanna... come in the back, chill in the break room for a minute?

KIM. Am I allowed in the back room?

GORO. Hey, I am the seafood section assistant manager. I do what I want.

(GORO *helps her up.*)

You want some water, something to eat? Some like, soup or whatnot?

KIM. I think I just need to... sit for a minute?

GORO. There's a couch back there, and you can chill as long as you need to, and then whenever you want, you can leave.

KIM. That's – that's perfect.

GORO. Lemme know if you want me to call you an Uber, or whatever.

(*Pause.*)

Funny. I was just talking about you today.

KIM. Oh yeah?

GORO. Yeah.
Now here you are.

KIM. Here I am now.

(*They start moving toward the back room.*)

GORO. Hold up. Ima get you a smoothie.

KIM. Uh…

GORO. We got these new fruit smoothies – I'll get you one but you don't hafta drink it, if you don't wanna, but you'll probably wanna because that shit is delicious and it's probably good for your, your blood sugar and whatnot.

KIM. Okay. Thanks. I don't have my wallet with me but –

GORO. Don't worry about it – I got you. Be right back.

(GORO *exits.*
KIM *waits.*)

(CIO-CIO *san enters, sees the destroyed crab leg display.*
She sighs deeply.
She and KIM *see each other.*
A moment.
KIM *nods at her.*
CIO-CIO *san nods back.*)

KIM. CIO-CIO san smiles suddenly, a huge, bright, joyful smile that touches and warms everything in the vicinity.

She lifts a hand and makes some kind of vague circle motion in the air that encompasses the busted crab legs display, the seafood section, KIM, GORO, the whole store, the whole world, and which means:

'Every day we must begin anew.
This is what it is to be alive.'

(*She and* KIM *smile at each other.*)
(*Muzak plays, maybe 'O-o-h Child' by The Five Stairsteps.*)

(*Blackout.*)

(*End of mutherfucking play.*)

The Bruntwood Prize for Playwriting: A Timeline

2005

The inaugural Bruntwood Prize for Playwriting was held at the Royal Exchange Theatre, Manchester, in 2005.

Chris Smith MP was Chair of the 2005 judging panel. Fellow judges included actor Brenda Blethyn OBE; Artistic Director of the National Theatre Nicholas Hytner; actor and playwright Kwame Kwei-Armah; founding Artistic Director of the Royal Exchange Theatre Braham Murray and Chairman of Bruntwood Michael Oglesby.

Bruntwood Prize for Playwriting: *Pretend You Have Big Buildings* by Ben Musgrave (Produced by the Royal Exchange Theatre, 2007)*

Second Prize: *Monster* by Duncan Macmillan (Produced by the Royal Exchange Theatre, 2007)

Third Prize: *The Cracks in My Skin* by Phil Porter (Produced by the Royal Exchange Theatre, 2008)

Under 26 Award: *Sixty Five Miles* by Matt Hartley (Produced by Hull Truck Theatre, 2012)*

North West Award: *Candyland* by Ian Kershaw

2008

Actor and director Richard Wilson was Chair of the 2008 judging panel. Fellow judges included actors Brenda Blethyn OBE and Michael Sheen; playwright Roy Williams; film director Roger Michell; Artistic Director of the Royal Exchange Theatre Greg Hersov and Chairman of Bruntwood Michael Oglesby.

The Bruntwood Prize for Playwriting 2008 was awarded to four joint winners: *Butcher Boys* by Naylah Ahmed

Mogadishu by Vivienne Franzmann (Co-produced by the Royal Exchange Theatre and the Lyric Hammersmith Theatre, London, 2011)*

Salt by Fiona Peek (Produced by the Royal Exchange Theatre, 2011)*

Winterlong by Andrew Sheridan (Produced by the Royal Exchange Theatre; transferred to Soho Theatre, London, 2011)*

2011

Playwright Simon Stephens was Chair of the 2011 judging panel. Fellow judges included actors Maxine Peake and Sue Johnston; writer Jackie Kay; Artistic Director of the Royal Exchange Theatre Sarah Frankcom and Chairman of Bruntwood Michael Oglesby.

Bruntwood Prize for Playwriting: *Three Birds* by Janice Okoh (Co-produced by the Royal Exchange Theatre and the Bush Theatre, London, 2013)*

Judges' Award: *Brilliant Adventures* by Alistair McDowall (Co-produced by the Royal Exchange Theatre and Live Theatre, Newcastle upon Tyne, 2013)

Judges' Award: *Britannia Waves the Rules* by Gareth Farr (Produced by the Royal Exchange Theatre, 2014)*

Judges' Award: *Shadow Play* by Louise Monaghan

2013

Broadcaster Dame Jenni Murray was Chair of the 2013 judging panel. Fellow judges included award-winning playwrights David Eldridge and Tanika Gupta MBE; Associate Director of the National Theatre Marianne Elliott; actor Suranne Jones; theatre critic Benedict Nightingale; Artistic Director of the Royal Exchange Theatre Greg Hersov and Chairman of Bruntwood Michael Oglesby CBE.

Bruntwood Prize for Playwriting: *Yen* by Anna Jordan (Produced by the Royal Exchange Theatre; transferred to the Royal Court Theatre, London, 2016)*

A TIMELINE   485

Judges' Award: *The Rolling Stone* by Chris Urch (Produced by the Royal Exchange Theatre; transferred to the Orange Tree Theatre, London, 2015)

Judges' Award: *Bird* by Katherine Chandler (Co-produced by the Royal Exchange Theatre and Sherman Cymru, Cardiff, 2016)*

Judges' Award: *So Here We Are* by Luke Norris (Co-produced by the Royal Exchange Theatre and HighTide, 2015)*

2015

Former Artistic Director of the National Theatre Nicholas Hytner was Chair of the 2015 judging panel. Fellow judges included Artistic Director of Actors Touring Company Ramin Gray; Bruntwood Prize-winning playwright Vivienne Franzmann; writer and broadcaster Miranda Sawyer; playwright Bryony Lavery; actor and writer Meera Syal CBE; Artistic Director of the Royal Exchange Theatre Sarah Frankcom and Chairman of Bruntwood Michael Oglesby CBE.

Bruntwood Prize for Playwriting: *Wish List* by Katherine Soper (Co-produced by the Royal Exchange Theatre and Royal Court Theatre, London, 2016)*

Judges' Award: *How My Light is Spent* by Alan Harris (Co-produced by the Royal Exchange Theatre, Sherman Theatre, Cardiff, and Theatre by the Lake, Keswick, 2017)*

Judges' Award: *Sound of Silence* by Chloe Todd Fordham

Judges' Award: *Parliament Square* by James Fritz (Co-produced by the Royal Exchange Theatre and the Bush Theatre, London, 2017)*

Judges' Award: *The Almighty Sometimes* by Kendall Feaver (Produced by the Royal Exchange Theatre, 2018)

2017

Broadcaster Kirsty Lang was Chair of the 2017 judging panel. Fellow judges included Bruntwood Prize-winning playwright Phil

Porter; screenwriter and producer Russell T Davies; playwright Lucy Prebble; director Lyndsey Turner; actor Alfred Enoch; Associate Artistic Director of the Royal Exchange Theatre Matthew Xia and Chairman of Bruntwood Michael Oglesby CBE.

Bruntwood Prize for Playwriting: *Heartworm* by Tim X Atack

Judges Award: *King Brown* by Laurie Nunn

Judges Award: *Plow* by Sharon Clark

Judges Award: *Electric Rosary* by Tim Foley (Produced by the Royal Exchange Theatre, 2022)*

Commendation: *This is Not America* by Joshua Val Martin

Commendation: *A Bit of Light* by Rebecca Callard

2019

In 2019 two awards were introduced:

- The Original New Voice Award, available to playwrights who had not had a full-length play professionally produced for twelve performances or more.
- The International Award, accepting submissions through partner theatres in Australia, Canada and the USA. Partner theatres can vary in each round of the Prize – to date, the Bruntwood Prize has partnered with Atlantic Theatre, Australian Plays Transform, Banff Centre Playwrights Lab, Belvoir Theatre, Berkeley Repertory Theatre, Melbourne Theatre Company, Playwrights Horizons, Stratford Festival and Woolly Mammoth Theatre Company.

Artistic Director of the Young Vic Theatre Kwame Kwei-Armah was Chair of the 2019 judging panel. Fellow judges included Artistic Director of Graeae Theatre Company Jenny Sealey MBE; Bruntwood Prize-winning playwright Anna Jordan; journalist, poet and critic Bridget Minamore; actor Shane Zaza; Artistic Director of the Royal Exchange Theatre Bryony Shanahan; Director of Social Impact at Bruntwood Kate Vokes and founder of Bruntwood and Chairman of The Oglesby Charitable Trust Michael Oglesby CBE.

Bruntwood Prize for Playwriting: *Shed: Exploded View* by Phoebe Eclair-Powell (Produced by the Royal Exchange Theatre, 2024)*

International Award: *untitled f*ck m*ss s**gon play* by Kimber Lee (Co-produced by the Royal Exchange Theatre, Factory International for Manchester International Festival, the Young Vic Theatre, London, and Headlong, 2023)*

Original New Voice Award: *Akedah* by Michael John O'Neill (Produced by Hampstead Theatre, London, 2023)

Judges' Award: *Glee & Me* by Stuart Slade (Produced by the Royal Exchange Theatre, 2021)*

Commendation: *Tambo & Bones* by Dave Harris (Co-produced by Theatre Royal Stratford East and Actors Touring Company, 2023)*

Commendation: *Ballybaile* by Jody O'Neill

2022

In 2022 the awards structure for the prize was streamlined to four sole winners: the International Award, the Judges' Award, the North West Original New Voice Award & Residency and the Bruntwood Prize for Playwriting.

The North West Original New Voice Award & Residency was introduced, available to playwrights resident in the North West who had not had a full-length play professionally produced for twelve performances or more. The winning writer received a year-long attachment to the Royal Exchange Theatre.

Diversity Activist Amanda Parker was Chair of the 2022 judging panel. Fellow judges included director Miranda Cromwell; actor Julie Hesmondhalgh; Bruntwood Prize-winning playwright Kimber Lee; Local Exchange Leigh Ambassador Farai Matekenya Nhakaniso; Artistic Director of the Royal Exchange Theatre Roy Alexander Weise and Non-Executive Director at Bruntwood Kate Vokes.

Bruntwood Prize for Playwriting: *Bullring Techno Makeout Jamz* by Nathan Queeley-Dennis (Co-produced by Ellie

Keel Productions, Paines Plough and The Belgrade Theatre, Coventry, in association with the Royal Exchange Theatre; transferred to the Royal Court Theatre, London, 2023)

International Award: *The Red Lead* 红铅 by Roshelle Fong

North West Original New Voice Award & Residency: *Leave the Morning to the Morning* by Patrick Hughes

Judges' Award: *Bindweed* by Martha Loader (Co-produced by Mercury Theatre, Colchester, HighTide, New Wolsey Theatre, Ipswich, in association with the Royal Exchange Theatre, 2024)*

2025

Celebrating its twentieth anniversary year, the Bruntwood Prize for Playwriting 2025 Awards Ceremony took place at the Royal Exchange Theatre on Monday 21st July 2025.

* indicates plays published by Nick Hern Books

www.nickhernbooks.co.uk

@nickhernbooks